Praise for

A LITTLE DEVIL IN AMERICA

"Poignant . . . Abdurraqib has written an important book on the transformative power of . . . love."

—*The New York Times*

"An absolutely brilliant book from a critic who's become one of the country's most essential writers . . . To call Abdurraqib anything less than one of the best writers working in America, and to call this book anything less than a masterpiece, would be doing him, and literature as a whole, a disservice."

—Minneapolis *Star Tribune*

"*A Little Devil in America* sheds light on repeated small acts of joy that lift us during traumatic experiences."

—*USA Today*

"Contemplations of legendary voices, sleights of hand, and charismatic choreographies are in dialogue with his own stories of grief, love, faith, and the search for freedom within the confinements of borders and a body. . . . Abdurraqib expands the conception of 'performance' to include the whole realm of behavior and culture. . . . Playfulness, seduction, artistry, and reinvention: Abdurraqib wants us to know that these devilish gestures have their place, too, among the saints that line the corridors in this tiresome, captivating, and essential struggle."

—*The Nation*

"[Abdurraqib's] books are soundscapes in print, and I was somehow listening to each sentence as if it were a breakbeat of personal narrative and socio-historical commentary. Hanif is one of the most exciting writers of his generation."

—*Los Angeles Review of Books*

"Abdurraqib, an award-winning poet, combines meditations on personal experiences—losing his mother, navigating the Midwestern punk scene—with affectionate studies of cultural moments and figures, beloved and under-sung alike. Abdurraqib views performance as an expression of life and a means of survival."

—*The New Yorker*

"Abdurraqib is an affable, generous host whose company is always a pleasure."

—*The Big Issue*

"*A Little Devil in America* offers a wide, deep, and discerning inquest into the Beauty of Blackness. . . . [Abdurraqib] has brought to pop criticism and cultural history not just a poet's lyricism and imagery but also a scholar's rigor, a novelist's sense of character and place, and a punk-rocker's impulse to dislodge conventional wisdom from its moorings until something shakes loose and is exposed to audiences too lethargic to think or even react differently."

—*Bookforum*

"An achingly personal reminiscence . . . . *A Little Devil in America* is [Abdurraqib's] widest-ranging collection yet, and yet also his most focused in the way he circles again and again around the theme of Black performance in all its layers."

—*The Current*

"Abdurraqib's book is a dance in literary form; he moves with us and entices us to move toward him, to engage in one of the most intimate of social interactions. . . . There's much joy in this book, as there is in the lives that Abdurraqib explores, including his own. We need that joy, that celebration, this book."

—*Chicago Review of Books*

"A brilliant, multilayered ode to African American genius."

—*Washington Independent Review of Books*

"Writing about joy is challenging; falling back on cliche is a constant temptation that Abdurraqib avoids in this insightful tome."

—*Forbes*

"The book, in the way Abdurraqib's work so often does, erects monuments to our should-be legends and our unignorable icons alike, and paints an expansive, deeply felt portrait of the history of Black artistry."

—*Electric Lit*

"Abdurraqib sees performance as a site of radical questioning, experimentation, and dream-making. This book is not a work of theory. It is sensual."

—*Vulture*

"Hanif Abdurraqib's genius is in pinpointing those moments in American cultural history when Black people made lightning strike. But Black performance, Black artistry, Black freedom, too often came at devastating price. The real devil in America is America itself, the one who stole the soul that Abdurraqib, through open eyes and with fearless prose, snatches back. This book is searing, revelatory, filled with utter heartbreak and unstoppable joy."

—MARLON JAMES, author of *Black Leopard, Red Wolf*

"Hanif Abdurraqib has a way of taking slices of our cultural landscape, examining them, and transforming them into observations and analyses that leave me underlining the entire page. In *A Little Devil in America*, Abdurraqib brilliantly braids together history, criticism, and prose so stunning that it makes you want to read every word out loud just so you can hear its music. Everything Abdurraqib writes is a must-read, but this is his best yet. It is one of the most dynamic books I have ever read."

—CLINT SMITH, author of *How the Word Is Passed*

"A rapturous exploration of Black genius . . . Whether heralding unsung entertainers or reexamining legends, Hanif Abdurraqib weaves together gorgeous essays that reveal the resilience, heartbreak, and joy within Black performance. I read this book breathlessly."

—BRIT BENNETT, author of *The Vanishing Half*

"Abdurraqib is one of the most brilliant writers I've ever read. *A Little Devil in America* needs to be on every bedside table, every high school and college desktop; in this age of revolution, this is that one book that everyone needs to read. It's pure genius. I'm not trying to get at even *some* of the brilliance Hanif gets to with this book—there is just too much. From Black exceptionalism to Josephine Baker to old heads, he brings it and clarifies it, then shapes it into every bit of medicine we need right now."

—JACQUELINE WOODSON, author of *Red at the Bone*

"Staggeringly intimate . . . Filled with nuance and lyricism, Abdurraqib's luminous survey is stunning."

—*Publishers Weekly* (starred review)

"Social criticism, pop culture, and autobiography come together neatly in these pages, and every sentence is sharp, provocative, and self-aware. Another winner from Abdurraqib."

—*Kirkus Reviews* (starred review)

BY HANIF ABDURRAQIB

A Little Devil in America: Notes in Praise of Black Performance

A Fortune for Your Disaster

Go Ahead in the Rain: Notes to A Tribe Called Quest

They Can't Kill Us Until They Kill Us

The Crown Ain't Worth Much

A Little Devil in America

A LITTLE
DEVIL IN
AMERICA

IN PRAISE OF

BLACK PERFORMANCE

HANIF ABDURRAQIB

Random House

NEW YORK

2022 Random House Trade Paperback Edition

Published in the United States by Random House, an imprint
and division of Penguin Random House LLC, New York.

RANDOM HOUSE and the HOUSE colophon are registered
trademarks of Penguin Random House LLC.

Originally published in hardcover in the United States by
Random House, an imprint and division of
Penguin Random House LLC, in 2021.

Permission credits can be found on page 287.

Library of Congress Cataloging-in-Publication Data
Names: Abdurraqib, Hanif.
Title: A little devil in America: notes in praise of black performance /
Hanif Abdurraqib.
Description: New York: Random House, 2021. | Includes
bibliographical references and index.
Identifiers: LCCN 2020023086 (print) | LCCN 2020023087 (ebook) |
ISBN 9781984801203 | ISBN 9781984801210 (ebook)
Subjects: LCSH: African Americans in the performing arts. | American
literature—African American authors—History and criticism. |
African Americans—Race identity. | United States—Race relations. |
African Americans—Intellectual life. | African Americans—
Social conditions.
Classification: LCC PN1590.B53 A23 2021 (print) |
LCC PN1590.B53 (ebook) | DDC 791.089/96073—dc23
LC record available at lccn.loc.gov/2020023086
LC ebook record available at lccn.loc.gov/2020023087

Printed in the United States of America on acid-free paper

randomhousebooks.com

3rd Printing

Book design by Fritz Metsch

For Josephine Baker

If you are not a myth whose reality are you? If you are not a reality whose myth are you?

Sun Ra

Think of our lives and tell us your particularized world. Make up a story.

Toni Morrison

Contents

xii]   CONTENTS

Movement I

PERFORMING

MIRACLES

On Times I Have Forced Myself to Dance

SAFE TO SAY none of the other Muslim kids on the eastside of Columbus got MTV or BET in their cribs & we do at my crib sometimes like after Pops got a promotion or after Grandma moved in & kept a Bible on her nightstand & had to watch the channel where her game shows ran 24/7 & so it is also safe to say that I was the only one in the Islamic Center on Broad Street who got to stay up & watch the shows on MTV that came on after my parents cut out the lights & went up to bed & it was only me & the warmth of an old television's glow & the DJs spinning C+C Music Factory for people in baggy & colorful getups & bouncing on a strobe-light-drenched floor & so it is safe to say that I only danced along the slick surface of my basement floor with the moon out & all the lights in the house out & the television playing hits & this wasn't exactly *practicing* dance moves as much as it was learning the different directions my limbs could flail in & there is no church like the church of unchained arms being thrown in every direction in the silence of a sleeping home & speaking of church to be Muslim is to pray in silence some-times even though the call to prayer is one of the sweetest songs that can hang in the air & there is no praise & there is no stomping in the aisles & there is no holy spirit to carry the blame for all manner of passing out or shouting or the body's pulsing convulsions & I do not want a spirit to enter me but I do want a girlfriend or at least a kiss from a girl at the Islamic

Center where we go on Friday afternoons in the summers for Jummah prayer & kick our shoes off on the carpet & slip into the hallway where the boys & girls would congregate briefly before being separated for prayer & it is absolutely safe to say that with my socks on the marbled tile of the Islamic Center on Broad Street I felt overcome by something we will call holy I suppose for the sake of not upsetting the divine order & this was the mid-'90s & so no one was really doing the moonwalk anymore & even when they did no one was doing it right & there is only one Michael & I am not that nigga & still with the girls at the Islamic Center standing in line for the water fountain I thought *Now is the time* & I was decidedly not in the dark of my basement anymore where I knew the floors & I understood every corner of the architecture & I slid back on the top of my toes & no one even turned their eyes toward me & so no one could tell me about the stairs I was sliding toward & so no one saw my brief moment of rhythm before it unraveled & just like that I was in a pile of discarded shoes & it is safest to say that there was no girlfriend for me that summer or the summer after & the cable at my house got cut off the year my mother died.

On Marathons and Tunnels

WHEN THE THICK fog of exhaustion set in on a room, it was desire that kept a dancer's body upright. When the desire wore off, it would be another dancer, pulling their partner up by the arms. In the photos from the Depression-era dance marathons, women sometimes appear lifeless in the arms of their men. In some photos, men lean their resting bodies on women who have their backs arched, standing and trying to support the dead weight of the person affixed to them.

Dance marathons began in the 1920s, largely in farm towns. As carnivals and fairs began growing along the American landscape, Americans became more obsessed with the impossible. Feats of strength, or human endurance. People attempted flagpole sitting, or long, horrific cross-country footraces. With the successful modernization of the Olympic Games in 1896, Americans became invested in the idea of world records. Even well before the establishment of the Guinness Book of World Records, everything was measured. Time and tenure were benchmarks for the impossible.

In 1923, Alma Cummings danced with six men in Upper Manhattan's Audubon Ballroom for twenty-seven hours straight. Cummings was a dance instructor who was interested in the body's limits on the dance floor. Her triumph sat directly at the intersection of the era's many fascinations: with excess, with endurance, with testing the limits of the country's tolerance for more liberal sexual expression. In the

only photo of Cummings taken right after she'd stomped and
spun along the wooden floor for over a full day, she's got her
feet in a small bowl of water. Her smile would appear to be
one of satisfaction, if not for our understanding of what she'd
just completed. With that knowledge, her upturned mouth
looks as if it might be tilting toward a type of madness, high-
lighted by her barely open and vacant eyes. In one hand,
Cummings holds the shoes she danced in. A hole is blown
clean through each of them, near where a foot might strike
the ground during a spirited movement. Both holes, wide as
two open mouths, in awe, in horror.

When word of Alma Cummings's accomplishment started
to crawl across the records-obsessed country, there was no way
folks were going to be outdone. People saw someone do something that had never been done before, and they wanted a
piece of that something too. Some churches still said dancing
was a sin, but there would be no sin greater than the sin of
sitting idle while a chance to carve your name into immortality was available. Cummings had her record broken at least
nine times in the next three weeks. In Baltimore, in Cleveland, in Houston, in Minneapolis. Stories of the hours people
danced spread through newspapers, traveling from town to
town. If someone hit thirty-one hours on a Sunday somewhere in Indiana, then surely someone a few states over
would be trying to drag themselves to thirty-two hours by
Tuesday.

The problem, as eager promoters saw it, was that no one
was capitalizing on this new obsession. Sure, the boom of industry in the early 1920s kept the people in urban centers well
fed and eager to spend their coin on whatever entertainment
they could find. But the people who lived in America's rural
corners found themselves pushed to dire circumstances. A
combination of boredom and a scarcity of resources engi-

neered the perfect opportunity for promoters to cash in on the growing excitement around the dance marathon. There was the space to do it—barns made empty by lack of use, or vast gathering halls that some of the more claustrophobic bigger cities didn't have. There was also, simply, the ability to capitalize on poverty and need. Organizers would offer cash prizes of a few hundred dollars for the winners, sometimes more. A good competition could offer a prize larger than a farmer's yearly income. In addition, dancers were lured toward the competitions by the simple promise of food and shelter. Food was provided during the marathons, and the dancers were given short breaks to eat, bathe, and shave. It was a grand alternative to hunger, or having to be immersed in the reality of one's circumstances. Anything the dancers put themselves through felt worthwhile, given what the marathon was taking them away from. Even if they didn't win, they still had a purpose for however long they could withstand the sleeplessness, or the blood-swollen feet, or the trembling legs, bent and unsteady.

Once the stock market crashed in 1929, dance marathons became a nationwide craze. Desperation is the great equalizer, after all. The pool of willing contestants widened and spread beyond rural America. People with no job prospects would fill up dance marathons just to get a consistent meal while attempting to bring home a payday. There were hard rules set in place: A dancer's knees could not touch the floor at any point, or else both people in the team would be disqualified. Participants were permitted fifteen minutes each hour to rest, but once the fifteen minutes were up, they had to immediately return to the dance floor. What dancing was and wasn't seemed to be debatable, in terms of actual movement. Dancers read the newspaper while dancing; some shaved while their partner held up a mirror. The rules just went that at least one dancer in a couple needed to be moving—one set of feet had to be attempting some directional rhythm. The hours that marathoners held the floor quickly ticked upward, far beyond the twenty-seven hours of Alma Cummings. Winning dancers in the early '30s clocked hundreds of hours on the floor, then thousands. Some cities, like Boston, banned the events when participants started getting injured—or would pass out and die afterward.

For the most extreme marathons, the dances would oscillate between spirited turns of energetic movement and lazy stretches of half-rhythmic walking. People would choose their partners not always by affection or romantic interest, but simply by the person they most trusted to keep them alive during the marathon's most unforgiving moments. Someone who had a body weight that was sturdy enough to keep a partner upright, but not too heavy to lift. There were dancers who entered marathons in December with the hope of dancing all the way until June. Two people—sometimes lovers but sometimes siblings and sometimes barely even friends—had to commit to each other and the pursuit of staying on their feet. This might have been less difficult in the evening hours, when bands swung into action to keep a room upbeat. But the real test was during the daytime, when a radio merely droned out some dry melody and the spectators were few.

Yes, the spectators, those who watched with cynical excitement. Particularly in the bigger cities, where the marathons were a larger draw, spectators packed the venues. Even among the desperate, there was a class divide. The people who were down and out but not down and out enough to subject themselves to the rigors of a dance competition would come and bear witness to the people who were even worse off than they were—the people who collapsed their weary bodies into each other for a chance at temporary shelter or a run of hot meals or a place to rest in front of an audience of people who still had a place to live, or enough food to get by.

I typed "dance marathons, black dancers" into a Google search bar, and all of the results returned with a disclaimer tacked to the bottom. "Missing: ~~Black~~." The results ask if the term "Black" *must be included.* And at least here, it must. It also must be said that yes, there were a few Black dancers taking to their own marathons in Harlem or other pockets of New York City. But the majority of the marathon dancers and spectators were white. The biggest prizes were granted to the white dancers. But make no mistake, Black people were dancing. They were dancing in jazz clubs and small bars and in living rooms. Black people were dancing with an interest in skill over endurance. Requiring a partner who might highlight them rather than hold them up. Some of these Black people were struggling just the same as the white people dancing for hours, toward the edge of death. They were immersed in adjacent desperations, but afforded different opportunities of escape and reward. The Black dancers who Lindy Hopped in segregated ballrooms or casinos were about celebrating their ability to move like no one else around them could move, for whatever time they could. Pushing themselves to the brink of a short, blissful exhaustion, as opposed to a slow, plodding, death-defying one.

After all, what is endurance to a people who have already endured? What is it to someone who could, at that point, still touch the living hands of a family member who had survived being born into forced labor? Endurance, for some, was seeing what the dance floor could handle. It did not come down to the limits of the body when pushed toward an impossible feat of linear time. No. It was about having a powerful enough relationship with freedom that you understand its limitations.

* * *

WHEN I WAS a senior in high school, there were sock hops in the middle of the day. It was an excuse for juniors and seniors to divide their days, to draw a line between life before sweat and life after. It was also the only way the school could keep those of us with cars in the building. Once administration got hip to the fact that we'd leave at lunch and return only half the time, a compromise had to be made. The midday sock hop was born. During the lunch hour, the school auditorium would allow the students to roll up the bleachers, bring in speakers, and create a dance floor. The school was old, and the auditorium was a cavern. There were few lights to begin with, and by the time bodies were packed into the place, what little light there was got swallowed. A cacophony of noise and shadows, for about forty minutes every afternoon. It was so dark that it didn't matter who could or couldn't dance, or who was grinding up against whom—or even what song was being played—as long as it was loud and had some bass that could be felt all the way out to the hallways. Teacher supervision was low, as most of them seemed to decide that this alternative was better than half of the school emptying out for the second half of the day.

For most of the young and overeager teenagers, the prime real estate was in the corners, where the darkness was even more all-consuming than the already dark room was. There, the boundary between dancing and indecency was thinner. If two willing participants wanted to make a little more of the heat their bodies defined, or if eyes had met across the class-room at nine in the morning with clear instructions of what might go down a few hours later, the corners were where those deeds were sacred. As private as one could get in an au-ditorium with half the school present.

For maybe the only time in my life, I preferred the center of the floor. There was something seductive about being in a mass of limbs that hadn't yet figured themselves out, as I hadn't. My high school was racially diverse, but mostly only the Black people danced. Only the Black people played DJ at these dances. Only the Black teachers would look after the dance, or turn an eye away from the dance when things got a little too spicy but not so spicy that it might become danger-ous. Others were invited into the space, of course. But it felt distinctly ours—young Black kids who were mostly too ner-vous to do anything but try to shake ourselves free from the confines of school, or parents, or sports, or any of the other responsibilities that we would later come to see as gentle winds in the oncoming hurricane of adulthood. I preferred the mass of bodies at the center of the floor, where the ability to dance was just an arbitrary thing in a pool of already arbi-trary things. There was barely enough space to truly move, and so what one did within the confines of their small cube of space was dance—and no one was really checking your poten-tially non-dancing ass anyway, because they had their small cube of space to tend to.

I have never felt more like a dancer than I did then, among other Black kids who either had the moves or didn't but still wanted to imagine the afternoon as a night without worries. When the music ended and the auditorium doors opened, the harsh light from the hallway would spill into the room, and we'd all walk out covering our eyes, as if we'd spent the last several days underground. It all feels so odd now. To go im-mediately from that scene to sitting in some desk and reading about Chaucer or a Brontë sister, sweat still stiffening on the back of my neck.

It occurs to me now that this was the real joy of dancing:

to enter a world unlike the one you find yourself burdened with, and move your body toward nothing but a prayer that time might slow down.

Before I learned this lesson firsthand, understood the way sweat could gloriously cloak a dance floor, I would go to my television as a child to watch Black people move. *Soul Train* would air live on Saturday nights on WGN, a station out of Chicago, where the show originated. In Columbus, even if you had just a few basic channels, you'd get WGN. In the early to mid-'90s, it was the thing to watch before *Yo! MTV Raps*. In that era, the live show was more than fine. But the real gems were in the reruns, which would sometimes come on during the day on Sundays, when most other channels were bogged down by infomercials or the NFL game of the week. The reruns showed clips from *Soul Train*'s most golden era, from the mid-'70s through the late '80s, when the weekly musical guests came from the greatest eras of Black soul, funk, R&B, and pop, and the outfits of the audience-turned-dancers were adorned with fringe and frill and gold, their skin dark but for the glitter or jewels along their cheekbones and eyes.

Soul Train was guided by Don Cornelius, who got his start as a backup disc jockey at Chicago radio station WVON. Cornelius was born in Chicago in 1936, as the era of dance marathons began to die down. He worked primarily as a news and sports reporter, but he spent his downtime emceeing a series of concerts featuring local Chicago music talent. On weekend nights, he would pack as many people as could fit into Chicago-area high schools and put on his show. He called the series "The Soul Train," and his shows grew in popularity during the late '60s, with people coming from all over the Midwest to dance to whatever Cornelius decided to spin.

In 1965, two dance programs were running on the upstart

UHF station out of Chicago: *Kiddie-a-Go-Go* and *Red Hot and Blues*—both targeted to young people. The latter catered primarily to Black audiences, playing on Friday nights, hosted by Big Bill Hill, a DJ and promoter in the city. *Red Hot and Blues* featured mostly R&B, and younger kids dancing with varying degrees of enthusiasm to the hits of the day.

This was the seed for *Soul Train,* but Cornelius was trying to make a show that was distinctly adult, and distinctly rooted in a type of cool that was being born at the turn of the decade, when Black people were redefining themselves once again, after talk of civil rights turned to talk of complete liberation. At his core, Cornelius was a journalist who was driven to journalism by a desire to cover the civil rights movement, with an understanding that the movement was inextricably linked to the music that soundtracked it. It acted as both a call for people to take to the streets and a reprieve after a long day of protest, or marching, or working some despised job. Cornelius was frustrated by the lack of television venues for soul music, and the lack of Black people being their whole, free selves on television, and so he created a venue for it himself. By the time a television deal came knocking in 1970, he'd already established an audience. A people cannot only see themselves suffering, lest they believe themselves only worthy of pain, or only celebrated when that pain is overcome. Cornelius had a vision for Black people that was about movement on their own time, for their own purpose, and not in response to what a country might do for, or to, them.

It did help that Don Cornelius was cool. His name itself seemed like something passed through a lineage of mother-fuckers who wore their hats low and kept lit cigarettes in their mouths that never burned all the way down. His full name— Donald Cortez Cornelius—might have been even cooler than the one he's most known by, but I suppose even the freshest among us have to give people a break sometimes. He was a lanky six foot four and walked with slow, long strides. Don Cornelius didn't dance much; he preferred instead to give the floor to the many people who spilled onto it during each taping of *Soul Train* once the show got picked up by television and became a breakout success. But you knew Don Cornelius *could* dance. There are people who you don't even need to see move to know that they are one with rhythm, and Don Cornelius was one of those people, in part because he always looked so well put together, but also not so put together that he might shy away from fucking up a dance floor. He'd wear velvet sport coats and keep his afro picked high and flawless. His round-framed glasses sat evenly on his face and never needed to be adjusted.

Beyond all of his aesthetic cool, Cornelius was a poet speaker, toying with melody and syntax in his introductions and interviews. At the start of each episode, the voice-over would introduce Cornelius as the camera zoomed in on him smiling easy. Then he'd take a deep breath before unfurling a long, winding sentence along the lines of

HEYYYY welcome aboard I guarantee yous'll enjoy the ride especially if you like your soul ice cold 'cuz we got none other than the iceman himself here and he's gonna be lookin' ya right D-E-A-D in your eyes after this very important message.

Or

Hey there it's time for another *sweeeet* ride on the soul train and you gotta hold right on to that spot ya got because you're not gonna wanna miss your spot we're gonna be here *allllllll* night.

It also helped that Cornelius didn't take himself too seriously. Like *Soul Train* itself, he was aiming to show the multitudinous nature of Blackness, and sometimes that meant he'd put on clown-shoe-sized basketball kicks to do a bit where he plays a game of H-O-R-S-E with a friend. His presence as host served the show first, without question. But he also gave enough of himself to the viewers at home to make them feel like they were in the room as well, no matter what time or era they were watching the episodes in. For a couple of hours on some scattered Sundays in my youth, I was there with the dancers in their thick ties and butterfly collars, or I was there with Earth, Wind & Fire playing "September" and an audience washing themselves with the sound like it was the sweetest thing they would ever hear. I was there, every time, at the end, with Cornelius giving his signature send-off:

> We'll be back next week and you can bet your last money, it's all gonna be a stone gas, honey! I'm Don Cornelius, and as always in parting, we wish you love, peace, and *souuuuuullllllll!*

A major feature of *Soul Train* was the Soul Train Line, which anchored the program. It was simple, on its face: two lines are formed, and two dancers peel off from the end of the line and dance their way to the opposite end, until the line naturally dwindles. The participants in the line don't have a long stretch of time to make their way down, and they have to do it smoothly. Everyone is watching, at home and in the line itself. As people move down it, the waiting participants clap to the music to help keep them on beat. The history of the line itself was born out of the Stroll, a dance that gained popularity in the late '50s and extended to the late '60s. "The Stroll" was a 1958 song by the Diamonds, and it hit big on

American Bandstand, where the dance craze gained momentum. Videos of the original Stroll don't bring forth much excitement. The two lines are far apart, and most dancers, upon meeting in the center, simply hold hands and walk somewhat melodically down, sometimes swinging an arm or two for effect. All of the dancers are white, and the waiting dancers kick a leg out from time to time instead of clapping. In the black-and-white videos, most of the dancers look like they barely even want to be there. Like this particular song demanded a labor out of them that they were never fully committed to.

Still, the line formation itself was of interest to Cornelius, and the concept, it seemed, could be better served with some small adjustments. If the space in the line was tighter, for example. Or if the line existed outside the concept of a single song that made the movements feel like an obligation. The Stroll was slow and a bit tedious, but there was something insistent about the Soul Train Line. The songs were faster, sure. But the people inside danced with a clear urgency. Showing off their best moves as if they might forget how to do them at any moment. The people on the ends beating out a percussion with their open palms. The hand and the voice and the body, the sweetest instruments. The instruments from which all other instruments are born.

The line was an instant hit because it afforded each person their own time to shine. There were dancers who returned multiple times, and watching reruns, I was always delighted to see them reappear in the line a few weeks in a row. But I was never as happy as I was watching a new person in the line for their first time, which could sometimes be given away with an excess of flourish, or an even greater urgency spilling forth from their movements. Someone who savored their time in the line, maybe twirling sideways for a bit in order to milk just a few more seconds before finishing their turn. Someone who maybe heard stories of the line's mythology and made a pilgrimage to see it for themselves. As the line evolved, people got more and more creative about how they chose to use it. Dancers began to bring props. The moves got more acrobatic. The couples began to coordinate outfits. The Soul Train Line became an essential part of the *Soul Train* viewing experience. Black people pushing other Black people forward to some boundless and joyful exit.

Folks who would become stars of the '70s, '80s, and '90s had their first big on-camera moments twisting and twirling within the wall of clapping hands. Fred "Rerun" Berry from *What's Happening!!* was a hit in the early Soul Train Lines. Jody Watley and Jeffrey Daniel were Soul Train Line partners before the world knew them as part of Shalamar. Columbus, Ohio's own Jermaine Stewart lit up the line with regularity all through '77 and '78. Once, in '77, Stewart and his companion popped and locked through the line in matching glittering faux tuxedos. In 1986, when Stewart was riding high on the Top Five hit "We Don't Have to Take Our Clothes Off," Don Cornelius introduced him to the *Soul Train* stage by saying, *He's made good, and we're all quite proud of him*, and there was Jermaine as beautiful as ever, his hair pressed and laid, a long and radiant black tuxedo jacket hanging off his body. In the '80s, Rosie Perez perfected the moves that would later serve as the opening to *Do the Right Thing*, her arms violently swinging at her sides, propelling her waist into short, measured thrusts. When Perez was really *on* in the line, she wouldn't even finish dancing all the way down. She'd stop a little over halfway through and then confidently stroll the rest of the way, locking eyes with the camera.

I consider, often, the difference between showing off and showing out. How showing off is something you do for the world at large and showing out is something you do strictly for your people. The people who might not need to be reminded how good you are but will take the reminder when they can. The Soul Train Line was the gold standard of where one goes to show out.

But perhaps my favorite clip of *Soul Train* is the one in which Don Cornelius dances. The Supremes were on the show, and Mary Wilson *really* wanted to dance in the legendary line. Cornelius, who had never taken to the line before, refused at first, but eventually he caved in. When he appears at the top of the queue, the crowd tips toward a wildness that had never before been heard. He busts a funky chicken, and then an ill-fated attempt at a split that still managed to look effortless and somehow magical. It was a tithe—another thing to add to the list of generosities Cornelius gave. If someone wanted to dance, he would find a way to get them to dance, even if he had to sacrifice his mystique in the process.

Don Cornelius saw in Black people a promise beyond their pain, and I was always saddest to come to terms with the idea that he could not outrun his own. In 2012, he shot himself in the head, because at the end of his life, he was suffering too much to go on living. Cornelius retired from hosting *Soul Train* in 1993, more than a decade after he underwent a twenty-one-hour brain surgery to correct a congenital deformity in his cerebral arteries. He was never the same afterward, suffering from seizures and struggling with cognitive functions. He kept producing the show until 2006, when it finally went off the air, and then he was largely reclusive until his death.

If people could leave the world in the way they gave to the world, I wish for a path to heaven lined with Black people clapping their hands. I wish Don Cornelius at the center, all by himself, showing out with all the moves we knew he was stashing the whole time.

I NEVER SAW my mother dance, and I never saw my father dance, though I did watch them lean into each other during a ballad by Luther or Ms. Patti. I remember them rocking back and forth while being cradled by a slow and sad melody, both of them looking exhausted, but joyful. For so long, I watched the Soul Train Line videos wondering if there was some past version of themselves that had been hidden. If they'd leapt among you, my dearest dancing ancestors. If my father might have been the man in the hat so low that when he bobbed up and down, it looked as if there was only a toothpick protruding from a knowing smile. Or if my mother would emerge as one of the many heaven-high afros from the '70s, jeans pulled up to her waist, twirling easily down the line and trying to contain her cool.

I haven't found them in those videos, so I've imagined them. I've imagined all of you, too. I am haunted by your radiance: The man in the ocean-blue jumpsuit drowning in silver who kicks his leg heavenward during Rick James shouting "Give It to Me Baby." The woman in a pink sweater with a bow and massive white collar swinging her hips and fanning herself with a church fan simultaneously during Michael's "Don't Stop 'Til You Get Enough." The couple coordinated perfectly, the woman in a white dress decorated with dark crimson flowers and the man in a dark crimson suit and white pants, his cream shirt held together by only one button at the bottom, his whole chest on display, both of them shimmying their shoulders in sync to War's "Ballero."

I play the clips of Soul Train Lines and wonder where these friends and lovers are now; if they are still living somewhere watching the scenes of their past selves cartwheeling and spinning and popping and locking with perhaps some strangers rooting for them. It feels like those are the moments that make a home inside a person. Maybe they don't, but I want for that to be the case. For me to point at these archives of what it once was to be Black and a person on television with no real message or no laugh track or no manufactured sitcom family. Just a song and a handful of seconds in a line and an outfit that maybe cost too damn much but looks good under the lights.

In the name of loneliness, I would watch the Soul Train Line videos. In the name of a very specific dislocation, when I moved to a city or visited a city where I didn't know anyone, or didn't see anyone who looked like me, I would watch the Soul Train Line videos. From a distance, with friends who lived where I did not live, we would sit in silence on the telephone and watch the Soul Train Line videos, and after each of them, we would fall into a spiral of naming each person dancing through, shouting out how you might be related to us if we were so lucky. I have claimed the fantasy of kinship with so many of you, my dear cousins from another life. I have watched your leather and your pearls spin down the rhythmic labyrinth of that immaculate nighttime. I have imagined you practicing in your mirrors, as I practiced in my mirror before going out to a place that I knew would have the song, the space, and the opportunity for me to once again revel in the sin of not being born with your rhythm. My distant loves, I have imagined you with your arms in whatever closets you had, digging for the most luminescent of outfits. I have imagined you unable to sleep or unable to work or unable to do anything beyond pray to still be alive and standing on the night when the bodies parted for you, and the song was a song you'd woven your body in between the notes of in some time before. Every time I take to a dance floor and can't keep up, I am looking back and praying you all will open up a path with some unbreakable light at the end.

IN BOTH THE dance marathon and the Soul Train Line, I am in love with the performance of partnership, and the boundaries that performance is pushed to. In the dance marathons, when people would gather their landlord's daughter, or an ex-co-worker's son, or a tall and sturdy-looking neighbor from down the block, they were attaching themselves to someone who could potentially be their only ally for a run of months. In a room where everyone was looking to beat them, these were the two people who had to watch over each other. Who had to hold mirrors for each other while fixing hair, or applying fresh lipstick for the evening crowd of spectators packing into the hall. In the old photos from the dance marathons, it is impossible to tell the relationships that couples have with each other. The photos I return to most are the ones that focus on the people's faces, particularly while their partner is slumped over in their arms, or while they're carrying their dance partner to a cot for a brief break. Sure, within their eyes remains the same frantic madness once in the eyes of Alma Cummings sitting with her feet in ice and her torn-through shoes.

But also there is care, concern, fear. An affection born out of having to make a home out of the confines of dance, or of physically holding up another person. A dream exhibit born out of desperation. I am obsessed with this, I imagine, because of how many times I have leaned into someone or something and called it love, because it had to be. Because if it wasn't love, then something else would crumble. Sure, the stakes were not a hot meal, or a warm and sheltered place. The stakes for me were sometimes depression, sometimes loneliness, sometimes a morning I didn't think I could make it to. I am in love with the idea of partnering as a means of survival, or a brief thrill, or a chance to conquer a moment. Even if you and the person you are partnered with part ways walking into the sunlight after exiting a sweaty dance hall, or spinning off-camera after dancing your way down a line of your clapping peers.

In the very early days of the Soul Train Line there were fewer coordinated pairs of partners and more people who perhaps just showed up in the line and ended up together. In these scenarios, there was no time to figure out choreography with someone, just those brief moments to lock eyes before being at the mercy of each other's movements. Then it was just the two of you, moving through a narrow tunnel of music and shouts urging you forward. The Soul Train Line is rigorous, with its small space for lateral movement. People have to dance their way out of the line's exit and they have to do it well, because everyone there can dance, and if you can't, there is no backstage to run toward in order to reinvent yourself. And so the dancers must rely on what they know of the body to figure themselves—and each other—out of the hot, pulsing room, with nothing but noise and instinct to guide them before they reach the end of the line and part, maybe forever.

And I think this is how I would most like to imagine romance, friends, or should I say lovers. In praise of all my body can and cannot do, I wish to figure out how it can best sing with all of yours for a moment in a room where the walls sweat. I wish to lock eyes across a dance floor from you while something our mothers sang in the kitchen plays over the speakers. I want us to find each other among the forest of writhing and make a deal.

Okay, lover. It is just us now. The only way out is through.

On Going Home as Performance

IN A MEMORY from a time long before this one, I am a boy holding a dead bird in my open palms. This was before I knew which birds looked like what, and so I am not sure of the species, just that it was a dead winged creature. I remember its feathers being cold despite the fact that when I found its lifeless body, it was cradled by two beams of sunlight in a field across the street from my house. The field was once peppered with tall, thin trees, until the retirement home next to the field complained about how the trees obscured the view of the sky from some of its residents. And I suppose, now, that this was a fair complaint. The trees themselves weren't particularly attractive. A mess of wiry branches and leaves that didn't even have the decency to grow beautifully in the spring or die beautifully in autumn. The retirement home made the argument that its residents had lived a long life and deserved a view of beauty in their final years. The trees were, after all, useful only to the neighborhood kids like myself, who could use them to cloak misadventures, or store some treasure from the outdoors, or build a shaky clubhouse. My first real kiss came nestled in between two of those trees, with a girl who I rode bikes with and snuck candy bars out of the Revco with on days when we didn't have any cash, which were most days. On one afternoon in July when there were still trees in the field, we sat our bikes down and wandered into the center of them, jumping over the assorted tree branches. We leaned

against some tree that was losing its bark, sticky with the sap
underneath. We kissed in the way that children find their
way to kissing: out of curiosity, not romance. Transactional,
almost. As if there was nothing to find out at the end of it. We
went back out to our bikes and sped around the block a few
more times before going home. She moved out of the neighborhood that next March, and the trees came down in April.
I'd carved both of our names into one, a fool for the romantics
of permanence.

On the day I found the bird it was in the summer after the
trees fell and I went back to the field for the sake of some
nostalgia, perhaps. The landscape felt sudden and naked without the hiding places me and my pals would tuck away in.
And there was the bird, a heap of black among the clumps of
brown dirt. I don't know why I picked the bird up. I was also
too young to know much about any type of illnesses the bird
could carry. I just saw it on the ground, pulled apart from the
sky, and felt like it deserved better. I dug it a small hole, somewhere that the trees were once at their highest. I covered it
and placed a small flower over the mound of dirt.

This was the first funeral I'd ever been to. This, perhaps,
is the moment I first learned to honor the dead.

THE ACT OF the funeral as revelry or celebration was a for-
eign concept to me for most of my childhood, because I didn't
attend all that many of them, and the most prominent funerals I did attend were Muslim funerals. In Islam, the body
must be buried as soon as possible—something that shifts depending on the means of those doing the burying, and on the
time of death. The post-death ritual is simple, and revolves
largely around a cleaning and then shrouding of the body in
a white cotton cloth before placing it in a closed and modest
casket. The funeral service is short, with a gathering of the

community to come together and offer their collective prayers for the forgiveness of the dead. My earliest funeral experiences were this: brief, without ceremony. An emotional severing before a send-off. After praying, carrying a body to the graveyard, where it must be placed in a grave angled toward Mecca, so that the body faces the holy city. According to Islamic law, the grave marker cannot be raised more than twelve inches above the ground, with no sprawling or decadent headstones, which are discouraged. In Sunni Islam, there is a timeline-based mourning period—fifteen days for loved ones and relatives and four months and ten days for widows. When I was young, after two or so funerals, I began to imagine the brief and structured funeral as a type of gift. A mercy placed upon someone who lived a life and now got to, perhaps, see whatever awaited on the other side of that life. I imagined the entire process of the funeral being quick as a service to the dead—to spare them being stuck here with our grief, and instead send them to the waiting arms of some heaven-like interior. Some endless sky where they sit and wait for everyone they've ever loved to join them, where the years feel like the mere passing of minutes.

IT IS HARD for me to find my mother's gravestone, because it does not rise above the ground itself. There is no stone landmark jutting out of the earth with her name carved into it. There are no notable monuments near it. If not tended to during an especially eager season, the grass and weeds grow over her tombstone, camouflaging it and making it even more difficult to find. One of the last times I went, I wandered the graveyard looking for my mother's name in the earth for nearly forty minutes, each time coming upon names that were not hers and apologizing to each one. The most recent time I got it down to twenty minutes. There's something I've come to appreciate about this kind of hunt—searching for a name on a stone and a conversation with the body beneath it.

I don't remember much about my mother's funeral beyond the dirt, which caked my shoes for hours after she was buried. I remember carrying the casket through what I believe was mud, wet from rainfall that had settled into the ground from the night before. I don't remember if I helped to shovel dirt into the hole once the casket was placed there, but I clearly remember watching people push shovels into the ground. This is the unromantic part of the funeral. The labor of lifting dirt or carrying the weight of the body, unmoving but eternally loved.

When my mother died, I was on the verge of becoming a teenager. I was growing and outgrowing everything in my grasp, and not wearing dress clothes often. Nearly a year after the funeral, I went to put on the dress shoes I wore the day of her burial. There was some banquet I had to attend and I had to look nice doing it. When I pulled them out of the top of my closet, dirt from the graveyard fell from the sole and landed on my right cheek.

THE FIRST TIME I attended a Black funeral in a church, I was seventeen and my legs ached from standing for more than twenty minutes straight. I walked with awe past the open casket, richly adorned with fabric and flowers. At the two-and-a-half-hour mark, I went outside to see a fleet of cars waiting to take the mourners off to a graveyard. There was singing, and wailing, and composure lost and regained only to be lost again. Prior to this, it had only briefly occurred to me that there was another way to pass someone on to the better, hopefully more righteous hands of a world other than this one. So much of my upbringing revolved around death and loss as a structured, reserved period, where the visible out-pouring of emotion was unique at best, and shameful at worst.

When I was twenty-one, I saw a funeral in a church some-where in the southern part of Alabama, and a woman screamed during the eulogy. Something that sounded both painful and prideful. She then took to the aisle and began to dance, and others slowly joined. The funeral itself was some-what of a fashion show. People came dressed in whatever out-fits came after their Sunday best, the dresses and jewels and shoes tucked in the back of the closet, cocooned in some pro-tective tomb until the highest of special occasions called. The woman in the casket at this particular funeral had lived a long life, tied to this community in ways I didn't fully understand, having not lived there. The funeral was hours long, stretching into the night when, after it was all said and done, there was food and more dance. It struck me because no one seemed particularly sad. Every movement around death I'd come to understand in my youth told me that the acknowledgment of it needed to be somber and silent. Something one moves through with decorum and then never looks back on again. A funeral was a task, not something to make a memory of.

It dawns on me now that the funeral—particularly the Black funeral—is a way to celebrate what a person's life meant and to do it as if they're still here. To offer gratitude for the fullness of whatever years someone chose to have their life intersect with your own. I've been to Black funerals where people bring food that the deceased taught them to make, or they wear a wide hat that they picked out with the dead in mind and let it cast a massive shadow over their grinning face. People telling fond and exaggerated stories of the life some-one lived, well into the night. There is no trick to this, no de-ception. It is continuing in the tradition of Black Americans

attempting to protect and enlarge their own narratives. A tradition that has been present since being forced into America,
knowing that there were stories and history and lives to be
honored beyond this place.

WHEN MICHAEL JACKSON died, in the early summer of
2009, it was the kind of celebrity death that my particular
generation has become especially used to in the past two or
three years: a hero central to our childhood suddenly gone,
unexpectedly and out of nowhere. Death simply opening its
mouth to a wide yawn and drinking in a life that certainly
had more to give. While it isn't like Michael Jackson's was the
first shocking star death by any means, to my friends and me
it felt especially heavy. Many of us—namely, all my friends
who were born in the 1980s and came of age during the latter
part of that decade and into the early '90s—learned what a
pop star was from Michael. That's when he was at his most
performatively decadent: everything cloaked in gold, music
videos premiering in prime-time hours like news specials,
Neverland Ranch sprawling over endless acres. Despite the
fact that in 2009 Michael Jackson was far from the pop star
draw that he once was, his death still echoed for my corner of
people in a way that I can't remember any other death echoing. Jackson seemed, at times, to be immortal. Even amid the
controversies that surrounded him and his odd public behavior, he was still our pop star. The one we assumed would live
forever.

It was hot in Columbus, Ohio, on the day Michael Jackson's death started to circulate in the news. It was a different
time, in some ways. Twitter was in its absolute infancy, and
Facebook, much like it is now, wasn't the place to get accurate
real-time news. I scrolled through and refreshed a series of
choppy news reports on my laptop from bed while two fans

blew at full ferocity onto my sweat-slicked skin, which was soaking the pillow behind my back. I remember the heat by the way I sat forward in the moment when the news seemed most true, when several outlets were reporting it at once. I remember the heat by the way the pillow cover first stuck to my back as I reached for my phone, then slowly peeled away from the embrace of my damp skin. And I remember the heat by the way I ran outside to share the news with my neighbors, who were sweating on their porches, because it was slightly better than sweating in their non-air-conditioned apartments. And so I'm saying that the heat in Columbus was unforgiving on the day Michael Jackson died. I'm saying that everything in the air had bad intentions.

In Columbus, there is a bar called Hampton's on King, and it is largely unspectacular as far as bars go, except for its basement. The basement of Hampton's on King is a cave. It is one of those spaces that almost certainly should not hold people within it, and yet it does. There are no windows or ventilation, just space and opportunity, should a DJ feel compelled to bring the tables out for a night of revelry. On the night of Michael Jackson's death, a handful of DJs from Columbus dragged their equipment into the basement of Hampton's on King, and the bar called off every other purpose it served for one evening and told the city to come dance in the name of the King of Pop, workweek schedule be damned. And so we did. In the basement of Hampton's on King on the night Michael Jackson died, there wasn't enough space for the bodies to do anything except dance with the dance partner claustrophobia chose for them, and sometimes that was the wall, and sometimes you couldn't lift your arm to wipe your sweat, and so sometimes you just shook your sweat off onto whoever was in front of you or behind you, and that person didn't mind because I think what Michael meant when he sang "Don't stop 'til you get enough" is that a river must be built out of what the dancing can offer so that we might float once again off grief's island.

I know, I know I have again come to this specific feeling— one that you might know and one that you might have enjoyed at the opening or closing of some summer of unbearable heat. There is something about the way the night air purses its lips and blows a gentle respite over damp skin that does it for me. I want the feeling of walking out of a hot, sweat-drenched dance party and into a cool night bottled and sold. The first few moments of the breeze hitting you, carrying you to a cooler freedom. In Ohio, the humidity has teeth. But once it subsides, the night air is a blessing. In the early hours of the day after Michael Jackson died, my friends and I stumbled out of the basement of Hampton's on King at two-thirty in the morning and dragged ourselves home singing along to the cars and their open windows blaring Michael's old hits. *This is how one should be laid to rest*, I thought. Loud, and with memories of their voice making the sky tremble.

IT TOOK EIGHT full hours and a band of preachers and their many-armed gospels and singers slipping out of their shoes before shaking the church walls down and old friends pacing slow through old memories and Cicely Tyson's hat casting a wide shadow over her eyes while she read a repurposed poem and showed she could still hold a room in her steady palm, Cicely, our forever Godmother, who was helped off the stage by three men so a viewer might do away with the lie of her defying time. It took dancing in the aisles of a church, and men hollering affirming cries—a "Go 'head!" or a "Don't stop now!" when a speaker caught a good groove. It took even the non-preachers becoming preachers—anything spilling from a mouth in service of the moment becoming gospel. It took all of this, but Miss Aretha Franklin finally made it home on a Friday evening, as I watched the service live in a hotel room in Atlanta. Other viewers spent a full workday and then some, glued to their computer monitors or sneaking sips of television glances to see what might come next. I fought back tears when former NBA player Isiah Thomas told stories of how Aretha helped raise him into a better man than he was, and yawned when Clive Davis lovingly droned on about the mechanics of Aretha's singing, and cringed during the sprawling fifty-minute eulogy by pastor Jasper Williams, Jr., that spanned everything from Black-on-Black crime to the ways single mothers were failing to raise their Black sons, spoken while Aretha Franklin—a single mother of four boys—rested right before him.

When all of the preaching had been preached and almost all of the songs had been worn down to echoes and every memory had been rebuilt wide enough for every listener to crawl into, there was Stevie Wonder, Aretha's dear old friend, singing one last tune before she was carried out of the church and on to her final resting place.

In those last, swelling moments of Aretha's homegoing, I thought about what it is to send someone home properly. How even that, when done right, can be a performance on par with a person's living. The Portuguese soccer player Eusébio was given a towering gold casket that was then carried in circles around the Estádio da Luz in Portugal, where he played for years. Michael Jackson's casket was plated with 14-karat gold and lined with velvet for a three-hour ceremony that filled the Staples Center and left a crowd outside waiting. In March 1827, tens of thousands of people marched in the streets of Vienna, bearing torches in the name of Ludwig van Beethoven. As Aretha's body and services were being prepared, John McCain's casket traversed the country he once served, having a funeral service in Arizona and then another in Washington, D.C.

The joke many Black people made on the Internet as Aretha's service dragged into its fifth, and then sixth, and then seventh hour was that we all expected this. As some tuned out and tuned back in only to see the ceremony still going on, as some scanned the preprinted funeral agenda to see that nearly every guest speaker and performer had gone well over their allotted time, there were some who kicked back and said *Of course, of course.*

I suppose we should have expected a long-drawn-out affair, although deep down I think many of us knew that this number of hours was a bit more than even our most extravagant celebrations. At this point in my life, I have attended far more non-Islamic homegoings than Islamic ones, so I'm no longer shocked by how time can tick away in honor of someone's living, how—in the moment—it all feels like the least one can do to honor another. But even the most seasoned of my kinfolk knew Aretha's homegoing was equal parts too much and still somehow not enough. Too long and too full of people with too much to say, but still, it kept her with us. Some of the reverends dozed off and some of the church women's heads leaned all the way back in their pews while their mouths hung open in the eighth hour and some of the people left early and so many of my people clapped their hands together with joy and said, *Look what we can do.*

IN THE LATE summer of 2018, an orca whale named Tahlequah swam around the Pacific Ocean carrying the corpse of her dead calf under her fin. The calf had died a few hours after its birth. Tahlequah was first spotted attempting to push it toward the edge of the Pacific Ocean between the United States and Canada before deciding to just carry the calf with her, which she did for over two weeks. Observers and scientists called it a "tour of grief." The length of mourning was—to that point—unprecedented. It was always a question of letting go. If the whale let her calf go, it would sink to the bottom of the ocean and become a memory.

Once, I had a conversation with a poet who also lost their mother. As we charted out our shared grief, the poet told me something they had learned from another poet. "Well, we have two mothers," they began to tell me. "The one we keep with us in our hearts, and the corpse we can't put down."

There is the putting down of the metaphorical corpse, and then there is the carrying of the physical, but the hesitation to part with both comes from a similar place. A mother who has lost a child carries with her not only the corpse of that child, but the potential for what that life could have been. I mourn both the actual body and the potential for the whole person it held. How much better my time in the world could have been spent with all of the once-living people I've loved, still here.

The drawn-out funeral, or the pictures on the wall, or the remembrances yelled into a night sky are all a part of that carrying. It is all fighting for the same message: holding on to the memory of someone with two hands and saying, *I refuse to let you sink.*

And so yes, I was sad, watching Aretha Franklin's homegoing and knowing it had to sometime end, or knowing I'd have to tear myself away from it, because that meant I would finally have to say goodbye to one part of my grief: the part that held on to Aretha as an earthly being. And perhaps all elaborate, prolonged measures in homegoing are this: an attempt to stretch out a person's time on earth for as long as we can, whether it be driving a casket around a soccer stadium or flying a body across a country or slipping off shoes and drawing out every last note of a song while onlookers flood the aisles of a church and raise a single hand in praise. Even now, far away from the moment, I am clinging to Aretha Franklin's casket and trying to bring it back for just a little bit longer, even though I know it is gone. I am trying to recreate what I know I saw in hopes that the memory echoes and you and I are both transported back to a time when she was still being celebrated by a people who never wanted the celebration to end.

BELOVEDS, I COME to you today in a month when I have buried no one! I come to you having buried no one for a whole year, and this is worthy of celebration, too! I come to you with stained knees from that old and familiar dirt again, but this time the stains are from a fall I took after wrapping my arms around a loved pal I had not seen in a good while, and upon our embrace, were both carried to the ground by our happiness, and then decided to stay there for a bit and stare upward. I come to you stained with the remnants of happiness in a bad year, and a bad year it has been! A year when no one I love is buried still can be a bad year, but in it, I came to want to celebrate the smallest corners of my love for the people I do have love for. I got another year older and therefore one year closer to kissing the edges of whatever my end might be, and yet I am still here. Hopefully for another season. I have fallen so in love with the leaves, who do the duty of making their death beautiful, bursting from otherwise unremarkable branches before the cold browns them and grinds them to dust. May the performance of each funeral be like the leaves on the trees outside my apartment this late November. The leaves that were first a kaleidoscope of colors and then simply a fading but satisfying orange. The leaves that held on while all of the trees around them became barren. The leaves that, as I write this in mid-December, are just now giving in to the cold and wind and slowly making their tumble down to earth. After all of this time, I can hold them. I can whisper into their vines. *You did all right for yourselves.*

An Epilogue for Aretha

BECAUSE I STILL couldn't let Aretha go, I walked to a movie theater in Pasadena in the spring of 2019. Of course, I knew she was gone and believed she was gone, but there was an opportunity to see her young, and living, and so I took it. The documentary *Amazing Grace* hadn't yet been released widely, only in scattered theaters along the coasts, and I happened to be near one on a Sunday, and so I took myself to get saved.

In an interview as part of HBO's 2008 documentary series *The Black List*, the playwright Suzan-Lori Parks used some of her time to talk about Black people and our tendency to be active participants in our entertainment, regardless of the venue. She recalled how, when her 2001 Pulitzer Prize–winning play *Topdog/Underdog* first hit Broadway, Black audiences showed up late and didn't turn their phones off. They wore baggy jeans to Broadway and shouted at the action unfolding on the stage. Recalling the zeal of these crowds, Parks insisted that we need to celebrate and encourage such moments, and to treat them with as much reverence as whatever is prompting them from the stage or screen.

I like this idea—that it's noble for Black people to react viscerally to work that is created for us, and to respond in a language we know well. There is something valuable about wanting the small world around you to know how richly you are being moved, so that maybe some total stranger might

encounter your stomp, your clap, your shout, and find themselves moved in return.

Aretha Franklin did not want the footage of her *Amazing
Grace* live recording to be released. It's worth mentioning this
because the film that documented the recording process
glosses over it during the opening, with a small mention of
how "the footage was shelved"—which is true, but doesn't
tell the entire story of why the movie was never released until
2019, a year after Franklin's passing.

In January 1972, Aretha went to Los Angeles to record an
album of gospel music over the course of two nights at the
New Temple Missionary Baptist Church, accompanied by her
old friend the Reverend James Cleveland and the Southern
California Community Choir. The recording of the album
was filmed by Warner Bros. and was slated for release around
the same time as the audio recording, to be screened as a double bill with the film *Super Fly*.

The first problem was that the film's director, Sydney Pol-
lack, didn't use a clapperboard before each take while recording. The process was unpredictable and free-flowing,
sometimes improvisational. And so there was no seamless
place to start and restart takes. As a result, the sound and picture were not synchronized, and because there was no easy
way to restore it at the time, the film sat in a vault until 2008,
when it was turned over to producer Alan Elliott.

It took Elliott two years to synchronize the film, and he
had designs to release it in 2011, but Aretha, by that point in
her late sixties, did not want the film released unless she was
guaranteed proper compensation. When Elliott attempted to
screen the film at festivals, she sued repeatedly. (Aretha
wanted a large share of the profits that the film was slated to
gain, and that seems fair: she was the basis for whatever suc-

cess the film might have and therefore had a legitimate stake in trying to control how it appeared and got distributed.) After a final lawsuit in 2016 kept the film shelved, Aretha said: "Justice, respect, and what is right prevailed, and one's right to own their own self-image."

After Aretha died in 2018, Elliott was summoned to Detroit by a friend of Aretha's surviving family members. He was asked to show her family the film, which none of them had ever seen. And just like that, the clouds that had obscured this magic for forty-six years slowly began to break.

Amazing Grace is a singular album, even without film footage to bring it to life. It's not just an excellent collection of songs, it's an album that Aretha didn't have to make in the first place. By 1972, she was established as a star. She'd had a run of massive success, with ten singles in a row landing in the Top Ten of the R&B charts. She'd headlined major venues like the Fillmore West. Still, there was little risk in her decision to make an album showcasing a return to the church. As a child in Detroit, she had first come into her voice at New Bethel Baptist Church, under the guidance of her father, the Reverend C. L. Franklin.

With a voice like Aretha's, the distance between soul music and music of the soul is short, so, at worst, *Amazing Grace* was slated to be an album of great singing that might read as a departure for some of her new fans, and a return for some of her older ones. Yet it became, and remains, Aretha's bestselling album of all time—and the bestselling live gospel album of all time. It won Aretha a Grammy in 1973. With the album's phenomenal success in mind, I think about the small but important distance between gospel as popular music and gospel as a vehicle for salvation: how it is possible to take in the music without much concern for salvation, but still be carried off to a place that feels holy.

The songs on *Amazing Grace* are traditional gospel songs. Some are reworked or reimagined, but they're not like many of the contemporary gospel songs you can hear on the radio today, in which the lyrical gestures toward the beloved could be of a spiritual nature, or else something more earthly and carnal. Aretha sings "What a Friend We Have in Jesus" and "Mary Don't You Weep" and "Amazing Grace," and her renditions of these songs are not about extracting the divine for the sake of vague romanticism, but rather about finding new ways to get the divine into the bodies of each listener, even the ones who might not have been expecting it. This is Aretha, at the height of her game, coming back to see if she could still match the swelling voices of a choir; to see if the words of a hymn could still move her to tears midsong. It is good for a person to be remembered for the songs they choose to sing when they could've sung anything else.

Still, as spectacular as the album is, it must also be said that you do need to see the film, all two hours of it, start to finish. It proceeds with an emotional momentum that makes it feel much shorter than it is. There are too many delicious moments, even outside the songs. Oh, the entrances. On night one, Reverend Cleveland summons in the Southern California Community Choir, and from the church entrance a row of glistening silver vests sways down the aisles. On night two of the recording, Aretha shows up to the church in a glorious sprawl of a fur coat, and the beams of light from above trip over themselves in an attempt to light her path to the stage. On that same night, Mick Jagger, tucked away in the back during one song, stands up and realizes that he has no choice but to clap along, anxiety leaping to his face as he recognizes he might not be on beat. Choir director Alexander Hamilton, through precise wizardry, pushes the choir to an exuberant, emotional tipping point before knowing just when to fall back. Throughout, you are transfixed by Aretha herself, wearing an immovable and immaculate afro like a crown, that tricky and generous light once again dancing on each hair like a concerned parent, keeping it in place.

Aretha doesn't speak much during the film. Most of what the viewer hears from her is that unmistakable singing voice, which now, I will say, feels to me like an arrow to the heart. Even after a lifetime of hearing the voice of Aretha Franklin, to hear it again is to hear it anew. There's a bright spark of joyful pain to see it coming directly from her body, which is no longer tethered to this fragile and faulty earth. Aretha was one of those singers who sang with her whole face. Her face was generally stoic (and maybe a bit nervous) during the parts where she had to hold back, and when she sang, her cheekbones rose into small mountains that the corners of her mouth attempted to scale but never quite succeeded. If the film had no sound, perhaps, in such moments, it might appear as though she were in the throes of laughter with an old friend.

This is a theme of Aretha's performances on film, in which a viewer can see the mechanics behind her natural ability to draw out a song. The church setting furthers this instinct of hers. It's the improvisational nature of the spirit: If the voice calling the words out is good enough, any words will do. A song can go on forever.

And some of them feel like they might. The title track, for example, unfurls for nearly eleven minutes, breaking into a sort of spiritual chaos in the middle that carries until the end. The choir members themselves lose all composure and break out into fits, jumping up and down and throwing their hands into the air. At one point, Reverend Cleveland takes a moment to sit down and put his face in his hands, overwhelmed by the impossibility of it all. "Amazing Grace" has been sung

and heard in countless renditions, but never like this. The entire last minute and a half of the song is Aretha doing Aretha,
finding a new note to carry into another, even more powerful
note, while the audience shouts—half at her to keep going,
and half at the Lord to keep pushing her forward.

Toward the end of the second night, Aretha's father, the
Reverend C. L. Franklin, delivers a few words. He recalls
someone telling him they'd seen Aretha on television, and
that they'd be glad when she came back to the church. At this
point, he pauses for a moment, steps back from the mic, and
smirks. "And I told them, listen baby . . ."And, with that, the
audience spills over again with cheers and shouts, because
they already know what is coming next. It was the declara-
tion of what the night had proven, of what they'd already
understood: Aretha had never left the church. She'd been
singing with the spirit the whole time. The camera bounces
again to Aretha, who has maintained a quiet focus onstage
while her father praised her. She lets out a little half-smile.

The final song of the film is "Never Grow Old," which
takes nearly ten glorious minutes to get through. At the very
beginning of the song, C. L. Franklin rises from his seat to
gently wipe the sweat that has gathered around Aretha's forehead and eyes, while she remains singing, not missing a beat.
Later, Aretha's idol, Clara Ward, will scrunch up her face and
roll her eyes back in ecstasy at one of Aretha's impossible
high notes, a gesture many of us know to mean you better go
ahead—a reverent disbelief when all other emotions fail.
Then there's what some may think is the end of the song, but
real ones know is just the middle, when audience members—
who, by this point, might as well be choir members—begin
flooding the aisles and holding on to the edge of the piano to
keep from passing out. As great as the entire film is, it all
comes down to these ten minutes. Everything it had been lift-

ing a viewer toward is here: the complete and joyous unraveling of a room brought closer to something holy, and Aretha in the middle, doing her best to draw it out for as long as she can.

Some concert films focus solely on the stage and nothing else; take *The Last Waltz,* during which a person watching could at times forget that an audience is even in the building. Others, like Jay-Z's *Fade to Black,* offer large, sweeping shots of the crowd and the stage in almost equal measure. What is fascinating about the filming of *Amazing Grace* is that its makers seem to have understood that, in the gospel setting, the audience is a part of the stage. The audience, through its engagement, cannot be separated from the experience, or from the document of that experience. The footage is raw, which means that there are cameramen scurrying around and all kinds of helpers moving in the background. But what that also means is that, in its purest form, there is an audience of Black people in direct conversation with what they are witnessing, uninhibited and unafraid of anyone who might demand that they quiet themselves.

And here I say that I surely wept though I did not know when my weeping began. It may have been in those early moments, Aretha walking briskly down the church aisle. It may have been in the middle, during the behind-the-scenes footage, when Aretha and the choir stumble and stumble until their stumbling becomes a synchronized sprint. It could have been during the footage of the second night, watching C. L. Franklin sit in the front row watching his daughter, nervous and fixated. I just know that at some point, I touched my face, and there were tears. In the small theater, through what light the screen blessed the room with, I saw white tissues and handkerchiefs dabbing the Black faces in the audience as the film came to a close. And I realized then that this was yet another funeral. I was reminded, once again, that our grief decides when it is done with us.

And I saw this film in a room with people who were truly there to worship—some folks who gathered outside the theater on a Sunday in outfits that looked like they were either coming from church or going there after or maybe counting this as their holy excursion for the day: wide hats and striped suits and shoes shiny enough to see my reflection in. When people on the screen in front of us caught something resembling the spirit, these people expressed their own version of it too: laughing loudly at all of Reverend Cleveland's jokes and throwing their hands up in praise when Aretha bent yet another single-syllable word into several seconds of beautiful sound. Upon leaving the theater, we all stood and exhaled a bit before parting ways without speaking, because what could we say to each other anyway? What could we speak out loud that, between us, wasn't already known?

Movement II

SUSPENDING

DISBELIEF

On Times I Have Forced Myself to Dance

NO ONE WANTS to be the kinda Black person that white people drag out when they get caught up in some shit & gotta carve out that wide escape route of having a Black friend & I must say here that it is odd to keep seeing that parade march down the same old American streets & it can be argued that it never worked & it works even less now, when all manner of Black folk peep the game & maybe have been unwillingly subbed into the game & all of this is to say that I sometimes think about the white people from the time I spent at my almost white college & how I could tell which ones had never been around any Black people before by how they tried to imitate what they thought was cool & it is funny how easily the fake can jump out once you've seen the real & I mean the slang too & the swagger too & the way one nods their head to music & I'm talking about all of it & how I sat mostly silent in the back corner of dorm parties & watched it all unfold silently with the small handful of other Blacks exiled to this liberal arts island where we decided that we were certainly not going to be responsible for teaching these white people how to dance or sing or clap on beat & still me & my crew went to the parties on the nights we didn't want to sit in our rooms & play rap music loud & rap along with the word *nigga* without also scanning the room & seeing who else was or wasn't saying the word *nigga* & my roommate was this white kid from a side of town where there were Black people who kept his ass real

close because his pops was a lawyer & had gotten some folks
outta some real shit & it is funny, I guess, how the interactions
become transactional between those we decide are our people
and those we decide are not & my roommate would sometimes
walk through campus with the Black kids & sit at the cafeteria
table where all of the Black kids sat & would sometimes skip
out on the house parties to wander around campus alone in the
darkness & I think now that there is probably a difference between wanting to be Black and wanting to be down & I imagine this is a difference that echoes especially if you come from
a place where you were already down & then thrown into a
place where you look like everyone else who is decidedly not
down & I am not talking about sympathy for the single outsider here but rather sympathy for not knowing the singular
joy of understanding that you are already down among a
group of people who think they're down but are not at all &
maybe the truest Black superpower is the ability to see through
the bullshit & I have kept myself alive & relatively happy by
peeping game from generations away & one night at the end
of fall, I went to one of those corny ass parties with my roommate & we took over the stereo & we played some shit that
would get a party started in our respective corners of the world
& when the white kids in their Hollister & Abercrombie shirts
saw us with our hands up in the middle of the house, they
stopped the music & pointed at my roommate & asked all of
the questions someone asks when they think a person who
looks like them is behaving out of pocket & I maybe should
have jumped to the defense of this kid I knew & had grown to
love & had seen longing for some small connection within this
limbo & instead I shrunk back into a corner & while I didn't
laugh I was still silent & that silence itself rattled the walls &
in the spring my roommate went back to his old neighborhood
for a weekend & never came back.

This One Goes Out to
All the Magical Negroes

TO UNCLE REMUS in *Song of the South*, the magical negro from whom all other magical negroes were sprouted. The rib from which each magical negro was built. The magical negro who was actually magic & solved little Johnny's problems with folktales & at least James Baskett got some honorary Academy Award in '46 for playing Uncle Remus & he was the first Black male actor to get a gold statue & I guess that's some kinda magic too & in the mid-'60s, Bobby Driscoll—who played little Johnny—couldn't find any more acting work & took to the drugs & the drink & died on a cot in an abandoned building in the East Village surrounded by religious pamphlets but not before he told a reporter, *I have not found that memories are very useful.*

But back to the magical negroes.

This one goes out to my man Robert Guillaume, who was magic as a cartoon in *The Lion King* & lifted that baby lion over a cliff & made the stars take the shape of home after that coward Simba ran away from home to go eat bugs with a couple miscreants while his mom & relatives were under the rule of cackling & foolish hyenas who, as it turns out, were voiced by some negroes but still not magic. This one goes out to my man Robert Guillaume again, who was not a cartoon on the ill-fated Sorkin concoction *Sports Night* but was solving all of the problems nonetheless & he had a stroke during the filming & the entire show just couldn't carry on without him &

the production was falling apart & so he came back with his slurred speech & his cane & his weary eyes, staring into the expanse of white despair. Shoutout to Whoopi in that *Ghost* movie & Carl Weathers who was decidedly not magic enough to avoid getting beaten to death by Ivan Drago but who was magic enough to teach a hockey player how to play golf before dying onscreen & becoming a spirit guide of sorts.

This one goes out to all of the magical negroes who helped their wayward white pals find love in the vicious underbellies of romantic comedies. To Dave Chappelle, who helped Tom Hanks catfish Meg Ryan through both capitalism and America Online. To Will Smith in *Hitch*, who did the very common service of teaching his white friend to dance so that he might score a date with a model. To Daryl Mitchell, who was the woke teacher at the mostly white school in *10 Things I Hate About You* and then was the wisecracking and all-knowing Black person in the otherwise white small town in *Ed*. This one goes out to Gabrielle Union in 1999! To Bubba in *Forrest Gump*, who revealed his love of shrimp to Forrest during the war & talked about how he wanted a shrimping boat & then died so that Forrest could come back home & start a shrimp company & there is a Bubba Gump Shrimp Company in *real life* & it was started by some guy named Tim & Bubba is maybe the most magical of them all for what he allowed the world to receive. Shoutout to the magical negroes who were also God or who could have been God-like. Shoutout to Eddie Murphy & Morgan Freeman & kind of Laurence Fishburne too but not Laurence from '91 when he went by Larry & was in *Boyz n the Hood* talking that real shit. This one goes out to all the Black people in *O Brother, Where Art Thou?* & Djimon Hounsou & Magic Johnson I guess & Stacey Dash both now and then but never to Stacey Dash running for her small and brilliant sliver of bright freedom in that Kanye West music video & this one goes out to Michael Clarke Duncan, may God rest his soul & may God also be Black and in heaven solving the insurmountable problems of the dead who should be at peace but almost certainly will not be.

This one goes out to my boy Trey, who could have gone to the public school on the eastside but his parents wanted him to get a *good* education & so they sent him to the mostly white Catholic school around the block & he was a star on the basketball team & the football team & he wore a shirt & tie to his classes & had the cool sneakers & stopped hanging out with us all that much once he could get invited to parties in the suburbs & answer all of the questions about why the hood is the hood & why he wasn't like everyone else who looked like him & some would say we've all got a little magic inside & it just takes the wrong mix of people and imagination to bring it out & this one goes out to both the magic performance itself & the audience, waiting with held breath & not realizing they're in on the ground floor of the trick.

IN 2006, THE movie *The Prestige* was released, based on a 1995 novel of the same name by Christopher Priest. In both the book and the novel, the magic trick is deconstructed into three parts: The Pledge, you are shown an object that appears ordinary—a deck of cards, a bird, the body of a living person. You, perhaps craving the feeling of being fooled, might haphazardly inspect the object to see whether it is unaltered, ignoring the signs suggesting that it is. Next, The Turn, the ordinary object becomes or does the extraordinary, right before your eyes. The deck of cards dissolves into shreds, or the bird calmly vanishes into the folds of a scarf, or the body becomes a doorway through which you can enter and find yourself absolved upon exiting. Finally, The Prestige, simply, the moment where the extraordinary something returns to its ordinary state, but slightly altered. From underneath a palm, the cards reform into a tumbling parade of bright red hearts, the black card you picked resting right in the middle. The bird explodes from within the unfolded scarf, but this time the bird is a cardinal, or a dove, or something more fluorescent than the death-dark feathers of the crow. The body, of course, appears somewhere different than it once was. Somewhere it can be briefly useful again for the sake of an audience's awe, then forgotten until it can perform the next trick.

There is the version of this in which I vanish before the eyes of classmates and teammates and old friends, only to reappear somewhere else and perform the same act over again. The college I went to rested at the center of a suburb. The suburb was encased by two Black neighborhoods, which were largely neglected by the suburb itself. Almost all of my college classmates were white. Those of us who were Black were mostly there to play sports and pass knowing looks to each other in the cafeteria line or shuffling from one class to the next. Some of us bonded, of course. But it was a bond formed through a need for survival. A bond like that isn't always substantial enough to transform into something extraordinary beyond the boundaries of wherever surviving takes place. Many of the white students stuck to the campus and the few-block radius of calm that the suburb afforded them. The suburban residents and my college classmates would lament taking the short trip down the street to the Kroger, because the Kroger was, decidedly, a part of the more undesirable neighborhood—a neighborhood I knew well, and grew up a part of. No one around me on the school's soccer team acknowledged this when, after practice, they would groan about having to go to the ghetto grocery store down the street. I was there during the practice, I was there with the ball on my foot, or when someone needed tape to secure their ankles. But then, just like that, it would be as if the wind kissed me into translucence.

Spring '03 was the season of the Diplomats spilling out of open dorm windows and pouring into the hallways during morning showers. America was going to war again, and Cam'ron, Juelz Santana, Jim Jones, and Freekey Zekey adorned themselves in the aesthetics of empire, accessorizing with American flag bandanas haloing their heads or dripping out of the back pockets of their descending denim. Their logo, an eagle with its wings sprawled the same way the eagle wings sprawl on the Great Seal of America. The cover of their 2003 debut album, *Diplomatic Immunity,* showed their faces against a red and white backdrop, inside a circle of stars. Few things beyond their choice of visual presentation suggested the group had any strong relationship with patriotism. If anything, in 2003, they made music that was distinctly antagonistic toward the country. The album itself was littered with pushback against the post-9/11 American Narrative. On the song "Ground Zero," the group declared that they made "9/11 music." The member of the group who seemed most interested in toeing the line between the American Aesthetic and the Antagonizing of the Country was Juelz Santana. Who, on "Gangsta," rapped both "I'm the realest thing poppin' / since Osama bin Laden" and "I ain't mad that the towers fell / I'm mad the coke price went up / and this crack won't sell."

There was one Santana line that was adjusted before the album was released. On the album version of the song "I Love You," listeners hear Santana rap solemnly about broken pieces of towers being the graves of many. But in the original version of the song, the line he rapped was in praise of

Mohammed Atta, one of the 9/11 hijackers, praising him for his courage.

Someone, somewhere, decided this was a bridge too far, and the line was altered and replaced.

None of this mattered in the enclave of wonder and fascination that was the dorm halls and house parties of my college campus. White students pulled American flags around their heads and rapped eagerly along with the lyrics on *Diplomatic Immunity* about how the streets were sometimes war, streets that these people at house parties might be afraid to walk on. Streets that they liked to imagine themselves walking on nonetheless. Ryan from a few suburbs over had a picture of the Diplomats on his wall, and his parents, without listening to their music, thought that it was about time rap music got some real patriots speaking to young people. My classmates wore long, baggy T-shirts to classes in homage to the Diplomats dress code. It was a fascinating transformation that took over at the end of the school year. So many of them, who had made a fantasy of an idyllic America, or who cheered in March when the president declared war, now seeing themselves in a group of rappers who looked the part from afar, and only from afar. No one listened to the songs as much as they loved the refashioning of age-old iconography into something that was newly dangerous for them. Iconography that, for me and some of my Black homies on campus, had been dangerous for years, in its original form. Before it had been made into something extraordinary.

There are moments when I question what I am taking in with my eyes and ears, and if it is vibrating at the same pitch as what everyone else is taking in with their eyes. And then I am reminded of the Vanishing Man. The central tension that threads through the entirety of *The Prestige* is the dueling

magicians attempting to outdo each other in the name of re-
venge, which plays out most viscerally in the goal of perfect-
ing the Vanishing Man trick. On its face, the script of the
trick plays out simply. The Pledge, a body appears. The Turn,
a body vanishes. The Prestige, the body reappears. In seamless execution, however, it is a trick that would be difficult to
pull off even now, let alone in the 1890s, when *The Prestige*
takes place. The trick required too much of the performer,
and too much of the audience's suspension of disbelief. In the
story, the magician Robert Angier tried to create a lookalike
out of a stranger on the street, so that when he vanished underneath the stage, the lookalike would appear, smoothly. The
problem was both that the lookalike was an unreliable drunk,
and also that Angier craved the audience's applause—the
look on their faces when the unexpected leapt out.

The solution for this was Angier enlisting the help of
Nikola Tesla (who, in the film, is played by David Bowie).
Tesla creates a machine that duplicates anything placed inside it, including a person. The trick of the machine is that it
would clone and recreate a person, just a short distance away.
What this also meant was that in order to effectively pull this
trick off, Angier would have to become a new person each
night, while the more original version of himself met a quick
demise. The newly cloned Angier would appear on a balcony,
arms open to drink in the approval of an audience, while his
slightly older original drowned in a tank beneath the stage.

Magic tricks all have extremes, but there is so often some
movement of the trick that requires sacrifice. A field of dead
crows; a trashcan full of playing card fragments. Or the com-
mitment to killing off your whole self so that another version
of you can live for an audience's approval. Until people don't
think of the physics of it all. Until the people who have been

aching for a vision see only that vision and nothing else. You know that trick. I'm sure you've seen it a hundred times.

SINCE WE ARE talking about vanishing men and the 2000s, this one goes out to Dave Chappelle once again. Who, after he worked his magic in *You've Got Mail* but before he worked his magic in *A Star Is Born,* found out that in his particular line of work, the laughter of white people was both currency and conflict. A long and loudly echoing purgatory with no exit. *Chappelle's Show* had a brief but singularly brilliant twenty-eight-episode run between January 2003 and July 2006, though that final July season was partial—only three episodes aired, after countless delays and the news that Chappelle was stepping away from the show and the tens of millions of dollars Comedy Central was offering him to continue it.

There was always the sense, for some, that the white people who found themselves so enamored with the show didn't exactly know which parts of it were carrying them to the furthest limits of their laughter. So much of the show's energy was driven by Chappelle's mindset at that time, which was using the sketch and the screen as a type of cultural funhouse mirror, stretching out ideas both of Blackness and of how whiteness impacts Blackness. This wasn't all the show was, of course. But at its heart, it seemed to have a desire to lead people to a less flattering reflection of themselves, for the sake of something in between absurdity and introspection.

It took white people loving *Chappelle's Show* for it to become worth as much as it was to a network, but it took white people laughing too loud and too long—and laughing from the wrong place—to build the show a coffin. Quoting the jokes during parties, or dressing up like the characters during Halloween. I'm not sure what it takes to refuse to understand oneself as a target. There was the "Niggar Family" skit, for example. On the surface, the joke is that this white family in the 1950s has the last name Niggar, which invites their ability to look at a picture of a relative's baby and say things like "She's got those Niggar lips."

The real joke, though, is in Chappelle's milkman, who is introduced by the father of the family as their "colored milkman." The joke, too, comes somewhere late in the skit, when Chappelle's character and his Black wife run into the kids from the Niggar family at a fancy restaurant. The white host calls out, "Niggar, party of two," and Chappelle and his wife go to the podium, with Chappelle exclaiming that they didn't come out that night to be disrespected before realizing that the host was calling for the two white children from the Niggar family. Chappelle remarks, "I bet you'll get a finer table than any nigga's ever gotten in this restaurant before," and he and his wife throw their heads back in exaggerated, pained laughter while the three white people in the scene gleefully laugh along. The joke plays out in black-and-white onscreen as it did in homes across America in real, live color—in the bedrooms, basements, and living rooms of people gathered around their televisions. The joke, always, is in the nuances of pronunciation and what a single letter can allow. When white people talk about a desire to mimic—to say "nigga" with no repercussions—it is, of course, about power. But it is also about access. About the thrill of getting away with something. This particular part of the show understood that, even if the white people watching it didn't. With the laughter in the skit dying down, Chappelle's character exclaims, *Oh, Lord. This racism is killing me inside.*

But it was the Black Pixie skit that was Chappelle's personal undoing. The skit, in retrospect, aligns pretty clearly with every other movement of the show's goals. The setup is simple, then accelerates by its brash fearlessness. The scene opens with Chappelle seated on a plane, where he's soon approached by a flight attendant asking which meal he'd prefer: fish, or chicken. When the word "chicken" leaps out of the attendant's mouth, a smaller, pixie-like Chappelle materializes on top of the airplane seat. Black Pixie Chappelle is in blackface, adorned in a bellhop outfit and twirling a cane. "Chicken!" he exclaims. "I just heard the magic word! Go on and order you a big bucket, nigga, and take a bite! Black motherfucker!"

The whole conceit plays on the furthest extremes of stereotypes, and how they can haunt how Black people move in mixed company. Chappelle wrestles with the choice between fish and chicken, while the pixie urges him to indulge himself in what he truly desires. When he orders the fish, only to find out that the dining cart is out of fish, he nervously asks how the chicken is prepared. It's fried, he's told, and Black Pixie Chappelle conjures an olden banjo tune and dances in celebration. This is one of those Chappelle skits that almost certainly was made for him and his Black friends to laugh at. It skirts the line between comedy and discomfort, and doesn't do it as well as many of the other skits in the show's oeuvre. Most of the joke rests on the absurdity of the blackface pixie shouting encouragements at Chappelle laced with phrases like "you big-lipped motherfucker." The actual expression of Chappelle's hesitation and discomfort isn't acted out in a palpable enough fashion to force the narrative beneath the joke to land. All that's left is a shouting, smaller version of him, painted blacker than he already is. But, of course, whether or not Chappelle himself executed the performance well was, by then, beyond the point. The people who knew they could sometimes painfully laugh along with him and the people who knew they could laugh at him were already two clearly defined lines.

In 2005, Chappelle told *Time* magazine that while taping the skit, he noticed a white man on set laughing louder and longer than everyone else. That was his signal—the clear sign that told him he needed to take a break. He went to make Hajj. He spent time in South Africa. When he returned, he slouched into a chair on *Inside the Actors Studio* and lit a cigarette, and the crowd cheered. He rambled with the clarity and intensity of someone who went away, became a myth, and then returned. "People were here calling me a crackhead in the country I'm from," he said, leaning forward with the ashes dancing off the cigarette pressed between his fingers. "But in South Africa, people were feeding me. Making sure I had a place to sleep. Taking me to the mall. It made me feel good. It made me feel like a normal person."

Depending on who you are, when your Black friend goes to Africa, you don't ask what part. You maybe just wave them off, talk about the continent as if it is a city. Chappelle got to be everyone's Black friend for a while. The one that stays at a comfortable enough distance but still provides a service. There is a reason the idea of white people bringing up a Black friend when faced with accountability for some small or large racism doesn't resonate. It's because the Black friend exists only to give permission, and then absolution. Not that this would offer absolution, but it is never about the framing of a relationship's interior, or gratitude for having loved and being loved by, paired with grief for whatever trust has been portrayed. It is just the naming of someone who has breezed through a life in some past or current moment.

Chappelle was unique because even through what appeared to be a deep love for his people, he still fulfilled this particular fantasy of permission granting. It is something that rests beyond my control. I say I love my people and I mean there is a language that is only ours, and within that language there is shelter. But when I speak that language into the world, I know how eager the world might be to bend it to its own desires.

In 2017, I was reminded of Chappelle, and the laughter of white people, and all of the jokes about niggers. Halfway through *Three Billboards Outside Ebbing, Missouri*, there is a joke, really just a gag on the model of Abbott and Costello's "Who's on First?" Frances McDormand plays Mildred Hayes, a grieving mother who looks to town authorities for answers about her daughter's unsolved rape and murder. Sam Rockwell plays police officer Jason Dixon, a character presented as somewhat oafish at first. The first thing we learn about Dixon is that he was responsible for the torture of one (or more) of the town's Black residents while questioning them. No details are given, and the viewing audience doesn't actually see the torture, but the understanding is that Dixon has tortured Black people and still kept his job as a police officer. The gag goes like this: In the midst of being questioned by Dixon, Hayes shoots out, "How's the nigger torturing business, Dixon?" Dixon, flustered, offers a response along the lines of "You can't say nigger torturing no more, you gotta say people of color torturing." They go back and forth like this, Dixon becoming more and more flustered as Hayes eggs him on, before Woody Harrelson's Sheriff Bill Willoughby enters the room. When Willoughby asks what's going on, an exasperated Dixon exclaims: "Sheriff, she asked me how the nigger torturing business was going, and I said you can't say nigger torturing business anymore, you gotta say people of color torturing."

Willoughby excuses Dixon, only slightly annoyed. When Dixon leaves, Willoughby explains to Hayes that Dixon has a "good heart" and if all police officers with "slightly racist leanings" were removed, there wouldn't be any police officers left.

During the "nigger torturing" scene between Dixon and Hayes, almost everyone in the theater around me laughed. It was, of course, supposed to be comic relief. I don't know how many Black people were in the theater with me, just that the laughter trembled the walls close and pulled the ceiling low until I was in a room all my own. Few reviews of the movie mention this exchange even now, two years after the film's release. I haven't seen any review that asks about the joke's purpose, or who the punchline might be serving. The joke is that the white cop who tortures Black people is trying to stop calling them niggers. Or maybe the joke is that McDormand's character, the righteously angry white protagonist, has a Black friend but still thinks provoking a joke about niggers is funny. Or maybe the joke is that if we got rid of every racist police officer, we'd have no police at all.

I wondered, then, how many people in the theater had Black people they were close to, and how many of them might spend time with them later that day and talk about the movie we were all witnessing. And I wondered how many might omit that part in their description of it, because to voice how they reveled in the moment is an implication that wouldn't play as well with the lights of the theater up. I wondered how many of them were the type of people who asked their Black friends questions about the minutiae of everyday Blackness— what is good to say or not say, to listen to or not listen to. Questions, I imagine, that rarely get volleyed back in return, as to know whiteness is an infinite task.

Dave Chappelle is back now. He's doing stand-up again, which he always insisted was his best medium. His jokes are sometimes as layered, nuanced, and sharp as they used to be, but he often struggles with weaving in effective subject matter. He drifts into punching down, targeting queer and trans folks, or victims of sexual violence. His comedic style remains committed to walking the thin line between brash, extreme presentation and a palpable underlying message, but the line too often blurs itself and he, like other comedians of his era, gets caught up in being a victim of the times and their demand for evolution around gender, language, sensitivity. Chappelle himself hasn't changed all that much, but the era has. The people who craved permission from him haven't changed either, it's just that the permissions themselves have shifted. The same people who missed the message in his old jokes and laughed because it was funny to hear white people saying "Niggar" are the people who now, like Chappelle, feel as though they are being censored from expressing the truest version of themselves. In doing what he imagines as flying in the face of critics, Chappelle is once again confirming those who wish to be confirmed. Showing people that someone can say whatever they want, however they want, privileges and all be damned.

There are many ways to vanish, and there are many ways to reappear somewhere else.

THIS ONE GOES out to the magic trick I love most. This one goes out to the magic trick for our folks, so this one goes out to Ellen Armstrong.

In 1920, before Black Girl Magic was an idea up for consumption and debate, Ellen Armstrong was a Black girl who did magic tricks in her father's show. John Hartford Armstrong was a rarity—a Black magician who could pull in Black audiences in the early 1900s, performing along the Atlantic Seaboard from Florida to Philadelphia. He was called the King of the Colored Conjurers, a nickname he'd gotten from other Black magicians. Armstrong was known mostly for making things either appear or disappear. Coins would materialize from behind the ears of eager children, doves would burst from beneath a cloth and stretch into the sky while an audience gasped. His magic was not particularly singular for the time, but his audience was eager to see something that appeared to be impossible. Not just as some escape from their lives, but, I imagine, also to see someone Black performing miracles. John Armstrong didn't have to sell the show, or necessarily convince the crowd. He just needed to give them something exciting to look at for a little while until they went back to their lives. For this he was lauded. His show packed Black churches, where he would court audiences who had already placed their faith in the unseen.

About a decade in, John Armstrong's act became a family affair when six-year-old Ellen joined her father's show as his assistant. She added some of the showmanship that he lacked, and as time went on, she got her own segment. She would parade around the audience, insisting upon reading the minds of the people there. The gag was that she would touch someone on the head and then say what they were thinking about the person next to them. The audience member would stammer, embarrassed, and the room would erupt in laughter.

By the time Ellen was a teenager, she took on a larger role in the show, doing a routine called Chalk Talk, which involved her telling stories solely by drawing characters on a chalkboard. The trick this time was that the chalk was magic. And so, with only a few strokes here and there, each picture would completely change, adding to the story, or shifting it entirely.

John Hartford Armstrong died unexpectedly in 1939, when Ellen was twenty-five years old. People assumed his show would stop, because no Black woman had ever toured headlining her own magic show. Ellen could have easily latched on to another magician and kept doing her routines within the little bit of time she'd be afforded, but she already had the tools she needed to pick up her father's show and expand on it. And so, when she made posters for her own show in 1940, she kept her father's old tagline: GOING FINE SINCE 1889. Underneath this line, Ellen appears in a seated portrait, stoic and barely smiling. Wide ruffles of fabric cascade down her shoulders. Her long fingers spread out over a table in front of her. She looks equal parts nervous and determined.

Ellen Armstrong helmed her own show for the next thirty-one years, performing mostly at Black churches and schools up and down the East Coast, largely for all-Black audiences who were still looking for something brief and impossible to turn their eyes toward. She continued her magic chalk trick, and added to her routine things like sand frame illusions, in which she would miraculously produce a photograph from sand. The pictures would often be of Black icons, like the boxer Joe Louis. If she felt in the mood, she'd still bounce into the audience and pretend to read the occasional mind.

She also pulled from her father's tricks, mainly the ones involving coins. She perfected the Miser's Dream, a trick in which the magician makes coins appear seemingly out of thin air, then drops them into a metal bucket. Of all of Ellen's tricks, I think about this one most. Rather, I think about making money appear out of thin air. A trick my Black mother and Black grandmother would say was impossible when I pointed at something I wanted in some store on a week that was not the week of payday, even though that thing I wanted might show up in my room the next day or a few days after. I think about the way a coin sounds when it hits a metal bucket, especially if that coin did not exist mere seconds before. Ellen Armstrong was performing for her people. Black people who worked hard and believed enough in miracles to trust a magician to make some coin appear. The magic of it all. The literal magic, that which exists to give a suspension to belief. That which exists to wash away the knowing of a wretched world and replace it with another. What appears when there was once nothing. What miracles a love for our people bends us toward.

Ellen Armstrong eventually retired to South Carolina, and her show retired with her. She's not often discussed in the history of groundbreaking magicians, but I think about how she chose to take to her work. In the years when Black magicians were getting in front of integrated audiences and doing larger stage shows, she still chose to carry on the mission of her father's show. Her father, who performed to Black audiences because he had to, yet took pride in doing it. Ellen Armstrong kept performing in smaller rooms, to crowds without as much money or social capital. The idea, it seemed, was about offering a sense of wonder to those who may otherwise have been denied it. To make something small spectacular. Magic relies on what a viewer is willing to see, and what a viewer is willing to see relies on what the world has afforded them to be witness to. Ellen Armstrong was performing for some people who had seen both too much and not enough. She made a life out of this. Drawing cartoons of people and telling their secrets and sometimes releasing some white birds into the freedom of a black night swirled with stars.

I AM THINKING, today and always, of invisibility.

I have wanted more than anything for a problem to cower and grow silent in the presence of you, or perhaps a past version of you, my most magically endowed problem solvers. When the summer of my worst depression set in, I wished to drown myself in the shouts and jokes and card games of whatever jubilant corners I could find to keep myself alive just a bit longer. I know this isn't the same as an industry or an institution or a film trope or a white author looking to be absolved or shown some light by the brief appearance of a wise old Black person who fixes them and goes about their way. But I am simply saying I know of that desire to be solved and absolved. I know that in the moment, it might not feel as if you've fashioned a tool out of someone breathing and living a whole life outside your reckless agony.

According to the rules of the Prestige, the magic trick doesn't work if that which was vanished never reappears. If in place of the vanishing is more vanishing. I tell my friend that I'm done writing poems about Black people being killed and he asks if I think that will stop them from dying. At a suburban farmer's market, the white fruit vendor looks past a Black woman in line and asks the white guest behind her what she's interested in. I pass a storefront on the walk back to my car and the store is selling T-shirts with BLACK GIRL MAGIC flourishing across them, though no one working in the store is Black. If there is some kind of loophole in the rules of magic, it might be this: the one where a person is able to be invisible until they are desired. Where they are an echo of nonexistence until they can fulfill a need, or tell a story, or be a thread in the fabric of someone else's grand design. The flawed magic of desiring a body more than an actual person. The magical negro is so replaceable that there is nothing left of them to mourn.

So, this one goes out to you, most of all. You who might read this or hear this or stumble upon it and hope to find some answer or some absolution within. Shoutout to the things that I hope haunt you beyond whatever you might be searching for. This one goes out to the answers I do not have for you, or for myself, and this one goes out to the sins I cannot crawl myself out of in order to forgive the ones you might be buried under. This one goes out to all of the best stories I have never told. The ones I will hold close until I can pass them down to someone else who might pass them down. I have no real magic to promise any of you. I am praying for the most unspectacular of exits.

Sixteen Ways of Looking at Blackface

1

MAYBE FIRST THROUGH the eyes of Charles Dickens, who took to the road in January 1842 to write a travelogue that turned a critical eye toward North American society. In the book, *American Notes for General Circulation,* Dickens wrote as an observer, reporting the news of wherever he was to the imagined audiences who were anywhere else. He began in Boston, then went as far south as Richmond and as far west as St. Louis. He made his trips mostly by steamboat but would take the occasional trip by rail, or coach. Dickens would then visit prisons and mental institutions to get a grasp on what he felt was an entryway to the human plight, and how that shifted in geographies. He wrote, perhaps a bit too much, about the sanitary conditions of cities, waxing poetic about his affection for Boston, for example, due to the cleanliness of it. Toward the end of the book, Dickens writes about slavery and violence as the two most major flaws in the fabric of American society, insisting that slavery corrupted both whites and Blacks, and that the free states were happily complicit in the system because of their inaction. Due in part to America's comforts with slavery and violence, he stated, there is a universal distrust in anything other than individualism as a pathway to survival in the country. The path to success for the American, he observed, meant to carry a healthy desire to set oneself apart from the ideals of others.

Because Dickens was fairly popular at the time of his undertaking the project, he struggled to find the peace to be able to work on it. He was often mobbed in the streets and followed by fans. It led to his searching out late night performances in bigger cities, in places where he might not be noticed. One example was a visit he made to Almack's, a dance hall in Manhattan's Five Points neighborhood. There he came upon William Henry Lane—then known as Master Juba—who had been performing in minstrel acts since at least 1838 but who had never been documented by anyone before Dickens set eyes on him.

William Henry Lane was born a free Black man in Rhode Island in 1825, and he took to dancing for spare coins as a young teenager in the rough saloons and halls that most young dancers were too afraid to set foot in. One way to make a name for yourself is to conquer the places your rivals are too afraid to touch, especially if those places do not particularly want you around. Lane could play the tambourine and fiddle, and he had the ability to easily mimic all the moves of the best dancers of the time and then improve on them. In the Manhattan section of his *American Notes,* Dickens writes:

> The corpulent black fiddler, and his friend who plays the tambourine, stamp upon the boarding of the small raised orchestra in which they sit, and play a lively measure. Five or six couples come upon the floor, marshalled by a lively young negro, who is the wit of the assembly, and the greatest dancer known. . . .
> . . . Single shuffle, double shuffle, cut and cross-cut; snapping his fingers, rolling his eyes, turning in his knees, presenting the backs of his legs in front, spinning about on his toes and heels like nothing but the

man's fingers on the tambourine; dancing with two left legs, two right legs, two wooden legs, two wire legs, two spring legs—all sorts of legs and no legs— what is this to him? And in what walk of life, or dance of life, does man ever get such stimulating applause as thunders about him, when, having danced his partner off her feet, and himself too, he finishes by leaping gloriously on the bar-counter, and calling for something to drink, with the chuckle of a million of counterfeit Jim Crows, in one inimitable sound!

2

SINCE THE ELECTION, white people have been pretending to be Black on the Internet. To be entirely fair, I suppose there were white people pretending to be Black on the Internet before the election, too, but now people are talking about it. People are talking about it in part because the white people who are pretending to be Black on the Internet are so bad at it. My friend wonders what it says about Black people that we can so easily recognize a slang that is not leaping from the tongues and fingers of one of our own, but I maintain that it's the pictures they use. The obvious stock photos of Black men in suits with bad hairlines, or Black women with one raised eyebrow and with forced smirks affixed to their faces, in the direction of both no one and everyone. Sure, I do also peep the use of dated slang and the belabored nature of the language's haphazard arrangements in the tweet or the photo caption. Anyone who speaks a language inside a language can see when that dialect is presenting a challenge for someone who perhaps had to google the correct word to use and the placement of it. Or when it is coming from someone who watched a movie with a Black person in it once and then never saw a Black person again. It would be humorous or fascinating if it wasn't so suffocating. I would laugh if I was not being smothered by the violence of imagination.

3

I WISH THERE could be a living soul to come here, in this space, and tell of any time Juba wiped the floor with the fool John Diamond, the Irish American clog dancer who wowed the boring white audiences at minstrel shows all through the free states because he combined elements of Irish dance and then stole elements of African dance from street and tavern performers and that other fool, P. T. Barnum, put him in the damn circus. Diamond was known for rapid footwork that required little movement above the waist, and—despite his being seventeen years old—Barnum told audiences that he was twelve, a little white boy with his face painted black, dancing like people had never seen before. And the thing about white minstrelsy is that it was all a lie anyway, so what's one more.

After a short time, Barnum had grown tired of Diamond's attitude and unpredictable behavior off the stage, and so he kicked him off the circus tour and replaced him with a young dancer in either 1840 or 1841—William Henry Lane. This is where Juba was given his stage name, and got his reputation for how easily he could transform the moves of other dancers to complement his own. Diamond's moves were the last to show up in Juba's set, as he would close the show by imitating the clog dancer's steps and then blending them into his own movements.

Diamond, fed up and wanting to cling to a wave of relevance, began challenging dancers to duels. His challenge materials read:

Master Diamond, who delineates the Ethiopian character superior to any other white person, hereby challenges any person in the world to trial of skill at Negro dancing, in all its varieties, for a wager of from $200.00–$1,000.00.

He did, of course, successfully sweep through all of his white rivals, but then there was Juba. Juba, who had mastered the moves of Diamond so well that he outdanced Diamond doing his own shit before Diamond even had the chance to get a turn.

No one has lived long enough to tell the nuances of this moment. How the crowd maybe gasped when the Black dancer dismantled the white dancer with weapons of the white dancer's own making. How, when the world outside determines worth, it might be vital for the marginalized to find an arena in which they can unmistakably dominate. As to be expected, Diamond requested rematch after rematch. Their battles lasted well through the mid-1840s, with Juba waxing Diamond in every challenge—save for one, in Boston's Boylston Gardens. However, in their most famous clash, Juba bested Diamond in New York in 1844, pocketed $500, then had the last laugh when he returned to Boston as "King of All the Dancers." Next was a two-week residency in which Master Juba faced off against another white minstrel dancing contemporary, Frank Diamond (no relation to John).

Juba was there in the right time and place, but I'd like to propose the idea that any old Black dancer worth their salt could've made a fool out of that fool John Diamond. And what it must be like, John Diamond. To have worn the black on your face for so long in front of white audiences that you imagine yourself better at what they called "negro dancing" than the actual people they called "negroes."

4

THERE'S THAT SCENE at the end of *8 Mile* that everyone loves where Eminem's character is in the rap battle to end all rap battles against Papa Doc, his longtime foe. In the scene, Eminem goes first in the battle and ticks off all the predicted insults he believes Papa Doc has stashed, ready to unleash on him. When he's done, he tosses the mic to Papa Doc, who stumbles over a few words before being buried under waves of applause in celebration of watching someone triumph by rendering their opponent immovable.

5

THERE ARE A lot of things white people get wrong about blackface, but the one I think about is the way they slather the makeup on their faces, as if they've never seen a Black person before, usually pitch black and wildly uneven, or smeared haphazardly over the skin, with no attention to detail. I have thought before about how this feels like an additional insult positioned atop the obvious one. How even an attempt to mimic cannot be done with enough care for the skin of the mimicked.

Because I cannot take off my skin, I ask my homies for a skin care routine, and the group chat sprawls with names of products and links to them. I wander a Whole Foods and ask Safia exactly *which* exfoliating loofah glove I should purchase, sending photos of my findings in the group chat. Jayson tells me I can't go wrong with Cetaphil as a base. All I know is that I've had the good fortune of having largely great skin for three decades, with no real work put into it, and I'm looking to see what might be the fullest potential for my skin's immortality. I come from an ageless people, after all. At most Black functions I've been to, someone pulls me aside, points at some alleged elder, and asks me to guess how old this elder is.

When I guess too young, they throw out some age bordering on the absurd, one that seems even more foolish as the sunlight gallops across an absence of wrinkles during a vigorous dance, or a laugh that rattles the wind. I most love the mythology of the ageless Blacks, how it truly doesn't crack unless you give yourself over to do the bidding of some evil. Like we've all been blessed but might have to sell ourselves to the devil, who surely will want his, and in return, the aging process starts and accelerates. Stacey Dash didn't look a day over twenty-five when she was running in slow motion through the Chicago airport, trailed by Kanye West in a music video. But one year working for Fox News, and the people say she's looking every minute of her age, and the decade she kept at arm's length all that time has finally come, and lord, did it come to collect. All I know is I'm gonna be on the wrong side of thirty soon, and I'm trying to keep my skin and my spirit clean.

And so I spend way too much money on way too many products that I've never seen and don't understand. I apply my own facial mask, slathering on the white cream unevenly, too aggressively on my cheeks and forehead, but lightly around my eyes, my hands guided by even more anxiety than usual. From underneath my coated eyelids, I scroll through some social media timeline or another. Black people on the Internet are upset about a party at some school. The theme was "the hood," or some iteration of what white people think the hood is. None of the participants were Black, but most took measures to make themselves Black. Darkness was achieved by what seemed like all measures: shoe polish, makeup, even markers, faces sloppily colored in. The partygoers wore large fake gold chains, and massive white tees swung to their kneecaps. They twisted up their fingers in homage to the gangs of their wildest imaginations. Sunglasses and sneers adorned their white faces, hiding poorly behind the splotches of brown. And what a predicament, me, looking upon this with my face caked in some white substance, which promises to keep my skin young. And boys, younger than I was in that moment, throwing whatever they could on their young skin to make it darker.

Despite its history and its harm and the many echoes of violence it summons, the thing about blackface that most clearly stung arrived in this moment, looking upon this scene of recklessly adorned white skin while taking delicate care to help my own dark skin flourish.

This is what they think we look like.

6

CRITICS AND SCHOLARS struggle with the Dickens paradox: how he seemed very in line with many liberal causes and ideas but still managed to be racist, nationalist, and imperialist in his work. How he had sympathy for the plight of African slaves, for example, but still publicly supported the American South, due to being unconvinced that the North had a genuine interest in the abolition of slavery.

In *Oliver Twist*, the character Fagin is referred to solely by his racial and religious origin over 250 times in the first thirty-eight chapters. Fagin is Jewish, and an archetypical villain, who is wealthy but also hoards his money and keeps children close so they can do his bidding—usually pickpocketing. Fagin, despite his wealth, does not particularly care for or look after the children he dispatches to fulfill his duties. The character, some say, is the most egregious example of the anti-Semitism present in the work and ideas of Dickens.

There are historians who say that Fagin was based on Henry Murphy, a free Black Londoner who was known in the time of Dickens as Henry the Child Stealer. Murphy, like

Fagin, would hold children at a hideout and send waves of them into the streets, forcing them to beg or steal, then return the profits to him. There are historians who say that Henry Murphy was Fagin in real life but that Dickens, out of whatever sympathy he held toward Black people, decided to make the Fagin of *Oliver Twist* a Jewish villain.

And no one knows what to make of this, really. What to do when someone has committed themselves to sympathy, but not to mercy.

7

WHEN I SAY that Black performers used to wear blackface while performing in minstrel shows, I will not give you what you want. I will not give you the metaphor that ties it all to how easy it is to switch one's Black self into all of the things America imagines but doesn't want. I will not talk about crows or blackbirds or feathers or wings. I have no image of a night sky and a row of white teeth. You have had enough metaphors, and I've got a sneaking suspicion that's how we got here in the first place. The "we" being you and I, reader, or the "we" being you and I, America.

When performing in Southern towns in the 1860s and 1870s, all-Black minstrel troupes were forced to stay in character, even offstage, dressed in slave rags and smiling from ear to ear while being shot at by white audiences on their way out of town. But this was the only way for white people to take in what they came to view as real African-inspired dance, and not what had come to be seen as the imitations, done by white dancers. Consume what you can never become, and then kill it before it continues to remind you.

And so none of us deserve the metaphor here, but to say that Black performers used to wear blackface when performing for white audiences, so that nothing but the movements of their feet might be present in the room, everything else too black to be visible.

8

I HAVE HAD the dream where I hold Al Jolson wearing a dark coat of blackface under the water of an old bathtub. I do not know how I arrive in the scene, but I arrive with my hands on his shoulders, pushing him down below the water, which seems endless from my angle. In the dream, he's wearing the brown suit he wears while playing piano in *The Jazz Singer*. That movie was in black-and-white, as is this dream, but I know the suit is brown. I know the suit is brown because I have, in my waking hours, stared at the poster from the film, which is painted in color. I know the suit is brown because on the poster, Jolson's face is not brown. The suit is the only interruption of white on his whole body. In the dream, Jolson does not struggle when I hold his head under the water. His eyes stay open. I scrub at his face with my hands until the scrubbing becomes clawing, trying to remove the layer of caked-on dark skin, to address the man underneath. In the dream, I don't know what I would say to Al Jolson if I could peel the mask from his face, but I keep peeling, and Jolson does not fight, even as I swipe fingers across his eyes. Eyes that, surrounded by the darkness of his makeup, gleam from underneath the water. When I push him down far enough, his face vanishes entirely, or at least I think it does. In a dream, nothing is tangible, even in a dream that arrives and arrives again. Only the smallest details remain: I know the tub is old—it's one of those with massive claws as feet. In the background, a version of "Blue Skies" is probably playing, but in this dream, I have convinced myself that it isn't Jolson's version because it is being sung by a woman. Which means I tell myself it is Ella Fitzgerald. Who, I imagine, would also want me to scrub the black makeup off this white man's face. In the dream, I think I hold Al Jolson down because if I can't detach him from skin that looks like my skin, I at least want his eyes to stop glowing from beneath it. But the further I push his face down into the deepest parts of the water, I am left only to search the water for my own reflection, which looks dark, darker than I've ever been. So dark that it creeps along the water's surface like a shadow's dancing limbs. And then, as I lean closer to the water, I feel Al Jolson's suit snap itself empty, and I am not holding a body anymore, and then I wake up and in the darkness of my real life bedroom, I can't even see my own hands.

9

MOST OF THE Black people knew that woman was white from the moment we heard her, stumbling her way through that interview. Can't say much for what the eyes know. There are many ways to look Black and be Black, so I just can't call it. Some of my skinfolk sure did, though. Some of them—the ones from places that get no sun—insisted that they could tell a bad tan when they saw one. The Black women I know said they knew the whole time because if she *was* Black, no one would let her go out of the house with her hair looking a mess like it did. But hey, she was the president of the NAACP and that CP still stands for Colored People, last I checked! But also, it was the NAACP in Spokane, Washington! I was in Spokane, Washington, once. The Black people were so invisible that everyone else would attempt to walk straight through us. So it's tough to tell, really. But, even given every benefit of the doubt in regards to aesthetics, I knew the woman claiming to

be Black was not Black when the interviewer asked her: Are
you actually African American?

I don't . . . I . . . I don't understand the question.

10

HISTORY IS NOT always kind to ideas around what is or isn't
shameful. As time passes, the societal grasp on what the sins
of the past were become clearer and more set in stone, laid
down as markers of what not to repeat—even as some of
those sins are repeated. Now, it is shameful to imagine that a
Black dancer once painted his face even blacker and danced
for white audiences. But I would like, now, to offer some small
praise for Master Juba, who, in his time, stole the stage from
white men who could only pretend to be from where he was
from and know what he knew. Master Juba who spent half of
a decade embarrassing the same white dancer over and over
again, simply because the white dancer had the nerve to consider himself a descendant of a people who could *truly* move.
Juba was born a free man, but of course being born Black in
the time he was born in meant that even his freedoms weren't
all his. Freedom when contrasted against the option of bond-
age, sure. But not freedom like everyone else's freedom. And
so I get it. The echoes of minstrelsy impacted the landscape
of American entertainment well after Juba and several other
Black minstrels were dead and gone. I can't say they'd change
the course of their lives if they knew how far the reach of
their performances would arc into the future. It ain't up to
them, anyway. Blame the country they danced upon and the
people who could not stop watching. The dancers were simply
the dancers, and they would've danced somewhere, for someone. America made the dancing a weapon. All I'm saying is

that somewhere along the line Juba took what he could back
from the white dancers who claimed some shit they weren't
really about. And even if the tools were shameful, some small
corner of a stolen mythology was dismantled.

11

IT IS BLACK History Month and everyone is deciding now
would be a good time to admit that they, too, once wore blackface in college. At a party. Trying to dress up like a rapper, or
a pop star, or some actor from a sitcom. It was the '80s, after
all. Except when it was the '90s. Except when it was the
2000s. Except when it was last month. Some people on the
Internet know blackface is bad but don't seem to be entirely
sure why. It's just one of those things that white people
shouldn't do. I wonder about the benefits and failures of this:
how far the country has gotten laying down the framework
for societal dos and don'ts while not confronting history. If it
is possible to ground a true behavioral shift without attacking
the root of blackface. The fact that there will always be an
audience wanting a Black face, but not necessarily a Black
person. The problem with approaching history in America is
that too many people measure things by distance and not by
impact. *When I die*, Al Jolson said, *I'll be forgotten.*

Still, I tell myself, at least people get it. Except when they
don't. Someone says they don't see why blackface is such a big
deal. How else can homage be paid, and all that? In response,
another person says

If you're so cool with blackface, why don't you wear it
to your job tomorrow?

Onstage at a press conference with his wife, the politician
who put on blackface to dress as Michael Jackson in the '80s

fields a question about whether or not he can moonwalk. He insists he can, and then turns to his wife, who tells him that now is not an appropriate time to break out the old dance. Despite the absurdity, I find myself wanting to see him do it.

12

THERE ARE NOT many popular drawings of Master Juba, except for three:

1: From the night in Manhattan when Dickens saw him for the first time, there is a drawing of Juba surrounded by white revelers. In the drawing, one can see a portrayal of Dickens in the background, sketched loosely so that it looks as if he is half-smiling. At the center of a circle, the dancer's feet are lifted slightly off the ground. His arms are flung out at his sides, and his head is thrown back, as if he is consumed by song. To his side, a white woman watches. In the sketch, her eyes almost look like they're glowing.

2: In the caricature, Juba is mostly lips. It is hard to see the actual person beyond the lips, with the way they take up the entirety of the photo. But venturing past them, there is a small sliver of a white eye, which stands out only against the overwhelming darkness of the skin. The dancer is in a suit and his feet are once again lifted off the wooden floor, but it is hard to take in the small details of this picture aside from the way the lips protrude well beyond Juba's face and small body. The artist's work was meant to render the performer other-worldly. Dark and disfigured, so that even while performing his most spectacular action, a viewer can imagine that they are watching someone not human.

3: If you go to Master Juba's Wikipedia page, you will see the photo. A straightforward rendering of the dancer not in motion. Juba is in a sports coat and what appears to be a white shirt. A scarf is tied around his neck, and a clean part runs

through the right side of his head. He looks stoic and somewhat overserious. The portrait is not dated, but it is refreshing
to see the human, and not the overexaggerated idea of the
human, or the human an audience saw. It brings a little joy to
imagine that through the lens of another artist, Juba was
whole, worthy of a most honest portrayal.

13

ON THE WAY to her family reunion in Birmingham (that I
am invited to just by virtue of being in town with some free
time) my pal tells me that she notices the way she and her
people dance differently when white people aren't around, or
when they truly don't care if and how white people are watching. She jokes about our other pal, who dated a white man and
had to teach him how to electric slide at one wedding some
summer ago, and we laugh at the image: her standing over
him like she's coaching the final play of a high-stakes game,
laying out the moves herself, while he looked down at his feet
and tried to connect the dots.

There's a difference between not being able to dance and
the ability to fake being able to dance just well enough so that
people won't notice. I participate most heavily in the latter,
which is why the traditional line dances are perfect for me.
The kinds where the entire framework of the song relies on
laying out instructions for what one should do with their feet.
I'm fine on any dance floor, but I love best when a room folds
together in unison. It is almost impossible for anyone with
any semblance of rhythm to make a mistake if they just move
in the direction the room is already carrying them in, and I
suppose that is something like love, or something like trust.

At the family reunion, there is one of these moments.
Aunties and uncles, grandbabies and so on and so on, filling

up a hot backyard after the food and revelry had died down, playing a version of the Cupid Shuffle so extended I was sure it had to be looped. And again, after a few rotations, there is everyone clicked together on beat until it appears there is one single body moving as one.

I watched from afar and did not join in. Even within the comforts of shared Blackness, there are deeper, unshared comforts. Ones that demand witnessing, and not participation. Tell that to the world. There is some movement too golden, too precious to be interrupted.

14

IT IS SAID that Al Jolson truly loved Black people. That he wanted, in many ways, to form a closeness with Black people and every corner of him they influenced: from music, to language, to dance. It is true that he gave Black people places to perform, even if they had to join him onstage while his face was colored darker than any of their faces. At his funeral, Black performers lined up to pay respects. Tap dancers and background singers and jazz composers. It can be said that the very presence of a white person in the world of jazz fostered a type of closeness with Black people and their lives in that era, when dependency and artistic exchange was a more high-stakes game than it is today.

The thing I find myself explaining most vigorously to people these days is that consumption and love are not equal parts of the same machine. To consume is not to love, and ideally love is not rooted solely in consumption.

I have never seen Al Jolson cry while singing the song "Mammy," but Black jazz composer Noble Sissle says there was no sight like it. What Jolson had was the palpable and physical presence of passion. Before being cool was what sold.

Noble Sissle says Al Jolson cried while singing "Mammy" and it was one of the most beautiful things he'd ever seen. A single tear rolling slowly down Jolson's face while he crooned the old lyrics about Black servitude, a woman who leaves her own family to care for another. The tear streaking through Jolson's black makeup and creating a clear border. Who Al Jolson was, and who he was dreaming himself to be.

And while we are here with our hands in the aesthetics, I wish you would talk more about how frightening it all is. By you, I suppose I mean anyone, but let's say I mean you, non-Black reader or scholar of history. I wish we could get down to the bare bones of it all and talk about how blackface, beyond everything else, is such a horrifying look. When done with careful precision, the way it was done in the old days, in the black-and-whites. Black-and-white films interest me most when I think about how darkness is a currency.

It is said that black is not a color but the absence of color. Yet in a film with no color, that absence is how one knows there is potential for a shade. When white performers covered their faces with black paint in black-and-white films, and when they donned thick, nappy black wigs, from behind a screen, all a viewer can witness is the whites of their eyes, and the brightness of their lips, peeling back occasionally and giving way to a blade of white teeth. It is the kind of vision that stuck with me, as a child, watching from a hallway floor and peering into the room of my grandmother, who fell asleep with some classic movie channel network playing. These Black people were unlike any I knew, all standing in a chorus of shadows but for the small bursts of white leaping out from their mouths, or their open eyes. I looked at myself in the mirror with the lights off the next morning, just to see if I'd vanish. I smiled and opened my eyes as wide as I could, and yet I was still there.

15

RIGHT BEFORE THE Ronald Reagan crack era hit full swing, the man had to have an inauguration gala. January 19, 1981, at the Capital Centre right outside D.C. A long list of performers did their best to usher in the new president. Ethel Merman sang some show tunes, Ray Charles swayed like an energetic metronome during his rendition of "America the Beautiful," and so on and so on and so on. The decoration of these moments never changes, only the people in power do.

But then there was Ben Vereen, who was still riding high off his performance as Chicken George in *Roots* just a little over three years earlier. He'd already won a Tony Award by then, and his performance in *Roots* garnered him an Emmy nod. When Vereen was asked to contribute to the inaugural gala, he decided to stage a performance honoring the iconic Black vaudevillian Bert Williams. Bert Williams struck out as a solo act in the early 1900s after spending the latter portion of the prior century paired with fellow Black performer George Walker. As a solo act, Williams blackened his face to get a gig at Ziegfeld's Follies, his face as dark as his tuxedo jacket and top hat. His songs and dances were hits, and his mime routines kept audiences fixated. White writers at the time wrote about how Williams transcended race—how, upon the stage, he was almost detached from his race altogether. After his final Follies appearance in 1919, Williams had a hard time keeping his career going. He collapsed onstage during a performance in Detroit. The audience assumed it was a part of his bit. He was helped to his dressing room, where he smiled and said *That's a nice way to die. They was laughing when I made my last exit.* Williams died five days later.

And there was Ben Vereen in 1981, dressed as Bert Williams in long tails and a top hat, his face painted a dark black, darker even than it was when the sun was beating its palms down on it in *Roots*, when he was foolish and dapper. Vereen's lips were painted white and poked out far beyond his face. He sang "Waiting for the Robert E. Lee," a tune that good ol' Al Jolson shook some life into back in '47. The song is about a steamboat, coming to haul away cotton. But before he launched into the song, the cameras captured his entrance. Vereen shuffling about the stage in blackface, taking wide strides while the audience sits in nervous silence. As he arrives at the microphone, Vereen locates the camera. He pauses, and looks into it, wide-eyed, his face somewhere at the intersection of sadness and horror. After several long and quiet seconds, the camera shoots over to Ronald Reagan, laughing.

After the song and the rapturous audience applause comes the volta: Vereen, still in character as Williams, pretends to have an interaction with an imaginary bartender, offering to buy the mostly white, mostly Republican crowd a drink, as thanks. Then he turns to the audience and makes it clear that he couldn't possibly buy them a drink, of course not. He wanted to, of course, but the bartender wouldn't serve him, what with his skin and all.

To close out the performance, Vereen takes out a makeup mirror and sings Bert Williams's signature song, "Nobody," a song about the isolation that comes from being ignored. Vereen wipes the makeup off his face slowly while singing

I ain't never done nothin' to nobody, no time
So until I get something from somebody, sometime
I'll never do nothin' for nobody, no time

And then, with a towel covered in black paint resting in his hands, the song ends and Vereen's performance is over. The final five minutes are the important part. The makeup mirror and that particular song and the denial of service.

That's where all of the implication is. A demand, once again, to ask a white audience what the fuck is so funny. What, exactly, do they understand themselves to be applauding.

Before he went onstage, Vereen was promised that the whole performance would be shown by the network. It was crucial to the performance that all parts of it be shown. But the gala was televised on ABC and used tape delay. They cut out the back half of Vereen's performance, so that all people saw at home was the first part—Vereen shuffling and singing for a pleased white audience.

While I understand Vereen's aims and effort, I am not exactly in love with the idea of attempting to use blackface as a subversive tool for a white audience for a host of reasons—but most notably because it requires trust that said audience will understand themselves to be on the receiving end of the wound and not being invited to mock the wounded. Bert Williams collapsed to his near-death on a stage and a white audience laughed. Ben Vereen attempted to honor Williams and indict the institutions and structural racism that had plagued his life, and a white audience got their laughs, and then cut the cameras off. If there is nowhere for a joke to land, it floats and floats and then is forgotten.

16

OF COURSE, NO one knows how Juba died. Live a myth, die a myth. The stories are plentiful and layered. Most of them say he died in Europe, but the years and times and places have all become a cluster. Historians scatter his final records in a three-year window. Some say he last performed at the City Tavern in Dublin in September 1851, before he died two weeks later. Others say that he died in 1852 in London. Stories have been told about his skeleton on display in 1852 at the Surrey Music Hall in Sheffield.

But the most widely accepted date, the one supported by the Oxford Dictionary of National Biography, is February 3, 1854. It is said that Juba died in the fever ward of the Brownlow Hill Infirmary in Liverpool. He was buried in the free part of the cemetery attached to St. Martin's Church, which was later bombed during World War II. The cause of his death was unspectacular, most commonly attributed to the way his schedule slowly ate away at his health. He'd performed day and night for almost eleven years straight, sometimes working for scraps of food at taverns and sleeping very little. He was thirty years old.

It is less romantic to hear stories about someone who worked themselves to an early grave. I appreciate the many versions of finality that kind of life can offer, in a time with little to no documentation for a traveling Black dancer. An ending for every version of yourself that people eagerly consumed. Both unlucky, and blessed.

On the Certain and
Uncertain Movement of Limbs

NO ONE KNEW exactly what it was to *talk white* around any of the places I grew up. It was a sound that could be pinpointed, but the goalposts also moved, depending on what side of town you were on, or what school you went to. Many in my crew now might not admit it, but when we were kids— depending on where we grew up—to pin dressing white, or talking white, or acting white on someone who was not white felt like one of the most visceral of insults. Part of this is because the designation could mean any number of things, all of them likely something a Black person didn't want to be on the wrong side of.

It's not like any of my crew knew what code-switching was when we were rolling through our neighborhoods on bikes in the mid-'90s. Our parents knew it, even if they didn't know the language for it. Our parents who worked government jobs, or rang people up at the grocery stores in surrounding suburbs. My father, who would return home after work and sit in our driveway with the windows up on our old van, letting loud jazz fill the car's interior for a few moments before exiting. Like it was a bridge bringing him back to a more familiar self.

But in the small segments of world my crew and I inhabited, there was no need to code-switch or even understand the concept. Most of the neighborhood was Black. Most of our school was Black, and the kids who weren't Black mostly grew up around Black kids. Everyone at the corner store was Black. The cops in our neighborhoods were Black and sometimes one of them knew someone's older brother and might look the other way when a Snickers bar was swiped from the candy aisle.

In the *Cosby Show* era, our elders might tell us to *talk proper*, but no one, even them, had a clear idea of what that meant. No cursing, sure. But also a suggestion that we enunciate with clarity, or maybe not clip a letter off the backside of our words. That might play around the house, with someone you love pretending not to hear you unless you pronounced a word with a tone they wanted to hear. Of course, as easy as it is to paint these actions as shameful now, and as easy as it was to be annoyed by them back then, it is just another move in a line of moves that seemed invested in safety. In retrospect, I have sympathy for this concern, when it came from elders who I knew had these beliefs because of violence they'd witnessed, or been a victim of. Things they'd been denied access to. The idea that if only they'd sounded a certain way, or dressed a certain way, things might be different. If their family could be mapped onto a Black sitcom family, that might do the trick. One way trauma can impact us is by the way it makes us consider a polite proximity to violence and oppression as comfort.

And so, in rebellion, our familiar slang flooded school hallways. We cursed with impunity on basketball courts, letting the words dangle in the air long and loud after a missed shot, or a made shot, or a foul, or a pass skipping out of bounds. Any cause for frustration or celebration, punctuated with language our grandmothers would try to slap off our tongues. And, of course, when someone was mercilessly mocked for *talking white*, even when it was done with affection and not malice (which was often the case), we laughed, or sat silent. Foolish rebellion, but rebellion nonetheless. Our schools, tucked in the city's urban interior, might occasionally get a student who transferred in from the suburbs. Someone who had parents with luck that shifted in a different direction, forcing them to cut back on private school, or move to a smaller house. A student who, used to the confines of a uniform, would come to school tucked in, or with a tie. Someone would take the new kid under their wing, and within a week, the button-down shirts became monochromatic tees, the slacks became jeans, and the loafers became white Nikes.

I have thought often of these two contrasting acts of care, both performed in the hope that someone might conform safely and comfortably to their environment: our parents and grandparents gently nudging us toward a respectability they believed might save us in a world outside the confines of our neighborhood, and the coolest Black kids in a middle or high school putting an arm around someone new and not hip, showing them the ropes. Giving them music to listen to, or telling them what mall to hang out at on the weekends. All of this done out of (a sometimes misguided) love. A love that tells people that who they are isn't enough, but that they can at least perform in a way that will make others believe they are enough until an ecosystem fully embraces them. I think of this tension as a push and pull, between generations and histories and geographies. Between those who would try to convince us of a type of survival and those of us who would spend much of our adolescence detaching ourselves from those teachings, taking as many people as we could with us in the process.

Everyone putting on different masks for different worlds and calling it freedom.

* * *

FRIENDS, I MAY come to you under the cover of night, after the face of a wooden table has become well acquainted with a chorus of open palms slapping it after laughter, or on beat to some tune spooling out of a single speaker. I may come to you in the moments after the party, but before sleep. I speak of this moment, and you will know I mean the exact hour where the once-cold drinks sit half-finished, gathering a warmth in their pockets, the exact hour where people surely must go home so that their friends can go to bed but also do not want the night to end. I will come to you in this hour, when sleep paces the room like an eager dog, daring someone to make the first move. In this hour where things spoken can perhaps be passed off as fatigue and forgotten in the morning. The first time I ever told a girl "I love you" was on a couch at exactly 3:45 A.M. while her eyes were heavy, and she smiled and before drifting off to sleep told me, "We have to wake up in the morning," and we never spoke of love again.

I TELL YOU this to tell you that I might come to you at a time when you are eager for the night to erase the memory of a conversation, friends. And I will tell you what I know, and what I know is that Whitney Houston could not dance. I have made my peace with this and I beg of you to do the same. You may not know that Whitney Houston could not dance, but I am telling you that she could not dance to save her life.

I knew this first at the 1988 Grammy Awards, where the showrunners asked Whitney to open the ceremony with an elaborate performance of "I Wanna Dance with Somebody" and realized that there was no way to open the show with that song and have Whitney stand still behind a microphone, as she did the year before when she sang "The Greatest Love of All" at the 1987 Grammy Awards, barely moving but for the slight upward jerk of an arm for the sake of flair when the

song began to soar. No, in 1988, Whitney Houston would have
to sing "I Wanna Dance with Somebody" and she would have
to find her groove somewhere. Up to that point, Whitney had
largely been a stationary pop star. On her second album,
1987's *Whitney*, the pop landscape had shifted slightly. Whitney Houston's first self-titled album, released two years earlier, was awash with ballads, showing off her singular range
and vocal control. The album's cover is drenched in rich ma-
hogany tones, and Houston sits inside a square, an impossible
brown glow emanating from her skin, gently kissed by what I
tell myself could only be natural sunlight. Hair slicked back
into a tight ponytail. A single string of pearls sits calmly along
her neck. She appears both stoic and regal, far older than the
twenty-one years of age she was at the time of the album's
release. In some ways, this was what was demanded of the
career trajectory she chose. She didn't enter the game to compete with pop stars, she entered the game to compete with
traditional, big-voiced singers who were years older than her.

On the cover of *Whitney*, Houston's hair is massive, puffed
up to the sky and seemingly endless. Endless, the way one
might also describe the smile that stretched across her face.
She wears a white tank top and looks as if she is in mid-dance
move. The album's title, *Whitney*, is scrawled across the upper
left corner of the cover in a font that can best be described as
Miami Vice Cursive. It is really something to name your first
two albums after yourself, if you think about it. It is like entering the same room twice wearing a different outfit each
time, reintroducing yourself to everyone as if you've never
met them.

"I Wanna Dance with Somebody" is the first song on
Whitney, a statement choice. One that says, "Okay, we're done
with all that other shit, I have discovered the way feet echo on
a dance floor now." The song is essentially a more danceable

upgrade of the single "How Will I Know" from her debut album—cleaner, more direct in what it is asking. In the music video for the song, Whitney Houston doesn't really dance so much as she gives the illusion of dancing. Because the video is filled with trained dancers, Houston gets away with doing large, rhythmic gestures in short cuts of the camera. An aggressive head move, or a big swaying of arms. The kind of thing that almost any Black person immersed in music their entire life wouldn't fuck up. Those who might be a little more aware, though, notice the first sign: You don't ever see Whitney's feet during the parts of the music video where she's dancing, and I know enough to know that to dance well is a full body activity. Of the things that look fine above the waist, dancing is certainly among them, and I know this, as I have conned my way into making a flailing of the arms look romantic on more than one occasion.

It is possible that people at the Grammys did not think this through, or it is possible that Whitney Houston actually believed that she was a good dancer, because that is one of those lies it is easy to tell ourselves, because we are often not on the receiving end of the disaster. A lie that we are often none the wiser to, like *All of my jokes kill in every room* or any number of things that people will not put us out of our misery about by pulling our card.

At the 1988 Grammy Awards, her performance was so elaborate that it distracted from any of Houston's dancing failures. The stage was large, and producers chose to pack it with as many dancers as possible, each participating in separate but loosely synchronized routines. The idea was that if something was happening in every corner of the stage, Houston wouldn't have to be the central focus. They also decided that the performance would be massive, one of the longest of the night, divided into two parts. Whitney would come out and sing the first part of the song, and then go backstage during the bridge so that the Grammy Awards announcer could welcome the audience and give a list of presenters and performers that would flash across the television screen while the band and dancers remained onstage, dancing to the instrumental. To remove Whitney from the space and let the choreography without her be memorable for an entire two minutes, in hopes that it might make the first section forgettable if Whitney couldn't pull off the elaborate dance numbers. In the first part of the performance, which consisted of the more complex dance routines, Houston is dressed in high-waisted pants with a massive butterfly buckle at her waist. It is almost comical in appearance—'80s enough to pass, but so massive that when Houston was the focus of the camera, it is all one can focus on. She was in heels high and sharp enough to make walking along the slick stage tricky. She was tentative and tense. It is one thing to look fun and free in a music video, it is another to be one of the biggest pop stars in the world on a stage in front of all of your friends and heroes, being asked to conjure unfamiliar magic.

It didn't help that the choreography of the first section of the performance was rigid, confusing, and cluttered. An awkward stroll with two keytar players who were definitely not playing their instruments. Dancers rotating around Whitney in a circle of elaborate moves while she kind of half-shimmies and looks around at them with a mixture of concern and confusion. A supremely puzzling moment when Whitney and her dancers briefly put on sunglasses to do a few body rolls and then take them off, but have nowhere to put them down smoothly. And then, Whitney darts backstage, eagerly.

There is truly no person or thing that exits the room in one outfit and returns anew in an entirely different outfit like the butterfly, who first crawls listlessly along the landscape before spinning itself a bed, inside which it can become beautiful. A winged creature, even. What a mercy it must be, to be able to sleep oneself into both beauty and flight. A world that knew you, but then not at all. A space in which you enter a room and make the old versions of yourself forgettable. I look in mirrors each morning and all I have to show for myself is the same face I was born with and have carried through this world since I was born and I suppose it could be worse, it could always be worse. I don't need to carry beauty around, at least not on my own person. I want, instead, to fill my hands with whatever beauty I can steal from all of your best moments. All of the things we might watch together in shared love. Like the moment when Whitney Houston emerged from backstage at the Grammys in 1988 in a white dress, with slightly lower heels, her hair puffed up like it was on her album cover. The moment when Whitney left the room as Whitney Houston and reemerged as Whitney, sliding easily through a parade of dancers, kind of on beat but kind of not, but certainly no longer giving a fuck. When she gets to the very top of the stage, a tall Black dancer in a suit emerges, seemingly from nowhere. He extends his hand to her, and they spin and kick, he twirls her into his arms, and she puts the microphone by her waist and loosely and eagerly swings her arms and shakes her shoulders in his grasp. The moment lasts all of twenty-five seconds, but it is the entire performance, everything the song is asking for.

"I Wanna Dance with Somebody" is a song that is more about forgiveness than anything else. If we are to redefine the concept of love, and what we ask out of the people we love, and the people who love us, this is clear. What Whitney Houston is saying is that to leave the house and go looking for a dance floor is not necessarily done out of love, but the person you find willing to occupy your space for a song or two is your person, for that moment. You two are mutually linked by a decision to, if nothing else, make each other look acceptable in front of other thrashing bodies. Consider what it is to want to feel heat in a way that is not sexual, but perhaps born out of rituals of shared space. The way Black people danced in the basements of juke joints because those were the only places that were safe. Consider what it is to want to escape something on fire to summon a different kind of fire. But mostly, consider the chorus: I want to dance with somebody who loves me. I want to dance with somebody who might forgive me for my failure. I want to dance with somebody who will know, as I do, that there are songs that summon movement even out of those of us who cannot dance, and I want to dance with someone who loves me enough to lie to me, until a record stops.

IN 1988, THE naked ear can barely hear the boos rising up from the crowd at the Soul Train Music Awards. But they're there, peppered underneath the Santa Monica Civic Auditorium sound system playing Whitney Houston's "I Wanna Dance with Somebody" while a short clip of the grinning, hair-flipping Houston from the song's music video consumed a screen behind the stage. In 1988, one might have to work to hear the boos, fighting for their space in unison with some vigorous applause.

The next year, in 1989, the boos were far more pronounced, overpowering the announcement of Whitney Houston's Best R&B/Urban Contemporary Single nominated tune "Where Do Broken Hearts Go." If there had been any mistaking the displeasure from the audience in 1988, the following year left nothing to the imagination.

Don Cornelius created the Soul Train Music Awards in 1987. "Blacks tend to get taken for granted," Cornelius told

the *Chicago Tribune* that year, on the eve of the first show.
"We tend to get ignored as a group of creative people. Black
music is too big and too powerful not to have its own awards
show. It's overdue." And so it was. The awards show set up
shop in Santa Monica its first two years, and then moved over
to Los Angeles' Shrine Auditorium from 1989 until 2001. To
host, Cornelius tapped legends of soul: Dionne Warwick
hosted the first five years, joined by co-hosts Patti LaBelle and
Luther Vandross, with the exception of '88, when she did it
alone. The awards were created in *Soul Train*'s image, which
meant they were catering to a very specific type of Black
music: music rooted in soul, jazz, funk, and R&B. The categories didn't use words like "pop"; instead they were labeled
with language like "urban contemporary." This didn't mean
the categories were unforgiving of pop music, of course. Michael Jackson won multiple awards in '88 and '89, the years
Whitney Houston was booed. It also didn't mean that the
awards were explicitly for Black artists, particularly in the
early years of the jazz category. In 1988, the multiracial group
Hiroshima won in the Best Jazz Album by a Group or Duo
category. In 1989, when the Best Jazz Album category was
condensed to one award (as opposed to group/duo and solo
album), Kenny G won over Najee, Sade, and Bobby McFerrin.
And so it wasn't as if the Soul Train Music Awards were in-
flexible, it's just that the flexibility needed to come on their
own terms. The awards show was sold to eager and excited
fans as a celebration of Black music—a type of democratiza-
tion of the awards show that allowed for prioritizing fans of
music that had, by that point, been largely neglected by the
mainstream award industry. In a way, this made fans enthusiastic gatekeepers of what they would or would not let into the
utopia.

Whitney Houston became an even heavier subject of scrutiny among Black music fans in the summer of 1987, coming off her second album. Part of this was due to the album's more aggressive shift toward formulaic pop. The album received largely mixed to negative reviews, with (mostly white) critics lamenting how restricted and safe the album sounded. How Houston sold the promise of her first album and her golden voice short by committing to overproduced tunes, transparently salivating for the charts. An emotionless roller coaster, with all the assumed heights and dives of excitement but none of the actual risk. What drew more frustration and cynicism was the fact that the manufacturing of the album worked. Its first four singles topped the *Billboard* Hot 100 chart, which had never been done before. The album remained at the top of the *Billboard* album charts for eleven consecutive weeks. The machine had turned out a sparkling album, golden with its lack of daring.

The July 1987 issue of *Time* magazine offered up a feature on Houston titled "The Prom Queen of Soul." It opens by ruminating on Houston's looks. The subhead of the article reads: *Whitney Houston is sleek, sexy, successful—and, surprise, she can sing.* Its first paragraph refers to her as "a Cosby kid made in heaven." At several points throughout the article, the writer expresses surprise at both her looks and her ability to sing "despite" her looks. Houston is sprawled out across the first two pages in a red dress, the first page consisting of just her golden heels and her legs. There are photos of her in the studio, singing in an oversized blazer, hugging a teddy bear. The profile does what profiles do: dives into family, touches on Houston's relationship with Robyn Crawford. It strives to separate Houston from the current stream of R&B stars bending into pop music. The article's central argument, in its own words, is that Houston represented an "overdue vindication of that neglected American institution: the Black middle class."

This was one of the many attempts to position Houston as an exceptional Black person, one who transcended race itself. Attempts that, in doing so, needed to detach Houston from any of the many struggles she endured in her life before becoming the pop star with the record-setting second album. Michael Jackson, titanic as he was by the late '80s, still had the luxury of being seen by Black music fans as someone who had struggled. What was known of his demons then could be traced back to the fact that many Black consumers of music who had lived long enough had gotten to see him as a kid, channeling a tortured childhood into entertainment. If they didn't grow up with him, they maybe knew someone who did. They saw photos or videos of him as a boy, immaculately dressed and gliding across a floor. They had a familiarity with the machinery of Michael Jackson, and had become so attached to it by the late '80s that there was no removing their admiration.

Houston didn't have this luxury, and it didn't help that she was, in some ways, groomed for crossover success. Between 1981 and 1985, only three Black artists hit number one on the album charts (Jackson, Prince, and Lionel Richie), and none were Black women. The charts were still largely segregated and awash with rock music. At Arista Records, Clive Davis set out to mold the ideal Black pop diva. In April 1983, a wide-eyed nineteen-year-old Whitney Houston signed her Arista contract beside Davis wearing a Levi's sweatshirt, jeans, and a curly afro. Davis spent the next two years undoing that image, crafting an entry for her into the world of music that would place a Black woman at the top of American popular music for years to come. He scouted out songwriters, producers, and musicians. Arista employee Kenneth Reynolds once remarked that Davis would send back anything that was "too Black-sounding." Everything was calculated, and unlike Jackson, Houston didn't have the tenure that might have undone some of the cynicism that greeted her arrival.

The conversation about Black art and Black audiences is often flattened, in part because it is hard for a people to articulate what they know they know. A people who are surely not a monolith, but are also not fools. Yes, Blackness is vast and varied, and there is no singular Black experience. But there are certainly Black people who know when they aren't being spoken to by a marketing campaign for a person who looks like them. There are Black people who, even in enjoying the songs of an artist, can see through the aims that that artist is (sometimes unfairly) burdened with. It is more difficult to talk about the never-ending failings of industry and what side of those failings our people usually end up on. There are Black artists who are not just packaged and marketed to white people, but—and more importantly—to the white imagination, and the limits of Black people within it. Sure, Houston had to look a certain way and sound a certain way, but this also required her being written about in a certain way. In order for her to take on the pop world like no Black woman musician of her era ever had before, she had to be written about in a way that placed her above and outside the narratives of other Black musicians. Consumers know when they aren't a part of the intended conversation, and they opt in or out, depending on that knowledge.

And so, at the intersection of all this, there were the boos that came raining down in back-to-back years at the Soul Train Music Awards. Houston was nominated for two awards during the show's inaugural year, but the crowd—perhaps still simply excited to bask in the newness of the show—

didn't react much to her name being called out then. But in the following two years, even though she won one of the three awards she was nominated for (*Whitney* won Best R&B Album of the Year), the crowd at the Soul Train Music Awards wanted to make their frustration known. By that point, some Black radio stations had decided not to play her otherwise all-over-the-place hits, claiming Houston wasn't "Black enough" for their listeners. The understanding was that if the establishment was choosing to place Houston outside the circle, she could stay outside the circle.

WHEN BLACK PEOPLE tell stories about how listening to "alternative" music in their youth drew the ire of other Black people around them, it is something I often find fascinating. Fascinating in that it so frequently seems as if it is striving to place importance on the storyteller's Black uniqueness at the expense of everyone Black they grew up around. Fascinating, also, because that experience felt so far outside my childhood orbit. My neighborhood was Black, and the schools I went to were mostly Black, and so the school buses I was on were filled with Black kids with headphones, and from underneath the metal playground structures at school and in the neighborhood there were Black kids sitting cross-legged and bobbing to something pouring out of headphones, and at the park there were Black kids riding around with speakers haphazardly affixed to their bicycles, and in my Black home there were multiple stereos that worked when nothing else seemed to.

And I do admit that coming of age in the '90s with older siblings might have helped. In the early to mid-'90s, there was an exploratory nature to most of the older Black music heads I knew. So many of them were still grounded in hip-hop, R&B, and sometimes jazz. But the same disaffections that held up an interest in '80s anti-establishment hip-hop and the same disaffections that seeped into many of my beloved neighborhoods were also the disaffections present in the frenetic drones of grunge, and in the booming rattle of metal. They were even present in the mopey indifference of '90s indie rock. And so, in the winter of 1992, Radiohead's "Creep" rattled out of the speakers weighing down the long trunks of cars. The Nirvana cassettes sold out of the record stores the day of release. There were no Black people who clowned me or any of my pals for listening to so-called "alternative" music, because the people who introduced us to that music were Black people. Of course, there were the hip-hop stalwarts, just like there were the overly devoted punk kids or metalheads who didn't really have much interest in crossing genres up. But these were not a malicious bunch—one simply respected the territory as needed. Keep a wide range of cassettes in a bag, so that if the fate of school bus seating shook you out next to the devoted rap heads, you'd have something to pass around and collectively nod to. And if you found yourself with a committed Black goth, you could pull the dubbed tape of Cure songs out of your back pocket. I first learned to code-switch through the musical movements of my people, and done among my people in this way, it didn't feel like a shameful burden. It felt like a generosity—a celebration of the many modes we could all fit into.

I think of this particular part of my upbringing when I hear other Black people reference what they grew up listening to or watching in an attempt to distance themselves from other Black people, or to make their experience exceptional or unique. A better and more interesting conversation to have, I think, is the one about how we are all outside the borders of someone else's idea of what Blackness is. To someone else Black, I am either too much of something or not enough of something else. The impulse when confronted with these facts, it seems, is to either attempt to assert whatever Blackness you claim and know well, or punish or deride those who might dare question your identity.

But if Blackness and the varied performance of it are to be embraced, then what also has to be embraced is the flawed fluidity of it. How the performance is sometimes regional, sometimes ancestral, often partially forged out of a need to survive some place, or some history, or some other people who didn't wish you or your kinfolk well. And yes, sometimes forged out of an ambition to appeal to the limited imagination of whiteness. The problem is that there is no way to prove oneself Black enough for every type of Black identity in the States, let alone the world. There is not always a way to prove (and possibly no way to trace) the how and why of your personal performance, until it becomes calculated. And in trying, high-profile figures often spiral further into being scrutinized by their doubters. I am thinking often on how crucial it is to love Black people even when feeling indicted by them. Even when that indictment is not out of love (which of course it sometimes is), but out of them clocking you for a standard you are not capable of rising to. I don't have any solution for this, but it has often seemed to me that even nodding and keeping it moving is an act of love when faced with the alternative of publicly debating the small or large nuances of specific modes of Blackness. And to not, in turn, make yourself a victim of Black people for the sympathy of a white audience.

This is not to say that Whitney Houston wasn't allowed to be hurt by her own people booing her at an awards show two years in a row. In a 1991 interview with *Ebony* magazine, Houston said: "My success happened so quickly that when I first came out, Black people felt 'she belongs to us,' then all of a sudden the big success came and they felt I wasn't theirs anymore, that I wasn't within their reach. It was felt that I was making myself more accessible to whites, but I wasn't."

What sits atop all of this is the understanding that massive, global success—then and now—does not come without non-Black people consuming an artist's production. And the fact that there is no perfect math on what tips the scale for Black people when a Black artist gets famous. Sometimes it is the artist's audience paired with who it appears the artist is performing for in an attempt to ascend to some higher ground. It goes without saying that Black folks are not fools. But, even with that knowledge, the game of authenticity is a foolish one to play. The boos didn't arrive out of nowhere in 1988. They came on the back of Whitney smiling, dancing, aiming for a second album that would dominate the pop charts.

Whitney, rightfully pained, was a single human target of a larger frustration. A frustration that was, at least a little bit, rooted in the hopes and dreams Black people had pinned on her at her entry point into pop music. When she was put through the sanitizing assembly line of Arista Records for her first two albums—but primarily the second one—Black people felt their excitement dwindle. It isn't worth litigating whether the frustration, in the moment of the awards show, was handled well or handled poorly. It is better to understand the frustration as something greater than just the moment itself. Frustration that came with decades of Black music fans seeing the artists that looked like them refashioned and re-purposed for an audience of people who did not look like them. Whitney Houston was just the container for the frustration in that moment.

There's the *Fresh Prince* episode so many of my folks have seen, in which Carlton is called a sellout at some frat party where he and his cousin Will are looking to pledge. The whole joke with *The Fresh Prince* is that we, the watchers of the show at home, know that Carlton is Not Like the Other Blacks. Even among the other children in the wealthy Banks family, Carlton stands out with his bow ties, his sweaters draped around his shoulders, his love of Tom Jones, and his conservative politics. Carlton dances off the beat, eschews slang, and is drowning in Ivy League ambition. He is most comical in how he is positioned next to the hypercool of Will, who gets into the Black fraternity with ease but is told by the president of Phi Beta Gamma that Carlton won't be admitted. *He's not like you and me*, the president tells Will. Carlton is not Black like they are Black. After a short defense of Carlton, Will goes to get Carlton from the dance floor where Carlton is winding his arms to a song other than the one that is playing from the party's speakers. On the way out, Carlton is tipped off to the reasons for his not being admitted to the fraternity. The president tells him they won't accept a sellout from Bel-Air into their fold. Carlton's voice lowers, and he speaks with a tone and rhythm his character hadn't been afforded to that point. "I'm runnin' the same race you are, so why you trippin' me up?" he says, mean-mugging the fraternity president. He closes with a flourish. "If you ask me, *you're* the real sellout," he says before sizing up the president's dreads and beaded necklace and patterned dashiki before walking out of the room to the studio audience applauding fervently. It is the most heavy-handed of '90s television messaging. Someone determined "Black" by way of aesthetic and someone determined "not Black" by a similar measuring stick, standing toe to toe over that merciless proving ground.

The episode famously ends with the Banks family gathered in a living room while Carlton recounts the happenings of the evening. The final words of the episode come from Uncle Phil, who puts a hand on the couch and solemnly asks,

"When are we going to stop doing this to each other?" before the graffiti-style end credits arrive on the screen.

The clip with Carlton at the party circulates on the Internet from time to time, often met with applause for how the show handled a difficult topic, even though nothing is really handled at all. Beyond the nostalgia of it, I find myself either celebrating or cringing at the clip from time to time, depending on what day it gets reshared. The complication, I think, is in my having to admit that I have been Carlton, dislocated from a specific set of Blackness but still attempting to feel triumphant. The harder part for me, and for so many Black people I know, is admitting that we've also been the fraternity president.

AND SPEAKING OF the way the voice can switch depending on the makeup of the room, or who is challenging the owner of the vocal cords or what era of life a person is immersed in, it must be said that Whitney sounded different in 1994. The evolution of Whitney Houston can, in part, be tracked by her voice. In her early interviews, she attempted charm and patient elegance. She was soft-spoken on the press cycle for her first album, anchoring each word with a smile and a gentle pause. Even in 1987, when she was interviewed for the *Ebony / Jet Showcase,* she turned on that same charm, even though her voice was a bit more assertive, and she clipped off the end of a consonant every now and again. In the '80s, she often spoke as if she were reaching toward an affectation of royals mixed with an attempt at everywoman charm. The whole idea was that Houston could be your friend, or your neighbor, even if you were a person who wouldn't live next door to anyone Black.

In 1994, Whitney Houston stepped onto the stage at the

Shrine Auditorium. She was back at the Soul Train Music Awards, accepting the Sammy Davis Jr. Entertainer of the Year Award. It felt like eras away from 1989, when Houston emerged from the storm of boos intent on rerouting her career and image. November 1990 saw the release of *I'm Your Baby Tonight*, Houston's third album. Upon its black-and-white cover, Houston sits atop a motorcycle. The motorcycle's license plate reads NIPPY, the nickname Houston was affectionately known by back in East Orange, New Jersey, where her family moved four years after Houston was born when race riots exploded in their home city of Newark. The cover was both a reentry and a reminder.

Houston tapped a production team including Babyface and L. A. Reid, with assistance from Luther Vandross. The songs themselves stayed true to Whitney's growing dance-pop interests, but latched on to funk and new jack swing as an unmistakable sonic backbone. The ballads swelled with the magic of Houston's gospel upbringing. The album had a duet with Stevie Wonder, "We Didn't Know," which the two performed on *The Arsenio Hall Show* with their arms around each other. The thing with Whitney from the start was that she was sort of a blank slate, more than capable of having any set of ideas mapped onto her creative output. And here she was, at the start of the '90s, having earned enough pop credibility to steer slightly in the direction of her people.

And yes, on the night of the 1989 Soul Train Awards, Bobby Brown pranced along the stage in an oversized white robe, singing "My Prerogative," dipping smoothly out of the outfit halfway through the song, occasionally falling into lockstep with his backup dancers. Bobby Brown, who knew the stage first as an extension of his own body, manipulating the surface with ease. He and Whitney met that night and fell in love soon after. Brown, a pop star who cultivated an image for his bold, brash attitude and his ability to find massive success but still remain engaged with Black audiences. He and Houston unlocked something in each other. For an America that imagined Houston as a pop princess, destined to be with a man of equally royal stature, for her to be linked with pop music's bad boy shook the foundation white America had imagined her into. The two were married in July 1992, a few months before Houston starred in *The Bodyguard*, a movie in which she falls in love with white Hollywood heartthrob Kevin Costner. In some way, the illusion must be maintained.

Onstage at the Shrine in 1994, Houston wears a blue headwrap with diamonds adorning the center. When she goes up to accept the Sammy Davis Jr. Entertainer of the Year Award, the crowd tips toward rapturous applause, leaping to their feet while a saxophone version of Houston's rendition of "I Will Always Love You" plays over the auditorium speakers. Houston turns to presenter Terry McMillan and, in a voice much evolved from her '80s days, declares, "Terry, that was truly a surprise, I want you to know, girlfriend." Houston then turns to the crowd, members of which are still shouting the occasional "We love you, Whitney!" among the final rumbles of applause. Houston throws up a gloved hand, flashes her signature smile, and shouts, "Wait a minute, y'all, I have something to say . . . lemme—umm—lemme say what I have to say."

It was Whitney at her most comfortable, facing her people. She gave a speech about Sammy Davis, Jr. How he performed in nightclubs for white people and had to enter by the back door to do so. Whitney, who by this point was a somewhat seasoned actor, knew how to play into her pauses. There were no more shy attempts at charm through her silences. Now, if she made an especially potent point, one that she knew the Black folks in the audience would relate to, she

might squint and shake her head with faux rage, or dramati-
cally roll her eyes like an exasperated auntie. During the
speech, she mentioned how Davis endured not only the humiliation of discrimination but also the insults of his own
people and goodness yes, when Whitney says *his / own / people* she cannot resist the raising of her eyebrows, and the
quick shift of her eyes scanning the audience to let them
know she was grateful but hadn't forgotten. The speech is
only about three minutes long, but it is brilliant, teeming
with ferocity. It reaches its peak after Houston unfurls her
long tapestry of gratitude for what Sammy Davis had afforded her. It's near the end, where she makes the abrupt shift
to the list of thank-yous. When she begins *Mommy and
Daddy, thank you. For helping me . . .* and when she trails off,
putting her head down briefly, and then throws it back up
again, gathering herself to make sure that this particular audience did not see her crying on this particular stage. And
then she finishes . . . *for helping me know the joys of being an
African American . . . as well as trying to protect me from some
of the pain.*

   I don't want to talk about the drugs anymore. I don't want
to immortalize the hotel room or the marriage, or all the
things Whitney could not be saved from. I want to talk about
Whitney in 1988, finding her way into the arms of a Black
dancer onstage at the Grammy Awards. I want to talk about
Whitney getting booed and then booed and then cheered. But
I mostly want to remember when Whitney stopped herself
from crying when she arrived at the understanding that no
matter how much our people love us, they cannot protect us
from all the pain that comes with living. I want to remember
Whitney holding an award with Sammy Davis, Jr.'s name on
it. Sammy Davis, Jr., who was gifted beyond belief but who
was a crossover star in part because it was known that he

wouldn't fight back. Because his relationship with the Rat Pack was fueled by his white friends being able to take the piss out of him without him throwing a fist. Dean and Frank cracking jokes about his Blackness the way white people at the bar wished they could, a consistent reminder that he was there, but only because they let him. At the Sands in '63, Frank tells Sammy he's gotta keep smiling, because he's a Black man in a black suit in a dark nightclub and at least his teeth were white. And so Sammy smiled his way through an era of knives.

I want to remember the Whitney Houston who, on the other side of her politeness, got to uplift Sammy in memory. Whitney who had maybe had enough of whatever limits existed within both the white imagination and the Black one and had fashioned herself into a singular star. Briefly beyond the reach of any sound born from any mouth.

Nine Considerations
of Black People in Space

1

TO BE FAIR, I cannot claim that I love the moon as much as all my pals and ancestors and peers. I maybe do not love the moon as much as other poets, who seem to love the moon for what it is capable of doing to the waters, or how it seduces the best or worst out of an astrological sign. I don't know much about astrology, but I do like the idea of astrology for what it brings out in my most creative and magically inclined friends. Elissa, leaning eagerly over a table to ask me if I know the exact hour and minute of my birth, so that we might do my natal chart and finally get down to the issue of what's going on with all my emotional rattling about. Madison, scrolling furiously through her phone over a dinner to see what phase the moon is in, or what planets are twirling ever more maniacally out of whack, so that she might explain to me why all the furniture in my heart's most precious corners has been overturned. Still, I can't say I'm much into what it all means, just that it means something. That we were all born under a different moon and a different sign. And I believe in it, I think. I have taken to waving a dismissive hand and telling a friend, "That's such a Virgo thing to say," even when I'm not entirely sure what I mean. And no one has corrected me yet, so either I'm right or I have surrounded myself with immensely kind people, which is probably a very Scorpio thing to say.

And besides, Robert Hayden loved the moon, and what a

fool I would be not to love what Robert Hayden loved—not to drink from whatever his palms offered. Robert Hayden so loved the moon that he decided to strip it of its magic entirely, so it was just the hanging & cratered glowing rock tasked with dividing up the darkness. Hayden wrote:

Some I love who are dead
were watchers of the moon and knew its lore;
planted seeds, trimmed their hair,

Pierced their ears for gold hoop earrings
as it waxed or waned.
It shines tonight upon their graves.

And burned in the garden of Gethsemane,
its light made holy by the dazzling tears
with which it mingled.

And I, too, dig the moon most when it is a question of its functions. How, for example, I might have once slid underneath it in some alley on a clear night to better see the face of a dear brother, or to skim a phone number scrawled onto a napkin after spilling out of some dive. I wish to view the moon as Hayden viewed the moon, an object that has a purpose rooted primarily in how it shines, and little more beyond that.

But still, I know that Black people in this country have long been obligated to a love for the moon, especially the enslaved who had to traverse the otherwise darkness in a search for freedom, aligning directions with the way the moon fell and following the shapes of stars. And so even if it is sometimes a bit of a show-off—every now and again puffing itself wide, sometimes blushing a gentle red—I do get the affection for the thing. Even when it is dragging me out of the house; interrupting a romantic movie night bending into the potential for more romance so that we can all go out and stare. Then again, who am I to judge? I've picked through my own closet and opted for the crushed velvet or the bright red on a day when I am dressing for someone else's wedding. I've shown up to the high school reunion in sneakers that have cost more than I made in a week of work at a job slinging books, so I suppose we're all the moon sometimes, depending on the occasion.

While we're here, though, I have to say that I also know nothing of the stars, but have lied about what I know many times. On the television once, a boy traced the constellation of freckles on a girl's face then pointed at the sky, and she gasped with joy. On a walk in my real life, holding hands with someone somewhere, I pointed up at the stars and pretended to know the shapes of them, and said something about eyes and a promised future, and the person I was with laughed. So okay, I suppose I don't know the stars well enough to lie about them comfortably, but I did have a telescope once, bursting out of my top floor window during a time when I lived in a city that got less clogged with smoky haze during its nighttime hours. And I would look into it every now and then, searching for all the shapes that everyone else saw. But with no luck. From under a campfire, my friend Kyryn said, *It's easy. The Big Dipper is right above us.* And then she traced it out with her finger, but all I saw was a series of tiny explosions that never vanished.

I have to have some sympathy for the moon, for all the foolishness I've projected onto it here, and all it is responsible for when it comes to making sense of the unexplainable human condition. But I also think about how lonely it must be up there among the darkness. Miss Zora, the truest of my ancestors and the only light pouring onto all of my unlit paths, says, *I feel most colored when I am thrown against a sharp white background,* which is true sometimes on the train and true sometimes at the birthday party and true sometimes in the office meeting. But what, then, of the sharp and dark background holding up the waning and waxing white, and all of its labor. What I feel is not sympathy, of course. A curious and thankful meditation, but still distance.

2

MY BOYS & I refused to believe it was Michael who didn't make it through the night even though the cameras strewn across the sky showed the mansion lawn specked with red sirens & from my own covers I imagined him to be simply asleep the way I slept with the red lights pouring into my bedroom windows in the summer of '97 while the medics decided that my mother's throat had closed & locked every door & they tucked her beneath a white sheet & to die in one's sleep must be to unfold a dream that never stops unfolding & then it is hard to say where sleep ends & death begins & how close to the edge each night drags the unassuming lives it holds in a trembling palm & there are news anchors saying Michael Jackson is dead on television today & I am late to work because it is 2009 & I overslept again & I can sleep my way out of a check & I can sleep my way into hunger & on the nights I dream of my mother the woman I rest my body next to tells me that I stop breathing in my sleep & inheritance is the gift of someone to spread the news of a morning you didn't wake up for &

it is a hot summer & I sweat through sheets I don't change & people haven't started filming Black folks dying yet & so I believe only what the casket tells me to & even then I watch for the dirt to jump & as a boy I lost a whole tooth trying to lean forward like Mike in the "Smooth Criminal" video & it skipped across the kitchen tile & my still-living mother gathered it in a white towel like a new child & here I learned to honor every hero with absence: an empty stomach or a smile like collapsed piano keys & it couldn't truly be Michael even after all of the pictures of his younger self flickered across the screen in memoriam & I'm wrecked with sorrow & not here to mince words & the moonwalk ain't got shit to do with the moon & how it hangs lazy & split into white beams over a hood where the streetlights flickered off once & never came back on

the moonwalk is all about trying to run from the past when its hands keep dragging you back & I have slept myself into exits & still woken to tell of each one & the cars outside my window start the dirge of *Thriller* hits from their open doors & the children too young to know anything but the call of rhythm run into the streets & kick puddles into small drops of water with their dancing & I suppose I also believe in death for the people it summons to dance & who are willing to sweat through a shirt for it & who are willing to stay out beyond the dark for it despite their waiting lovers or parents or children & who are willing to run into the fields screaming the one chorus they know without waiting for it to come back around & who are willing to fuck up a house party or just a house with a few idle hands inside & I remember now I remember in '91 it was my mother who stared at the man on television who was supposed to be Michael Jackson but he had paling skin & hollow cheeks & enough gold to be buried in & she whispered, *My god he looks like a ghost*

3

BUT FRIENDS, IT was not Michael who first slid backward across a slick floor on the tips of his toes. The first Black man to drift on some imaginary cratered surface was Bill Bailey, who probably invented the dance in the 1920s, but no one saw it on camera until 1943. *Cabin in the Sky* was one of the first films with a primarily Black cast. A film that attempted to veer away from many of the stereotypes and tropes that plagued Black actors of the era. An adaptation of the stage musical of the same name, it featured Lena Horne, Louis Armstrong, and the Duke Ellington Orchestra. Despite its best intentions, the film was met with mixed reviews, with Black reviewers stating that it still relied too much on Southern folklore, which meant that it trod too close to the racism it was trying to avoid.

But what did stand out was a brief dance interlude, performed by Bill Bailey, who had then garnered a strong reputation as a show-stealing tap dancer. Bailey had perfected both Bill Robinson's upright style of tap and also the paddle and roll tap style of King Rastus Brown. At the intersection of these movements, Bailey came up with something he called the "backslide," a move he'd utilize as a way to exit the stage. When his tap set wore down, he would slide smoothly on the tips of his toes, waving his hat as he slowly vanished behind a curtain. When he does it in *Cabin in the Sky,* it is the first time the move is captured on film. It happens fast but is impossible not to notice. Like Michael when he broke it out at the Motown 25 special in '83, the whole trick of pulling off the moonwalk is to spend all other parts of a dance routine training an audience to watch your feet. Before they can ask what is happening, the move is done.

Bill Bailey performed the move for years onstage, always at the end of his set. The way he saw it, the move was untouchable. Nothing could top it, so it had to be an exit. It seems this is where he and Jackson differ, as Mike would sometimes drop it into the middle of choreography, to drive people into a frenzy before bouncing on to something else. But I like Bailey's idea more. Providing a glimpse of something unbelievable and letting it rattle in the hearts and minds of people trembling in disbelief.

4

IT IS TRUE that my beloved mother did not live long enough to go to space, and even if she'd had the opportunity, she likely wouldn't have made the trip. But she did have an afro. And on the days she'd get home from work and take off her hijab, she would sometimes pick it out and let it sit high for a whole evening, and from a distance it looked like a whole black planet. And she'd sometimes sway in the kitchen and sing Miss Patti LaBelle, but it was never really the old Patti. The old Patti who in the early '60s tore through the Apollo Theater with Nona Hendryx and Sarah Dash, in a group that would come to be called Labelle, once the labels got hold of them.

Labelle could sing, but that was only the half, and the other half was about the *Look*, which they didn't always have. When they first started, they fumbled through a series of wigs that didn't always match their heads and sometimes drooped down during their most energetic performances. In the early '70s, they dipped a toe into the UK and started wearing tight jeans and massive afros while cashing in on some of the more political soul music of the era. But in 1973, the group was spotted by designer Larry LeGaspi.

I don't know when or where I first saw the video of Labelle in those silver space suits. I want to say I first saw the clip of them singing "Lady Marmalade" on *Soul Train*, but it might have been the clip of them singing the song on Burt Sugarman's *Midnight Special*. Both of those performances took place a few years before I was born, but I do remember watching them on some old and creaking VHS, with a label that had been written on and scratched out and then written on again. In the early '70s, Larry LeGaspi had become convinced that fashion was going to become obsessed with a futuristic, space-age look and that popular culture would follow. To get ahead of the curve, he began designing space-deco outfits for musical acts, the first of them being Kiss and Labelle. By the end of the '70s, the era of disco had taken some of LeGaspi's influences, and the country had found itself newly infatuated with the cosmos, immersed in movies like *Star Wars* in 1977 and the first *Star Trek* film in 1979, which capitalized on the era's space craze after the original television series fell flat after three seasons in the '60s. LeGaspi, it seemed, had been right all along.

Under the eye of LeGaspi in the early '70s, each member of Labelle had their own unique space look: Sarah Dash had a silver crop-top with wide, rounded shoulders and silver shorts, finished off with a pair of high silver platform heels. Nona Hendryx had a silver suit with an elongated diamond design dripping off the shoulder pads and stretching down to the pants. Patti herself wore a silver jacket with a massive, consuming collar and silver platform boots stretching almost all the way up to her waist. This wasn't their only look, but it was the most memorable. On nights they didn't take to the stage draped in their space suits, they did it drowning in massive feathers leaping out from every angle—from atop their heads, or flaring out from their backs. Some nights, they would mix the two aesthetics, accenting a space-themed top with bright, massive plumage.

In the most striking photo I recall, the trio is shot in black-and-white. Patti is in the center, flanked by Hendryx on her left and Dash on her right. The picture is from sometime in the mid-'70s, after Labelle finally had their big breakout

number one song with "Lady Marmalade," and their subse-
quent album, *Nightbirds*, became a hit. In the photo, Patti's
hair, thick and wavy, rolls neatly along her head. The light in
the photo makes her black hair glow. Nona's face is painted
with a triangle of small dots starting at the top of her forehead and dancing down to her eyes, which are accented with
eyeliner that sparkles even through the photo's lack of color.
Sarah's ears are covered with feather-like jewelry. They are
all wearing the half-smile and half-determined look that I'd
known the Black women in my life to wear before. It would
be hard to know if they were smiling at all, if not for Patti's
overabundantly defined cheekbones and Sarah's dimples,
which didn't need much temptation to make an appearance.

I found a framed version of this photo while antiquing
once in a place where not many Black people traveled and I
assume even fewer Black people lived. I am mostly assuming
this because I couldn't imagine any other reason the photo
lasted that long in the shop, especially for the price it was
listed at—a paltry two dollars when rung up on the loud and
rattling register.

I kept it on my desk in three homes. I realize that what I
like most about the photo is how, in that moment, they do
truly look like astronauts. Like perhaps underneath each of
their arms might have been a helmet. In the videos of all of
their performances during the space suit era, I marvel, even
now, at how smooth they made it all look. Wearing all of that
heavy silver, adorned in all of those feathers, they still moved
the way they did in their jeans and black sweaters.

I think when you are young enough and impressionable
enough, and you maybe don't know much about what rests
beyond the stars, you imagine anyone can just go. Including
yourself, or including a music group of Black women who
wore the costume well. Including a person you love, who sang

along to songs by a member of that group from time to time and surely danced to the group in a time before you were born. I guess I have tricked you into reading about my mother again, and how I do not know if she wanted to go to space but how I still wanted that for her. How, from time to time, I would catch her gazing at the stars. How, of course, I've held that old Labelle photo close because it reminds me of a sky my mother might be occupying now, picking out her black afro until it blooms and blooms, an endless dark. No one I love is immune to looking upward on a clear night. Within the vast and open possibility of darkness, though, I had hoped for a people to find a home, or at least a dream. Labelle, grinning in the width of their space suits, singing songs about lonely and powerful women. Songs about children going to space.

5

IN THE LATE 1980s and early '90s, if you spent any time near a radio or a television set, you almost certainly saw Billy Dee Williams or heard his voice. In those years, he was the magnanimous pitchman for Colt 45 malt liquor, and while I was too young to understand much of it at the time, I remember that Williams got a lot of criticism for being the face and voice of the brand. Some of the opprobrium centered on the liquor's slogan: "It Works Every Time," a juicily ambiguous tagline that led many people to think (correctly) that the brand was selling how easily it could get women intoxicated. The aesthetics of the advertisements didn't help either, with Williams in a suit and a woman draped on at least one of his shoulders. In one commercial, Williams simply cracks open a can of the drink and a woman rings his doorbell. She opens the door wearing a tight-fitting red dress and asks if Williams is free that night. He turns back toward the camera, grins, and waits a beat before speaking the tagline himself.

Another part of the criticism was how cheap Colt 45 was—swill sold from corner stores in low-income areas. Growing up, I would find 40-ounce bottles of Colt 45 broken on basketball courts, or empty cans of it piled up along the bike path. In movies like *Boyz n the Hood* or rap videos filmed on the West Coast, Colt 45 was the drink of choice—though some of these visuals came after 1991, when Williams stepped away from the brand. Colt 45 was what people in the hood drank, it seemed: what the gangbangers in movies drank, but also what the rappers in nice cars drank. It was a symbol of status that played to both sides of the fence. It was cool, in part because Billy Dee Williams spent five years saying it was cool. A Black man with a smooth voice and Black women in his commercials, all wanting a piece of what he had.

There are not many Black people in the film *Blade Runner 2049*. I think there may be only two, but, to be fair, I wasn't counting at my recent trip to the theater. If there aren't enough people of color for me to notice a significant number, I no longer do the work of counting whichever ones happen to pop up for scattered moments, or even the single one whose character has a name. I'm not fine with this, but I'm also less angry about it than I used to be. *Blade Runner 2049* was an entertaining, beautifully shot, captivating movie. It exists in a future where there are very few Black people. I laughed at this after walking out of the theater and back into the world, scrolling through news about Richard Spencer and his band of Nazis descending on a college campus. I was reminded that there are several geographies where Black people either don't exist or don't exist well, and I imagine this might not change in the coming decades.

But this ain't about 2049, and it ain't really about malt liquor all that much, and it *definitely* ain't about Nazis. This is about Lando Calrissian, and how I was young once and didn't know when *The Empire Strikes Back* took place, but I knew that it took place in some distant past that somehow looked like the future—a future not unlike that of *Blade Runner*— but in this universe, among the robots and the massive ball of fur with legs and the otherworldly creatures, was Billy Dee Williams. Not only a Black man in the future, but perhaps the coolest Black man in the future.

Lando Calrissian had great hair. I'm saying that Billy Dee Williams had great hair, and I imagine when he walked into auditions—if he even had to walk into an audition—the director and producers gasped at how his hair sat on his head. He had great action hair: the type that would barely move when he engaged in a tussle or a full sprint. Several Black actors have great action hair, which is why I think so many blaxploitation films focused on the aesthetics of things like an unmoving afro, or thick sideburns. Billy Dee Williams had both! And a cape! And he looked cool holding a gun! Not stiff like Harrison Ford, who was still great in many other ways.

Lando Calrissian was a Black man in the future with a moral code. I didn't know this when I first saw him onscreen, in part because I was simply in awe of his presence, and in part because I was too young to really grasp the plot of *Empire* (which is also, in part, because I watched the *Star Wars* films in a haphazard order, consuming *Empire* first). But in the film, Lando, after an admittedly shaky moral start, fights on the side of Han Solo and the good guys, freeing Princess Leia and Chewbacca. I imagined Lando Calrissian as the true hero of *Star Wars*, and no one else.

This, of course, is not true. The *Star Wars* universe is awash with heroes. But Lando radiated effortless cool, and I still imagine a future in which everyone gets to be as cool as Billy Dee Williams was in the '80s and '90s, just once. There he was in *Return of the Jedi*, rescuing Luke and fighting beside Han again. It seemed almost natural. The future is about imagination. The *Star Wars* galaxy exists long ago and far away, but the optics trigger the imagination to think about the future: the optics of space, lasers, machinery that travels at warp speed.

Afrofuturism exists as a genre because the white American imagination rarely thought to insert Black people into futuristic settings, even when those settings are rooted in the past, like *Star Wars*. Octavia Butler wrote science fiction that included aliens with dreadlocks. Nalo Hopkinson writes of a dystopian future in which Black people are trying to survive. I imagine all of these realities to be utterly possible, the same way I imagine that in an outer space civil war, there might truly be a Lando Calrissian. A single Black person in a large storyline, yes. But one around whom the story turns. One who does not die. One who instead destroys a Death Star.

Kids at college house parties on the suburban side of town in my late teens and early twenties would use their fake IDs to score 40 ounces of Colt 45 from the corner stores where no cashier gave a fuck if some nineteen-year-old punk got over on them for a cheap bottle of malt liquor. Colt 45 was still cheap, still coming in the same clear glass bottle with its iconic white label, which the white kids would tuck into brown paper bags and drink out of, like the Black characters in those '90s films and the rappers in those music videos. They would drink the malt liquor while listening to old rap songs and gesturing with their hands, their pants sometimes hanging below their waist. It was another performance. In the morning, they would go back to the quiet of their home in the suburbs, or their apartment on the outskirts of the hood, which was a place they would drive past with their windows up, or take a freeway around to avoid altogether. I would sometimes wake up on a couch, walk outside, and see the familiar sight of a Colt 45 bottle smashed into a constellation of glass along the sidewalk. I think about those moments now and consider the idea that maybe Billy Dee Williams was pointing us to the future all along. A future where being Black is so cool, everyone who isn't wants to try it on for a night. Just never for a lifetime.

6

AND SINCE WE'RE talking about it anyway: Look, I am certainly not one to project Blackness onto the fictional or cartoonishly ambiguous, and lord knows I don't want to upset the teeming masses of loud and affectionate *Star Wars* devotees, but it must be said that as a kid I had a sneaking suspicion that Chewbacca might have been Black, what with all the brown that hung from his body. Also the way my pal's dad would shout at the screen when *Star Wars* was on, about how those white folks who made the movie were trying to put one over, making the tall and incoherent beast *obviously* Black. And I don't know if I bought that as much as I bought the idea that so many of the Black people I knew would shout about all of their woes but no one would seem to understand what they were saying.

.7

WHEN THE INTERNET wanted me to believe that Trayvon Martin deserved to die, I was shown photos that were sometimes him and sometimes not. Photos of Black boys, shirtless and raising middle fingers, or photos of Black boys posing with weapons, or a Black boy blowing smoke into a camera. The idea was that they all deserved to die, I guess. If enough of them blur into the other one, a single bullet could do the trick.

To combat this, people began to circulate an image of a

younger Trayvon Martin, at Experience Aviation in Florida, from 2009, just three years before he was murdered. In the photo, Martin is wearing a replica of the blue uniform that the astronaut Michael P. Anderson wore in his official NASA photo. The same one that all astronauts wear. A rectangle with Trayvon's name on it is stitched into the chest, above NASA's logo: the earth, with wings.

Anderson was the ninth Black astronaut to go to space, back in 2003. The son of an air force serviceman, he was one of four Black students in his high school graduating class. After logging over three thousand hours of flight time in the Air Force, he was selected by NASA for astronaut training in 1994. He logged most of his hours for NASA on the space shuttle *Endeavor*, delivering goods to other astronauts on missions. Then he was assigned to the space shuttle *Columbia* mission.

The *Columbia* space shuttle launched on January 16, 2003. To prevent ice from getting into the fuel tank, the shuttle's main fuel tank was covered in insulating foam. During the launch, a small piece of the foam broke off, striking the edge of the shuttle's left wing and leaving a small hole. NASA scientists didn't notice the hole as the shuttle pushed toward space. The impact of the foam's damage is noticeable in launch videos. While the astronauts arrived safely into space, they urged NASA engineers to examine the wing and the potential damage the hole might cause. Engineers insisted that foam strikes were common, and the harm caused by them was minuscule.

In the NASA report that details the crew's final living moments, it says that upon reentry into Earth's atmosphere, superheated gases cut through the hole in the wing. The crew module was depressurized, and the shuttle went into a violent spin before some of the astronauts could get their suits and helmets back on. All seven of them became unconscious almost instantly. Their bodies flailed around violently. The ones who did get their helmets on had their skulls crushed by the force shrinking the helmet around the head. The shuttle disintegrated, and the bodies along with it. Debris stretched from Texas to Louisiana. A wheel here, a clump of metal there.

Black grass puffed out smoke for days after the flaming pieces landed on it. No bodies were recovered because there were no whole bodies to find. Farmers in Texas reported watching the bright blur drift across the sky and explode, only to see body parts raining down on them minutes later. An arm, or a foot. The stories became more and more sensational as the days wore on. One farmer reported finding a human heart, detached from any evidence of an interior. NASA insisted that there was nothing they could have done. Sometimes the disaster begins small.

Michael Anderson died a hero. No one insisted that he deserved what he got. No pictures circulated on the Internet of Black men who were not him. It dawns on me every time I see it that the Trayvon Martin Experience Aviation photo is so cherished because it offers him an adjacency to that dignity. It shows him in the replica of a suit heroes wore when risking their lives for the sake of curiosity. On Martin's birthday, people circulate the photo year after year. There is an idea that if Martin were still alive, he could have been a person who watched the skies and sought to climb into them. A person who looked down on the earth from somewhere above it and pointed to the state where he grew up. Or he might have done none of that. He might have gone to college and dropped out, or he might never have gone to college at all. He might have smoked and played videogames well into his twenties, working some job he hated. But he would have been alive to do it all, or not do it all. The whole thing with the Trayvon Martin Experience Aviation photo is that to see him like this, in contrast with seeing him as only a dead problem child, was to see that he was once perhaps someone who saw some promise and possibility in a world that would kill him and insist that he deserved to die.

The fundamental flaw, of course, is in this: proving to the public that someone did not deserve to die, or did not deserve the violence that chased them down. It is the worst instinct, and one that I fight against often, when I want to clear the name of someone dead who lived a life that was undoubtedly sometimes good and sometimes bad but always a life nonetheless.

At Michael Anderson's funeral in Arlington, the photo I recall most is the one of his mother, who broke the natural decorum of the space. There was, of course, a large picture of him on the stage. He is smiling in his blue suit in front of an American flag. The photo was positioned next to a casket that had no body inside it. In the photo I remember, his mother has her arms outstretched. Two hands reaching, as if she is trying to pull her son out of the still picture and back into the living world.

At Trayvon Martin's funeral, his mother, Sybrina Fulton, gently wiped tears from her eyes with a white handkerchief. America praised her for her restraint.

8

OCTAVIA BUTLER KNEW who would really survive when the sun set on this planet, or any planet beyond here. Butler was born to a maid and a man who shined shoes. Her father died when she was seven, which left her to be raised by her mother, whom she accompanied to work, entering by the back doors of white people's houses that needed cleaning. The Black

workers were only to be seen by what their labor could produce: a sparkling bathtub or a pristine kitchen. When Butler
was ten, she begged her mother for a typewriter, as a way to
isolate herself from her peers. Butler was shy and awkward,
and she struggled with schoolwork due to slight dyslexia. She
escaped to books and film, most notably the television version
of *The Devil Girl from Mars*, which was released in 1954 and
depicted a female alien commander descending on London in
order to bring men from Earth back to her planet, where the
men had been decimated by a gender war, making the planet's rates of reproduction drop significantly.

Butler, at twelve, imagined she could write a better story
than this one, and twenty-six years later, she released *Patternmaster*, her first novel. In it, humanity is divided into the
physically and mentally dominant Patternists, the Clayarks,
who were mutated humans suffering from an extraterrestrial
disease, and a group of enslaved humans who cannot speak.

Patternmaster—and the *Patternist* series that followed—
sits among my favorite of Butler's work, because it is where
she was most reckless in her attempts to see beyond the characters, beyond the landscapes she was building, and beyond
her own imagination, no doubt whirling with thoughts of the
unknown outer darknesses. It is a book, like so many of her
books, that tries to get to the heart of social and class divisions, kicking around the basic questions of what keeps humans apart and what is the responsibility of those in power.
These were questions far older than Butler's time on this
planet, which perhaps explains why she had to dream up new
worlds in an attempt to find an answer for them.

I return to the work of Octavia Butler for who survives,
and how they survive. Her stories are sometimes unkind to
humans, and the human body, be it through mutation, con-
tamination, sexual violence, or any other trauma or happen-

ing that shifts one's relationship with their ability to survive a world, and their relationship with how that world responds to them. In *Fledgling*, Shori's dark skin is a genetic modification—an experiment performed on her by her people in an attempt to make their kind resistant to sunlight. She was made dark-skinned by biological manipulation, and the society around her did the rest. Her own people, most of them white-skinned, discriminate against her. At the Council of Judgment, she is compared to a dog. Shori is a combination of human DNA and the DNA of the Ina—a nocturnal and long-living species similar to vampires.

The easy thing is that of course Shori's hybridity is something that dislocates her from her people. Something that causes her to be looked down on. But what Butler was doing with her other hand was showing how Shori's survival was inextricably linked to the things that may have gotten her exiled. Her mutation allowed her to be awake during the daylight, which made her able to avoid attacks. She was more adaptable to humans, and her venom was more powerful as a result of the mutation. There is a way that the book is speaking to what those in vulnerable and marginalized positions have always known: survival is sometimes how to adapt until something better arrives. Be who you must be in the job interview or in the college admissions essay or with the elder you love but don't respect. And then, as a reward for your survival, there may be a small world wherein you can thrive.

Octavia Butler came from a people who knew this brand of survival well. Who cleaned the shoes of wealthy people and entered through the backs of their homes. People who were invisible until they were needed, which is yet another type of hybridity. I give thanks, then, for the worlds beyond this world that Octavia Butler wrote. And for how, even in those worlds, there is a suffering like the suffering I understood. That even in space, or in futuristic landscapes, there are still codes to be switched. Still suffering that grows inside a person until it becomes armor. I give thanks for Octavia Butler, who still wrote Black people as human even when they were something greater.

9

SUN RA SAID it was a halo of light that appeared around him in 1936. Or maybe it was 1937. He was living in Chicago, or maybe he wasn't. There are no tactile details to the story that remain consistent. Just that there was certainly a light that consumed the body of Herman Poole Blount, who was from Birmingham, Alabama, and who was named after a vaudeville stage magician his mother loved named Black Herman. Black Herman died onstage in 1934 of a heart attack, but because one of his main acts was a "buried alive" trick, no one in the audience believed he was dead. His assistant, wanting to cash in on the act, charged admission for people to view Black Herman's corpse in the funeral home. The world is not done with you even when you are done with it. And Herman Poole Blount was not yet Sun Ra in 1937, but he was so done with the world that he embraced the strange light that drank him in and flew on up to a whole other planet. It was one he identified as Saturn. He was granted an audience with aliens who had one antenna over each eye and one on each ear. The aliens told him that he should drop out of college. That the world was dissolving into complete chaos, and they needed him to speak through music.

I don't like getting caught up in thinking about whether or not this actually happened. There are those who look at the history and timing and insist that there is no way it could have happened the way Sun Ra says it did. Flying saucers didn't become a part of the public discourse until the late

1940s. Sun Ra began telling this story in the '50s, still well before stories of alien abductions began to permeate the airwaves in the early '60s. It doesn't matter to me whether this story is true, because I have chosen to believe it is true. I have chosen to believe this because there is no other way I want to imagine the sometimes miraculous life of Sun Ra. Who moved north to Chicago during the second Great Migration and changed his name legally in 1952 to Le Sony'r Ra. Who shook off what he knew was a name from a slave family that was not his own.

His fashion began to shift in the late '50s and continued to bloom and transform with the unfurling of the decades. He wore voluminous and layered caftans. Headdresses festooned in gold and chains. He was often flanked by people wearing gleaming animal masks. It seemed most adjacent to the kings and queens of ancient Egypt, but still not entirely of Earth at all. Sun Ra's shoes were high platforms, giving him a few extra inches toward the sky. He often looked as though he were shocked to be here down on Earth among mortals. Like he was just visiting, doing the work he was tasked to do on Saturn back in 1936, or maybe it was 1937.

In interviews, particularly as his career wore on, Sun Ra made it clear that he was not from this planet. He never discussed his origins in clear or explicit terms, but he was certainly not who he was on his birth certificate. He had detached from all of that and achieved some higher plane of living. In 1989, he told *Spin* magazine he was from Saturn. That he was dropped down here like the rain, the snow, like anything else that came from somewhere else and ended up here. There was no place for him on Earth, which is why he couldn't fully give the world his music. Despite making albums for over three decades at that point, he insisted people were starting to lose an understanding of who he was and what he was sent here to do. To hold on—to keep steady until judgment day. Earth, he said. The kingdom of death. It's all make-believe.

When I think about Sun Ra now, I think of how fascinated I was with him in the late '90s and early 2000s, when I devoured his interviews and any videos of his live performances I could find. How I would wait on Napster while download progress on his albums ticked off about one percent every thirty minutes. What I loved was that none of it seemed outlandish. It didn't seem like a particularly excruciating performance, nor did it seem like the ramblings of someone suffering from some mental detachment. It all seemed very measured, calm, matter of fact. Sun Ra was from somewhere else, and he'd seen things none of us could fathom, and yet here he was, sharing what he had to give with us anyway.

In the early '40s, when Sun Ra was on trial for his conscientious objection to serving in World War II, a judge declared that he was fit to serve and would be at risk of being inducted into the military. He replied that if he had to serve, he would use whatever training he learned to kill the first military officer possible. When the judge exclaimed, "I've never seen a nigger like you before," Sun Ra quickly shot back, "No, and you never will again."

I am not concerned about the truth of whether or not Sun Ra ever went to Saturn, because if you can get good enough at convincing people that you are not of this world, or that you are capable of otherworldly things, then that act of convincing can bring you a little closer to a self-made utopia. Sun Ra was born in a violent and segregated place, was punished for not wanting to participate in war, and decided there had to be something better than this. I've run out of language to explain the avalanche of anguish I feel when faced with this world, and so if I can't make sense of this planet, I'm better off imagining another.

The Black people who try on the aesthetics of outer space, or who slide backward on a white floor until the white floor resembles the cratered rock, or the Black folks who write or sing or perform our lives into newer, better planets. Reminders that there is some place that lives in the imagination. A place beyond here, a moon or a planet for those who have only dreamed about what the stars look like up close. I tell my crew that I knew how to walk on the moon before I knew what an astronaut was, and they all laugh, knowing that so many of us pulled on socks and floated backward on a freshly mopped floor foolishly but generously left behind by our parents.

When this planet begins to drown itself and becomes unlivable, I might not be alive anymore. Some people might go to Mars, but I don't think many of my people will go there. My friend who has a flag that reads THERE ARE BLACK PEOPLE IN THE FUTURE hanging above her bed plays the new Janelle Monáe album for me in her car on a nighttime drive through a city neither of us knows well. When "Screwed" comes on, she puts a hand on my shoulder, wide-eyed, and tells me, *This is what our past will sound like in the future,* and I do think that is true, though it assumes we'll all be living and I don't want to get my hopes up. Still, there is a reason for this. This reckless and gasping pursuit of a world beyond this world. I am interested in what it feels like to imagine yourself as large and immovable as the sky. I have tried to love the unreliable moon, through its shifting and through the clouds coughing their way over it. That hasn't worked for me.

I don't want to go to the moon, but I do want to go to the place where Black dreamers stare at the moon and remark loudly about signs and stars in a summer that feels as endless as those old summers, which pulled me from the paltry responsibilities of youth. The planet within the planet. People dance in space suits and young Black boys fire rockets above the trees and they always come back down in one piece and sure, we'll crack some malt liquor for the drinking folks I guess. For as long as there is a future, there will be Black people in it, hopefully surviving in even newer and better ways than we are now. Circles of light opening their wide arms to briefly take our bodies somewhere higher. It will appear spectacular to everyone who isn't us.

Movement III

ON MATTERS

OF COUNTRY/

PROVENANCE

On Times I Have Forced Myself to Dance

IN THE LATE summer of 2019, at the BBQ spot in Memphis, I eat alone until the warmth of a shouted invitation makes its way over to me from across the room. A table of older Black folks had a spare seat, and they hated to see me eating alone, I was told. A woman with a few gray streaks in her hair smiles at me as I sit down and tells me, *We have to look out for each other out here,* and this is true. Sometimes the degree of looking out varies, depending on where the "out here" is, but today in the Black-owned food spot on the Black side of town, looking out just means not letting an obvious Black tourist eat alone. When I'm not from a place, I am often a dead giveaway. I take pictures of everything. I read local newspapers with a look of delighted confusion on my face. I sometimes forget to turn Google Maps off, meaning that my phone sporadically offers a loud burst of driving directions from my pocket. Today, it was the latter thing that tipped off this gracious group. Sitting down at this table feels instantly like being surrounded by concerned, caring grandparents. I've been thinking a lot about attempting to improve the ways I frame older Black folks—to not frame them as only ancestral or parental. I wish there was a better way to describe the feeling I got sitting down at the table, but this was it. We were not peers. There was a clear emotional and historical divide between us, and I imagine that's why they beckoned me over to the table in the first place, and why I made my way over to it. They asked me over out of care, and I responded out of respect.

Alonzo looks at my plate of fried catfish and mac & cheese and nods slowly while his wife, Emma, tells me I need some greens. I start to lie and tell her that I ate the greens already, but it feels like even the attempt would be doing a disservice to everyone at the table, including myself. Margaret tells me they've all been coming here for years. Through divorces, and deaths, new jobs, new marriages, kids moving home, retirements, all of it. *It's good to know you've always got a place that will have you*, she tells me.

Alonzo is wearing an Obama/Biden hat—one of the original ones, from the first campaign. Mary has on one of those faded flea market Obama shirts that situates the old president next to other civil rights leaders, Malcolm, Martin, Rosa Parks. I have an affinity for the shirt because it reminds me of the people on my old block who I used to see selling them, hustling them on their own outside the fried chicken joint, or the barbershop, or anywhere they might find a willing customer. Outside one of my old barbershops, the guy selling the shirts only took cash and claimed never to keep any change on him, an impeccable hustle that I admired.

I tell the table that I am there to cover a rap artist in the city, and our conversation easily spills into talk about old soul music, old bluesmen. They talk about the good old days of seeing bands for cheap at a small club in a part of the city where they didn't have to worry about getting shouted at from passing cars. Reginald thinks the world is going to hell. This president, he tells me. He's carrying us to hell and it's because people don't pay attention to history. Alonzo gestures toward his hat, says he misses Obama. Obama wouldn't have us in this mess, divided and endlessly fighting.

If this conversation were happening elsewhere—behind a

screen where I couldn't see the faces of the people speaking—
I might insist, loudly, that there is no such thing as a good
president. That this country has been careening toward new
hells with each passing year, and all that's happening now is a
slight acceleration. But here, at this table, I nod. I say "Sho
'nuff" when Reginald points a fork at me and tells me my
generation has to get out and vote.

In November 2008, I was in the woods, very literally. I was
working at an outdoor boarding school, which meant that I
lived outdoors for five days out of the week, getting weekends
off. I slept in a small house built from trees that I had to cut
down and strip of their bark. I rarely tell people about this
time in my life, because it doesn't seem real, even to me.
When I tell the stories of it out loud, I have to stop myself
from laughing. Staff were not supposed to have cellphones
with them while working. We were supposed to lock them
away when arriving on Monday and retrieve them only upon
leaving on Friday. On the week of the presidential election, I
snuck my phone with me into the campground. I knew I
could log on to Facebook and see the election results when the
time came, and so I did. Under my covers, so the light from
my phone could be somewhat hushed. When I saw Obama
had won, I held a small and silent celebration. I texted my
folks back home in Ohio, I messaged the Black kids I grew up
with. I reveled in *what it all meant.*

In 2019, at a table in Memphis, I can no longer unlock that
part of myself, but I still want to honor it. I'm thankful to be
surrounded by this optimism, coming from these people. People who have likely seen worse than I ever have in my lifetime but have definitely seen more. Convinced that their
nation is just one good person away from dragging itself up
from the depths and putting out all of its fires.

The Josephine Baker Monument
Can Never Be Large Enough

A COUNTRY IS something that happens to you. History is a
series of thefts, or migrations, or escapes, and along the way,
new bodies are added to a lineage. Someone finds a place
where they think themselves meant to be, and they stop moving. Had the first job my father interviewed for come through
at the start of the '80s, I would have been born in Providence,
Rhode Island, instead of Columbus, Ohio, where work at the
time was more plentiful. A city adorned with the name of a
violent colonizer, his statue looming over the center of the
downtown, his history a happening unto itself. I never asked
to be in this country, or this city, of course. But what we end
up with in the earliest moments of our lives can be beyond
asking. I think now about the story of my two pals sitting
down with their three-year-old only child and telling her that
she was soon going to be the older sister to a new, younger
child—the introduction of whom would require a halving of
attention. The child took all of this information in, sat quietly
for a moment, and then plainly replied, "No, thank you."

And speaking of youth, it was mostly in my younger days
when I heard people telling me to go back to where I came
from. It wasn't always done with what I thought was malicious bigotry at the time. It was most often broken out during
a school bus session of the dozens, when all else failed and I
managed to string together the right row of insults. Playing
the dozens is an art, like playing a song or writing a poem. So

much of it relies on knowing pace and tone. Land a joke that has multiple branches, or might benefit from descriptors. I won't just tell you who or what you look like, I will also embody the who or what, until the gathered masses are laughing so loud it doesn't matter what gets said next. But the exit strategy, when people had heard enough of my nonsense, was to fire back some generic and uninventive insult about me going back to where I came from, sometimes pinpointing a vast place without specificity, usually Africa.

Though not ashamed or even hurt, I was usually perplexed by the effectiveness of this return. It would end the exchange of jokes, seen as either too funny to be surpassed or a bridge too far, or too personal. As I got older and played the dozens far less, the insult was deployed in fewer situations, but with far greater velocity. During my brief stint as a bill collector, I'd introduce myself at a call's opening. The call would sometimes get hostile and irrational, as irrational as the work of demanding money from someone who doesn't have it so they can pay back a company that doesn't need it. And then I would be told to return whence I came.

Here, without being present in front of a person, it was still assumed that I was not of the land that happened to me. That I had to be returned to somewhere else. The place where my name obtained its uncommon cluster of sounds and characters. There are many ways to be of a place, and there are many ways to fade into the architecture of the landscape, until you draw the frustration of it.

THERE ARE STREETS named after Black people situated throughout America's cities. Most of the times, the Black people are dead. Sometimes the street bearing the dead Black person's name doesn't have many living Black people on it. And yes, it is so often Martin Luther King, Jr.'s name painted

on a green sign in a city far from where he lived and far from
where he was murdered. In St. Louis, Missouri, Martin Luther King Drive stretches for eight miles through the city.
Around the middle of MLK Drive's long sprawl, there is a
few-blocks-long street adjacent to it: Josephine Baker Boulevard, named in 1989. It isn't nearly as long a street, but it is a
street nonetheless.

In May 1906, a Black woman named Carrie McDonald
was admitted to an all-white hospital in St. Louis and pronounced pregnant. She stayed in the hospital for six weeks
and emerged on June 17 with a baby girl named Freda Josephine McDonald, whom the world would know as Josephine
Baker. Little is known of Baker's father, except that people
assumed he was white, due to McDonald's working for a
white family in the months leading up to Baker's birth, and
the fact that McDonald got to stay in a white hospital while
pregnant.

Josephine Baker grew up in a St. Louis neighborhood that
was dotted by movie theaters that split time as vaudeville
houses. Carrie McDonald had a dance act she'd do with vaudeville drummer Eddie Carson, playing wherever they could
find work. The two began bringing Josephine onstage when
she was just a year old, including her as part of their finale.
By the time she was a teenager, Baker had dropped out of
school and fallen out with her mother, who did not want her
daughter to drift into the life of entertainment. Baker began
waitressing for what little money she could get while also
staying out late and sleeping in makeshift cardboard shelters,
picking through garbage cans for food.

She would also make a meager living doing street corner
dancing, which eventually led to her being recruited to perform in the St. Louis Chorus vaudeville show, a traveling
troupe that made the pilgrimage to New York as the Harlem

Renaissance was beginning to unfurl and the city opened up its eager and curious arms to Black talent. Baker performed at the Plantation Club and got booked on some Broadway chorus lines, where she'd always play the last dancer in the line. Her gag was to act foolish, as if she didn't remember the steps she was supposed to be doing, until the group came back out for an encore, where she would take on the dance in a solo capacity, adding flair and complexity to its movements. Caroline Dudley Reagan first spotted Baker here, kicking up her legs and swinging her hips during an encore of *The Chocolate Dandies.*

It is said that whenever Josephine Baker was on a stage, there was no one else on the stage. All of the other bodies blended into whatever background was created by her furious whirling or sly and calculated romancing of an audience. It is possible to teach dance, of course. But it is impossible to teach a natural ability to calculate the many ways you can get an audience to watch you, mouths hanging open, unable to speak.

YES, JOSEPHINE BAKER left America, but it came on the back of several other leavings.

The chorus of telling people to go back to wherever they came from isn't new, and Black people wanting to prove themselves to a country that is at best annoyed by their presence isn't new either. At the intersection of these things, in the early 1900s, was war. In April 1917, the United States declared war against Germany, sparking its entry into World War I. In the States, segregation was rampant. Deemed not smart or skilled enough to keep up with the unpredictability and rigors of battle, Black people had, before that point, been routinely turned away from military service. But with the massive conflict of the world war looming, Congress passed the Selective Service Act in May 1917, requiring all male citizens between the ages of twenty-one and thirty to register for the draft, regardless of race. Young Black men signed up in droves, assuming that if they showed a willingness to fight and die for their country, their country might just love them back.

America drank in the enthusiasm of Black men to serve, and then took in even more beyond the enthusiastic. If some were willing to fight, it seemed, then they all had to be. Black men were drafted at rates far higher than their white counterparts. Draft boards that once turned away Black men were now pulling them in by the dozens, attempting to get as many as possible. In Georgia, one county exemption board discharged 44 percent of white registrants on physical grounds and exempted only 3 percent of Black registrants based on the same requirements. Black men who owned land and had families were drafted earlier than single white laborers. The army was particularly progressive at the time, allowing Black soldiers to serve in multiple capacities. Of the many questions sprouting from the body of war, one of them is the question of respect. And when soldiers are willing to fight for the idea of respect—both abroad and at home—it allows for exploitation by a country eager to remain powerful.

Over three hundred thousand Black soldiers served in some capacity in World War I—but the branches of the military didn't often know what to do with the bodies once they got them. Black soldiers became a problem for the military to figure out. Could they fight alongside white soldiers? Could they lead? Could they be trusted? Black soldiers were often kept separate from their white counterparts in the name of what some would call "racial tranquility," which led to a few all-Black combat divisions. But for a majority of other Black soldiers, they were simply relegated to menial and often isolating roles: as gravediggers, cooks, mechanics. Pushed to places where they could play a part in keeping the machinery of war going but still be out of the way, barely visible beyond the loud and trembling landscapes of war.

The all-Black combat divisions were the 92nd, 93rd, and the 369th infantries—the last of which nicknamed themselves the Harlem Hellfighters. These divisions were sent to fight primarily in France, alongside French soldiers. The idea was that the French would be more tolerant and open to fighting alongside the Black soldiers, partially because they were in such desperate need of assistance to hold back overwhelming German assaults deep in the forests of France. Black soldiers fought bravely and were showered with praise by the deeply thankful French nation.

Sometimes it is just the one thing, as the movies might suggest, insisting that with one tiny misstep—the death of a single butterfly—the eternity of the world shifts. But other times, there are several different parts all moving together to form a moment. Jazz didn't just arrive in Paris, even though the city took to it eagerly, wearing the sound and the trappings of jazz cool as if it was born there. But the first step was a country hungry for war but out of options when it came to the people on the front lines. Then it was the grasp for anyone Black and eager, and then anyone Black at all. And then, with the question of what to do with the collection of Black men who seemed like they actually could fight in this war, it was the positioning of those soldiers in a place America deemed the least offensive for them, with low enough stakes to survive.

At the height of World War I in Paris, Black soldiers would spend some of their downtime playing instruments they'd carried over with them. Mostly horns and guitars. Tables became drums. Eventually, casual collectives formed among the soldiers, groups that would go out to the Parisian music halls and play blues, jazz, and ragtime music. Jazz had begun to reach a heightened popularity in the States but had yet to break big in Paris. Once the locals got a taste of the sound, it carried through and beyond the war. Even after many of the Black soldiers went home to America, back to a country where they were not the heroes they were in France. Back to a country where they quickly remembered that being willing to bleed for a land doesn't mean the people of that land will require or desire your presence outside of that willingness.

Still, the impact of that brief burst of Black creation in Paris struck new chords. Paris became obsessed with American Black artistic culture, right as the Harlem Renaissance started to kick off in the States. Parisians were mimicking American Black culture, but also, after World War I, word got back to the States that Paris was a place where Black folks were treated well. Because the Black soldiers who fought in Paris were deemed heroes, the city revered its visiting Black artists as well. Black jazz musicians who couldn't play in all parts of America traveled to Paris to do a stretch of shows. Many didn't stay, however, which meant that Paris was left to try its best to merely mirror the experiences these artists gave to the city. Paris was ripe and eager for a Black artist to come and commit to its small artistic flourishing. Someone who could, perhaps, put their own stamp on what the city was attempting to offer.

And then, on a boat, arrived nineteen-year-old Josephine Baker.

I AM WONDERING always how one comes to love a country. Depending on who you are, or what your background is, or what trauma(s) you've inherited, it seems too complicated to unravel. It was not complicated for me to perform for a while, when I'd convinced myself in my teens and early twenties that my performance of love for a country would open itself up to some kind of safety for me and the people I held close. I also knew then, as I know now, that leaving felt immensely impractical. This is one of the biggest tricks of them all. You are burdened with a place, and then, by the time you realize that exit is a possibility, the options for exit can seem distant, or insurmountable. I love Columbus, Ohio, and wince when I speak the name into the air. I apologize for the massive bronze statue piling its way into the clouds when people come to visit, as if I had put it there myself. I love Columbus, Ohio, and I say this understanding that love would be mapped onto any place that I hadn't left, or stayed in long enough to build a shrine of memories. In this way, my love feels more like a matter of circumstance than a matter of politics, or at least that is what I tell myself.

I do envy Josephine Baker, who left America before it could persuade her to fall in love with it. La Revue Nègre—or the Negro Revue—had taken hold of Paris by the mid-1920s. The city's fascination with both jazz and Black culture had culminated in this show being created and centered at the famed Folies Bergère theater, in the heart of the city. The show began in 1925, when the artistic director of the Champs-Élysées theater, André Daven, began considering a route to a new, longer-running, more sustainable show. One that could cash in on the Paris obsession with Black culture by bringing actual Black artists to the city. A show played entirely by Black people, and not some of the less-than-genuine interpretations by the city's white artists. Daven connected with the American socialite Caroline Dudley Reagan, who went to New York in search of Black talent and came back to Paris with twenty artists: twelve musicians, seven singers, and one unique performer. A singer and dancer with a smile as wide and magnetic as her personality.

I first remember the photo of the banana skirt, which I found in some book in middle school that I had quickly taken away from me by a teacher. In what little footage exists of the original performance of Josephine Baker in this skirt, the grainy and warped shot zooms out over what is meant to be a jungle landscape. A fake tree with a thick, winding trunk is laid over the top of the stage, and fake plants burst up from the stage floor. As churning and ominous percussion rains down from the theater's speakers, in sync with drums slapped by shirtless Black men, Josephine Baker rises from the theater floor, her waist adorned with two layers of bananas.

The bananas on the skirt are bejeweled, though it is hard to tell how and with what, just that there are small circles on each one, reflecting the light. During the dance, the bananas are hardly visible. In videos, the footage is manipulated and slightly sped up, so it appears that Baker's hips are moving at an even more impossible pace than they were. The bananas themselves become secondary to the body tasked with carrying them as Baker swings her arms and widens her eyes, crossing them briefly before thrusting out her back, bending over, and doing a brief Charleston.

It is not difficult to manipulate the imaginations of men, with so many of us doing half the work ourselves before anyone else arrives with intentions of manipulation in mind. Still, for Josephine Baker, manipulation was part of the power. To manipulate the imagination of those men, and of that city, at that time, was a unique undertaking. Remember: Paris had saturated itself with ideas of Black art, Black minds, but not many actual Black people. For as liberal as the city was, there were still some who thought Black people were, by nature, primitive beings. To see the early performances of Josephine Baker in La Revue Nègre was to see someone taking the absurd stereotype and making it so absurd that it circled around to desire. The men laughed until they found themselves choking on all they wanted but could never have. The people who think they can never be played are the ones all true performers know to go after.

BECAUSE JOSEPHINE BAKER was a woman, and because she was a woman who captivated and controlled the imaginations of men, and because that means Josephine Baker was powerful, so much of the conversation around her career and existence revolves around her relationships, or her sexuality, or what her body was and wasn't capable of. A foolish thing is when writers, or curious people who hold information, insist loudly that they wish more people would be talking about a topic and then continue to withhold vehicles for the starting of that conversation. And so I have carried you here, beyond the history and the visuals of a twirling Josephine Baker in grainy black-and-white, to mention something else. The time during World War II when Josephine Baker—then well into her career and life in Paris—acted as a spy.

This part of her story is sometimes a footnote, which is almost fair. Baker had a wide-ranging career set against wide-ranging backdrops. She was a talent as interesting and engaging off the stage as she was on it. Once she got a large enough platform, she used it to set an eye on improving the conditions of her new home while criticizing the polices of America, her old one.

So much of the story circles back to war, the major enterprise of empire. Josephine Baker found footing as a performer in Paris in part because of a war. And then, when she had earned more than enough recognition in Europe, she took part in another war. I have no interest in weighing the morality of Josephine Baker with regard to this participation, but I find her willingness to put herself at risk for a country fascinating, particularly because it wasn't the country she was born into and unwillingly assigned. It was, however, the country of her rebirth. The country where she crafted the version of herself that felt most true to what she wanted. And I would think that that calls for a very direct kind of affection.

By 1937, Baker had married Jean Lion, a French industrialist. The marriage meant that Baker had officially renounced her American citizenship, after more than a decade living in Paris. Her shows still found massive success in the city, but they were often banned throughout Europe, making it difficult for her to tour. Her outfits and dancing were seen as threats to the morality of most republics. When she attempted to perform in Vienna, for example, churches rang bells during the concert, a signal to the audience that they were committing an act of sin by seeing Baker.

Because of both her newfound love and her reluctance to tour, Baker had become even more insulated in Paris. By 1939, when World War II was declared, Paris had begun to fill with refugees fleeing Germany. The city was rapidly populated, bursting with new people, many of whom had nowhere to sleep or consistently get a meal. Baker would leave theaters every night after performing and go to the homeless shelter on the Rue du Chevaleret. She made beds, bathed elderly refugees, and stayed hours into the night, comforting the people who had left their homes to venture into the unknown that seemed safer than the known.

Late in 1939, shortly before the Nazis invaded Paris, Baker was paid a visit at her home by Jacques Abtey, a captain in the

Deuxième Bureau, the French intelligence agency. Baker had become one of the most visible public figures in Paris and had offered to work for the French Resistance in any way she could. There were concerns about recruiting Baker as a spy, as France was only twenty-two years removed from the execution of the Dutch dancer Mata Hari, who, during World War I, was convicted of working as a double agent for both Germany and France, something that caused the deaths of at least fifty thousand soldiers.

Still, in the dark of a living room in her massive home, Josephine Baker told Captain Abtey to dispose of her as he wished. She had become a cherished child of the Parisians, she told him, with a hand over her heart. She was ready to give her life for the people who had given her life so much.

Many stories are told about Baker's time in the French Resistance. One is that she joined the French guerrilla freedom fighters known as the Maquis. It is said that the group took Baker underground and taught her to shoot in the darkness of the sewers beneath Paris, until she got so good behind the scope of a rifle that she could snuff a candle at twenty yards. But what is most widely known and accepted is that Baker's role as a spy was much like her roles onstage: she could seduce and manipulate the minds of men already eager to be manipulated. She could easily entice men in power to confide in her, in part because they viewed her as someone not intelligent enough to do more than entertain. Generals and diplomats would show her secret notes or whisper plans in her ear at parties.

Abtey, who would pose as Baker's agent while undercover, gave her invisible ink. She would scribble down information on sheet music or scraps of paper, pretending that she was preparing for an upcoming show. Then she'd pin these papers to her underwear to get the information across borders, under

the guise of touring. When Abtey would remind her, repeatedly, that these activities were putting her life at risk, she
would throw her head back, laugh, and exclaim, "Who would
dare strip-search Josephine Baker?" And of course it was true.
She was asked for autographs by patrols at borders.

When the Nazis invaded Paris, Baker hid members of the
French Resistance in the basement of her residence, a castle
on the Dordogne River. Nazis showed up to search the home,
but Baker stood in front of them, charming and flirtatious as
ever. By the time she was done entertaining them, they'd forgotten to search the lower level, and they stumbled out of the
castle under her spell, none the wiser.

Baker, having converted to Judaism with her marriage to
Lion, felt a heightened level of anxiety around her presence
in Nazi-invaded Paris as a Jewish Black woman. In 1941, she
moved to the French colonies in North Africa, claiming she
was ill. Baker was recovering from a bout of pneumonia, to be
sure, but she also needed to establish a safer base to continue
helping the French Resistance. She hid out in Morocco, making tours of Spain during which she continued obtaining information and passing it along to the Resistance agents. When
she did tour to play music and dance, she did it to entertain
British, French, and American soldiers in North Africa. No
civilians were allowed in the shows, and no admission was
charged.

I think most about the Josephine Baker who served a
country that was not her own during war. A country that first
found a need for her because of a previous war, when they fell
in love with all things Black. Not everyone might be as willing to give their life for a country. Unless, of course, that place
treated you in a manner that your home country could never
rise to.

*   *   *

ON FEBRUARY 3, 1952, Josephine Baker traveled to St. Louis to perform at Kiel Auditorium. She had returned to the city of her birth only a few times since 1919, and she had never performed there, because she refused to take the stage in front of segregated audiences. But she agreed to appear back in St. Louis because it was for a worthy cause: a local protest committee was raising money to fight segregation in schools. In Paris, Baker had become invested in being useful beyond what she was capable of producing for the public. But in America, she was still Black, and still an entertainer, and there are limits to what people would allow themselves to stand. By this time in her career, even as her work in Paris was uneven, Baker was still a powerful enough draw in the States to command an audience and to demand what that audience would look like. And so the crowd at Kiel Auditorium in 1952 was integrated, and they watched Baker perform two hours of songs in French and English, cycle through her customary elaborate outfit changes, and still charm a room as she did in her prime.

Much of the reporting at the time focused on the performance and nothing else. But at the end of her set, Baker launched into a long speech, balancing pride in her hometown with asking it to critically engage with its complicity in segregation and racism. She spoke of the good it did her heart to see Black and white people enjoying the show together, but then quickly spoke of her need to escape when she did:

> Strange, it seems just like yesterday that I ran away from home, not because I lived in poverty or [because] I was living in the slums for I have never been ashamed of my childhood surroundings. On the contrary, I have been very proud of my start, because it has made me remain human, and in that way understand my fellow

brothers of misery. Friends, did not our Lord Jesus
Christ live in poverty? Did he not? Then I believe it a
great privilege to have suffered during my childhood.

I ran away from home. I ran away from St. Louis,
and then I ran away from the United States of America, because of that terror of discrimination, that horrible beast which paralyzes one's very soul and body.
Those in this audience [who have] felt discrimination
know what I am talking about and those who understand human beings understand what I am talking
about too.

The hate directed against the colored people here
in St. Louis has always given me a sad feeling because
when I was a little girl I remember the horror of the
East St. Louis race riot. I was very tiny but the horror
of the whole thing impressed me so that here today at
the age of forty-five years I can still see myself standing on the west bank of the Mississippi looking over
into East St. Louis and watching the glow of the burning of Negro homes lighting the sky. We children
stood huddled together in bewilderment, not being
able to understand the horrible madness of mob violence but here we were hiding behind the skirts of
grown-ups frightened to death with the screams of the
Negro families running across this bridge with nothing but what they had on their backs as their worldly
belongings. Friends, to me for years St. Louis represented a city of fear . . . humiliation . . . misery and
terror . . . a city where in the eyes of the white man a
Negro should know his place and had better stay in it.

I think often of this performance in St. Louis. The one no
one writes about often because it's not as salacious as the ba-

nana skirts. I think about it because it is the best example of how to return to a place that made you, whether you wanted it to make you or not. Here she was, Josephine Baker, back in the city that she would forever be tied to because it was the city where she was born. The city where someone stopped moving long enough put down some roots. Here she was, beaming with pride, but also too proud to pass up the opportunity to put the people of the city in their place.

To look a familiar place in the eye and detail all of its old and unattractive blemishes—that, too, is a type of love for a place. A love not wedded to permanence or wrapped up in the memory of times past, as so much of my love is foolishly wrapped up in. To return to the site of the world coming into focus for you and offering newer, better eyes.

IN COLUMBUS, THE seemingly endless hands of summer are trimming autumn's once-long hair. The sun stays hungry well into September, which has become a more common occurrence in my adult years here. Soon, I imagine, the heat will tumble recklessly into October as well. If one doesn't think of the impending doom signaled by the rise in temperatures, it can feel like a welcome extension of our city's summer magic—a time when the town isn't bogged down by Ohio State students. But, as an exchange, owing to the heat and dryness, the leaves don't change until late in October before falling to the ground hastily, almost sprinting to their demise.

I moved back to Columbus after being away for nearly three years, following a relationship to New Haven, Connecticut. When the relationship ended, I could realistically have lived anywhere. I was working remotely, and for the first time in my life I had a little bit of money in a savings account. But I wanted to come home. Being from this place had become inextricably linked to my identity, and so I push myself to love it.

As the calendar ticked toward October and my days were still drenched in sweat, the signs began to appear on freeway overpasses. Large swaths of cloth with messages painted on them in black spray paint. Messages that are far-reaching and all-encompassing: YOU ARE LOVED hangs on the overpass right before the exit that used to take me to my high school girl-friend's house on the nights her parents were out of town. YOU ARE ENOUGH floating in a few gusts of thick wind on another overpass, the one before the exit that spits you out on the part of the eastside that bends into an insulated suburb where Black people from my hood couldn't hang out with much comfort despite living only a few blocks in either direction. I walk my dog over the highway near our apartment, which separates downtown from the brick-lined streets of German Village. We've walked only a few steps, but her tongue is out and she is panting heavily and squinting into the sun. The sign affixed to the fence reads, IF YOU'RE GOING THROUGH HELL, KEEP GOING.

I have never understood who these signs are for. I don't feel like the "you" that is being addressed by them, which might be a failure of my own imagination. Instead, I have begun to imagine that the messages are meant for the city itself. The city that breaks itself apart and rebuilds itself at the expense of often marginalized and often poor people. At the expense of their homes, their comforts, their history. YOU ARE ENOUGH, hanging from a freeway less than a mile from where the city decided one stadium wasn't good enough to keep a soccer team and so another one must be built, else-where, on new land.

And of course it bears mentioning that my mere presence

in this city—even in the parts of it I've long loved—is an act of painting over. Gentrification is undoubtedly a sin that comes with very tangible consequences. I have not loved to watch the way a city shifts at the whims of those with wealth and power. But the corner store I miss wasn't always a corner store. The basketball courts where I learned to shoot were built upon land that looked different than it did when they were completed. Much of our living is an act of painting over an existence before ours, and my understanding of that doesn't dim the pain I feel at the new unfamiliarity of spaces I've been in.

I maybe find myself envious of Josephine Baker because she was unafraid to leave. She did not need a city, or a country. She made herself bigger and more desirable than anywhere she could have been or been from. It is true that to love a place is as complicated as any other relationship, romantic or platonic. Perhaps even more so. A city's flaws can be endless, and reflect the endless flaws of the people who populate it. To attach identity to love for a place you didn't ask to be in, and a place that was not ever and will never be "yours," is a fool's errand, but it is one I have taken to. Because oh, how I adore knowing the corners of a place. Oh, how I love knowing a story of a building or a park or a church parking lot. A story that only a handful of people know. How I love hearing those stories from other people, from other pockets of this exhausting and dismantling city.

There was one overpass sign that didn't last. Another one on an overpass heading north. It read BLACK LIVES MATTER. It was cut apart and torn down within a week of being put up. In most coverage of the signs, this was never mentioned. All people wanted to talk about was the messages of affirmation being pumped into the city. How they revitalized and re-

energized the commute for residents. I am once again burdened by a love I inflicted on myself, and I fear it is too late to
detach.

A block-long section of Josephine Baker Boulevard was
removed in 2008. It was meant, at the time, to create some
additional space for Saint Louis University. The long arm of
gentrification knows little of resistance. White people in Columbus walk through areas that once housed people who
were displaced for the sake of an endless scroll of brick bou-
tiques. They bemoan the fact that new people are moving to
the city, insisting that the city will be ruined. It is easy to
build new borders when you are among the populations least
threatened by them, or the access they deny. Josephine Baker
lost a block, and I am reminded that just as there are many
ways to be of a place, there are many ways to slowly be erased
from it. One way or another, detached from the ground you
first danced on.

It Is Safe to Say I Have
Lost Many Games of Spades

SOMEWHERE ON THE road between Oxford, Mississippi, and Tuscaloosa, Alabama, my homie Jerriod looks at the cards fanned out in his hands. For anyone who has played enough games of spades and lost enough games of spades, it is known that you watch the moment directly after your opponent picks up their cards and assesses them. Some people sit stone-faced, staring at what they've got and nodding slowly, as if it could be anything. Some people make grand gestures about what it is they don't have and how bad the next few minutes of hand playing are going to be. The more dramatic, the bigger the potential for a lie. The person who throws an arm over their eyes, or pats away fake sweat from their brow while exclaiming something to their partner like "I don't know how we're going to make it out of this one. I'm going to need you to carry me."

We are among a group of twelve poets and peers, taking part in a weeklong fellowship that is requiring us to engage with the American South. Many of us have roots here, but the relationship is less tactile now, since the majority of us have scattered ourselves across the country in our adulthood. The days on the trip involve long, hot walks through paths lined with tree branches drooping under the weight of their own exhaustion. Sitting on porches of old homes and scowling at war monuments. The nights involve readings of our work for the communities we've landed in and engaging in panel dis-

cussions with one another. In between, we joke and swap stories and debate music and, of course, make threats about how
dangerous we are with a handful of cards.

During this particular game of spades we're in a white
van speeding through various shades of barren Southern
landscapes, and I am partners with Nate. Nate is from Chicago and probably better than I am at spades, though it isn't
ever worth saying that out loud. And it certainly isn't worth
saying now, as we are careening toward a certain loss. Nate
and I are vastly different spades players: Him, often operating
at the edge of risks that seem unlikely to pay off until they do
at the very last moment. And me, calculated, taking every
possible card into account and agonizing over the exact number of tricks to be taken before setting down safe bids. For
this, Nate and I are usually foes in this game, two players on
opposite teams during most get-togethers. But today, in a
twist, we have ended up as teammates. In a van with no table,
we make our own flat surface. The cards jump around on the
slick leather seats and we lean haphazardly over the rows to
throw down our offerings into the pile. We are hovering in
each other's space—too close, and not nearly close enough.

I see my friends best when I can see who they are during
a game of spades. How, in their playing, they become the
parts of their personalities that I most envy. Nate, with his
devil-may-care instincts worn outside his body. Jerriod, with
his quiet confidence. Danez, the fourth player in the game,
tucked into the corner of their back row seat, shouting out the
kind of quick-fire jokes they're known to unfurl when at their
most uninhibited. The kind of jokes that send us tucking our
cards into our chests and taking a break to laugh while Danez
continues to push the joke further.

The windows in this old van barely open, so the sweat begins to soak through our clothing. Nate dabs away at the beads

gathering at his forehead while I lean back to catch some of the stifling, humid air coming through the tiny sliver of opening in the window. But the heat doesn't mean a thing when the company is this good. To open these windows and let the outside world peel off a slice of our sweaty, laugh-soaked, echoing glory would make us too generous and too foolish. Better to let it stay where we can savor it all ourselves. Where every portion of it overflows and rests at our feet, an embarrassment of riches. Let the high cotton we speed past stay unpicked, if it means those who might be tasked with picking it get to remain inside and look at a good hand they were dealt and pretend it is a bad one.

And what I meant to say, before you indulged the reckless swelling of my heart, was about the moment when Jerriod, beloved and largely silent, looked upon his hand. One of the last hands of the game, a game he spent not talking much, but hiding behind his low hat and his always immaculate beard. In the few seconds after skimming my hand and realizing that it was, once again, entirely worthless to the cause, I watched Jerriod spread his cards real wide, the smile across his face matching their width. And in the silence of the van, without speaking, Jerriod takes out his cellphone, turns the camera on, and snaps a photo of the cards before him. After a split second of confusion, he shrugs and mumbles, "This hand so good that if I didn't take a picture, wouldn't nobody believe it."

And there we go, set off to laughing again, and slapping the leather seats and covering our faces with our bad hands, full of bad cards, as the van speeds into the open arms of the Alabama border.

Oh, friends—I most love who you become when there are cards in your hands. How limitless our love for one another can be with our guards down. When the first bit of shit talk rattles the chest and then gives permission for more, and more, and more until the talking of shit, too, is a type of romance. Anyone worthy of being taken down is worthy of hearing all of the ways they are being taken down. I meet my enemies with silence and my friends with a symphony of insults, or jokes that cut just deep enough for people to see them for a short burst of time but not so deep as to leave a scar. Dearest siblings, even in an ass-whupping, there's no place else I'd rather be.

"Joy" is such a flimsy feel-good word. I'm talking instead about what can be wrestled from otherwise uncomfortable circumstances and be repurposed, anywhere a flat surface can be fashioned. I want a gift like this at every entry to every unfamiliar place.

LIKE THE HISTORY of Black people in America, spades was born under one set of circumstances, but it came to life under another.

It is hard to say who first introduced the game to the world, but in my own mind's invention, I'd like to think they wore a low hat and chewed vigorously on something from the earth, though this is probably not true. There is no real history of the game but for loose ideas around time and place. The writer and card game scholar George Coffin traced the origins of spades back to Cincinnati, Ohio, bursting up from the dorm rooms of college students in the late 1940s. Students who came up on whist, a trick-taking game that rose to prominence in the nineteenth century and relied on simple methods and ideas: a partnership with another player, a hierarchy of cards, and the ability to take tricks based on that hierarchy. Coffin wrote that these college students improved on some of the minor functions of whist in an attempt to make the game go faster. Whist is a quick game in theory, but not often in practice. There were small holdups in the process, like a rule that said players could ask to review cards from the last trick taken so that they could remember what cards had been played and what cards hadn't been played. The idea around spades was to keep the game moving, since the students often had limited time to play it. The bidding system in spades is somewhat basic, though the stakes involved are high. The action moves quick, and the work of paying attention rests entirely on the players. If you fuck up, then you fuck up, and there are penalties dished out for your fucking up.

First seen as a regional game, played primarily by young people of the era, spades grabbed national and international hold under the umbrella of war. When some of those young spades players from Ohio became soldiers in World War II, the game evolved on battlefields and in barracks. Much of the general appeal of the game crossed over: it was fun and fast, rooted in the type of tactical strategy that might also serve a soldier during battle conditions. But beyond that, it was also a game that could be interrupted and returned to at a moment's notice. If something popped off, soldiers could lay the cards down and run toward whatever they were called to run toward, in hopes that they would all return later to complete the match.

In a standard game of spades, played with the fifty-two standard cards in a deck, the ace of spades is the most fortunate of cards. The one that promises at least one way out for you and your team. If you have the ace of spades and nothing else, you can be confident that you will bring at least one trick home. There will be some glory at the end of it all, no matter what other useless weeds may sprout out of a hand, how many red fours and sixes bloom from the interior. After a hand is dealt out in a game of spades, there are few feelings like sifting through the bouquet of unspectacular pasteboards until

166]   H A N I F   A B D U R R A Q I B

the ace of spades appears. And so, sometime during the Second World War, the soldiers of the 506th Parachute Infantry
Regiment of the American 101st Airborne Division began
painting the sides of their helmets with spades symbols, or
fastening the cards to their heads for good luck. Playing cards
more generally began to play a role in identification during
World War II. Regiments would paint varying suits on their
helmets to differentiate airborne divisions during combat.
But those who stuck the ace of spades to themselves were considered lucky. Promised to survive and at least bring themselves home to a team counting on them.

Another side of this was brought out nearly twenty years
later, during the Vietnam War. American troops believed that
the Vietnamese feared the symbolism of the spade, that they
thought it signaled death and ill fortune. So the military had
the United States Playing Card Company send them crates of
just aces of spades and nothing else, so that soldiers could
scatter them throughout the jungles and villages of Vietnam
before and after raids. The dead bodies of Vietnamese were
covered in aces of spades. Lands—entire fields pillaged and
burned down to the dirt—were littered with the card.

Power, as always, misused in the wrong hands.

IT MIGHT BEAR mentioning to you now that depending on
how you play spades, and where you're from, that li'l ace of
spades might not mean shit. On the eastside of Columbus,
Ohio, the ace might be the high card, but if you go a few
blocks north, them folks might take the red twos out the pack
and get the jokers into the mix. Travel in some other direction, and someone might play joker-joker-deuce-ace, and then
what are you going to do but pray you actually *don't* get that
ace of spades? But then someone might scrap the jokers alto-

gether and play deuces high, where the two of spades is the high card, and then the two of diamonds, the two of clubs, and the two of hearts all get run before you get to your ace, so you might as well just set it on fire if you get it.

Some would say there are as many ways to play spades as there are Black people playing it. I'm sure this is not true, but I still don't sit down at a table I've never been to without asking about the house rules. In some cribs, a person might not care if you and your partner have full coded conversations across whatever kind of table has been set up. But in others, even the slightest hint of table talk means you're falling into debt, two tricks or more, depending on how egregious the offense. In Atlanta in 2016, some older folk didn't appreciate my slick attempts at feeding thinly veiled metaphors to my partner to tip them off to what was in my hand and so they took two books the first time and then four the next, until my partner finally threw up her arms midgame and snapped, *Will you shut the fuck up*—which, oddly, cost us two more books.

There is no real consistency to house rules other than the fact that one doesn't question someone else's house rules. It feels, in effect, like questioning an ancestor or elder. Someone who likely is not there in their earthly form but who taught the game in a very particular way and demanded it to be played that way. And so the spades player must be versatile and willing to go with any rules laid down, even if they seem absurd, or unfair, or entirely whimsical. If the game is being played in mixed company in some neutral location like a hotel room or a basement bar, the house rules defer to whoever is from the place the game is being played, or whoever has some kin from somewhere closest to wherever the game is being played. There is no governing body that makes it like this, but there is a code of honor among the people playing.

Once, in Virginia, someone I was playing with attempted to trace their family's roots to Charlottesville just so that they could place deuces high when no one else wanted to.

What strikes me as most in line with the American Experience when it comes to spades, though, is the shifting value of a card's worth. How the red twos can either be dispensable or invaluable, depending on what city the game is being played in. How the ace of spades can be a symbol of ultimate power or a source of anxiety, depending on who is holding it and what borders they are sitting within. I like a people to be nothing if not malleable. A people who can open their nearly bare cupboards and pantries and still find their way to a meal for a week, or a people who can choose not to code-switch and still get the job. And because of the transitory nature of its earliest days, it makes sense that spades has so many different iterations, with nowhere to trace them to. Soldiers came back from war and taught the game to people who taught the game to people. Along the line, things got tweaked, new challenges got added, and now there is a card game in which the worth of a card in your hand swings wildly depending on where you've taken a seat.

It might also bear mentioning that I have had more than enough money in my pockets in cities where I've still managed to be invisible. In the middle of Texas, where the host at the restaurant nervously looked back toward some empty booths before looking at my road-weary attire of sweatpants and an old band T-shirt and said that there were just no tables for me at the moment. Everything was reserved, and I'd have to wait at least two hours, but potentially more. In New Haven, Connecticut, where I'd been living for well over a year, I return from a run to meet my mailman at the door of my apartment as he is preparing to place my mail in the slot. When I tell him I live in the apartment and can take it, he looks at me skeptically and insists that I can pick it up after he locks the slot again. When I protest, he slams the mail door shut and locks it. I am not particularly sad, or angry, about incidents like these, but I have been thinking about what it is for a person to shift in worth depending on who might be doing the looking and in what city they are doing the looking.

And so of course I love a game in which a card's value can change depending on which ancestor whispered some rules to another one. Spades isn't a game distant enough in history to pick up this many fluid iterations, and yet here we are. I most like to think that someone was dealt a losing hand one too many times and then they changed the rules to suit the bad hands they were getting. All of a sudden, a hand saddled with twos is a type of royalty. I play my game with the ace high because I just happen to be from a place where the people don't like to complicate a good thing as long as it stays good. Or, I'm from a place where if the people are lucky, they can live a life happily ignored without shaking anyone else's foundation. When people ask what I like so much about being from the Midwest, I get to tell them: I know the architecture of the wind. I know the violence it blows in and out. I like to keep my survival as simple as I can. It is so delicious to set your own rules and know that anyone who walks through your door has to bow to them.

THE ARGUMENT I hear offered up from time to time is that spades is not a game of skill, but is a game mostly of luck. That, like poker, it doesn't rely entirely on what you have, but what you can trick people into believing you have. I nod gently at this revelation but also know the major difference is that in poker, there is a choice to opt out if what you have in your hand doesn't suit your comfort level. With this in mind, spades is a game that rests somewhere in the middle between skill and bravado—of hyping yourself up even if you know your kingdom will crumble with each hand playing out.

I am maybe not the best spades player in the world because I am the youngest of four, which (in my case) means that I cannot conceal the excitement that comes with having some small bit of power over an outcome. I cannot conceal the joy of anticipation that comes with wanting to open my palms, draw someone close, and show them something I believe to be miraculous.

I am trying to summon a specific type of feeling here. The one that can best be described by the summer I got my driver's license, and the car I got the day after. The last of my four siblings to get either, having spent so many of my teenage years in cars with them, their own music blaring out of the speakers while I was forbidden to suggest or even hint at suggesting a song selection. I outfitted my car with a cheap stereo system within days of owning it, and incessantly asked my older siblings, all of them home for their summer breaks, if I could be the one to drive them somewhere, no matter how short the trip. I'd sometimes park in the driveway behind their cars, so that if they had to leave, I could suggest that I just take them where they needed to go, since I'd have to move my car anyway. All of these transparent attempts failed, of course. But it was the constant ache of wanting to invite my older and cooler siblings into my version of a world they'd already been living in on their own terms. It was me, bubbling over with excitement, wanting to turn up the volume in my own car with my own hands.

And this is why I throw that tricky ace of spades too early in every game. Or why, if I get dealt enough spades, I'll cut other cards early and often, sometimes throwing off a teammate's more sound strategy. I'm giving away all of my secrets here, writing about a game in which everything is a secret and then nothing is. Spades is not always a game for us who had to grow up proving ourselves to the more hip or more apathetic people in our lives. Every good hand is an opportunity to gain some ground on a past moment of flying uncomfortably under some coveted radar. To drown out the moments when your music rattled out of the open doors of a car, and no one came to join you.

So, yes, the secret is out and I am not great at spades. I am a fine player, probably the same as you or most of the people you know. I have rarely been the best player in the room, but I am always the player in the room most willing to play. I don't want to win as much as I want to draw a game out, long and loud. I want the rematches for losses I've endured, knowing another loss is around the corner. Bring me the people who can only kind of play and might lie to grab a seat at a table of old friends. Those may be my people more than anyone else, the ones I'd attempt to lift with me to an unlikely victory while the jokes rain down at our expense.

There is a type of love in that—how I've been carried by someone who adored me too much to allow me to look foolish. How, even when the van ride through the South ended, I looked at Jerriod and Nate and Danez and made them promise that we'd have a rematch later, even after a long and hot day that was unfolding into a long and hot night. How I knew we'd all drag ourselves out of a bar or out of a bed that night for the sake of rebuilding the moment from a few hours past, before it grew too distant in our memories.

THE BLACK PEOPLE I know let some cultural shit slide from our skinfolk, even if we sigh while doing it, or throw a hand in the air and laugh loud enough for the laugh to catch on with the other people around a table. Yeah, your cousin can't cook worth a damn, but at least they can play the dozens.

Yeah, your little nephew never quite grew into any dance moves, but the boy sure looks like he might be able to hoop.

For whatever reason, there is little scorn like the scorn of not being able to play spades, though I'm not exactly sure why. Perhaps because it is an easy task to pick up—one that comes, largely, with watching and paying attention. Or having someone who loves you show you the ropes at some point. Because it's a card game and so many of the Black people I know learned card games at the feet of an elder, not to know one's way around spades can seem like a reflection on their entire lineage. It is never that serious, of course. But the tells of the person who can't play spades but doesn't want to admit it are among my favorite subtleties of the game: the player who, upon getting their first hand dealt to them, sets the cards down on a table, looks around nervously, and then opens a sentence with "Okay, so just to clarify . . ."

Or the person who loudly announces how long it has been since they've played, before the game even starts. They haven't played since high school, or college, and they've only played a few times, but they remember the rules. Or at least most of the rules. They are certain they can recall a good portion of the rules. The important ones.

I've been the spades partner to these people many times, and I imagine that I get stuck with them because I'm forgiving, and perhaps too kind as a partner in spades. When a partner makes a glaring mistake, I insist that we'll get it back, even after the score tally tips firmly out of our favor. I think of this as a kind of foolish clemency, understanding that the wrong kind of mistake made at the wrong kind of table can lead to a spiral of ridicule that pushes a player into never playing the game again, or leads to them questioning the stability of their own identity. I'm not saying that I have made myself a savior of sorts, taking loss after loss with a smile for the benefit of wayward souls who never knew the game all that well, or at all. But I am saying that sometimes the game is just a conduit for something greater, or a window into a more vital community. And I suppose I can live with a less than stellar win-loss record if it means that I don't overturn the tables every time a partner of mine has made an error that might suggest they have no idea what they're doing but wanted to be close to where the laughter and the table slapping and the swift talk was coming from.

I have intentionally not dug my feet too deep in the explaining of the nuances of spades here, but to "renege" on something is an expression that has universal roots outside the game. In spades, to renege is a cardinal sin, but a sin that is easy to commit if you are the distracted type, or the anxious type, or the overzealous type. The thing with spades is that there is an order to things. A player can't just throw down whatever card they want, whenever they want. The suits on the table must be strictly adhered to. If a player, say, throws down a spade when diamonds are in play—and they have a diamond resting in their hand—that is going to cost. Eventually. Whenever the misdeed is figured out. It could be the next rotation of diamonds being played, or it could be the end of the game. And what it might cost varies. Some people confiscate four tricks, some even more than that. It is the kind of sin that can kick the legs out from under a pretty strong game. And it can happen so quickly, if one player briefly pulls their eyes to something beyond the game and looks back to the table after more than two cards have been played. In a life riddled with mistakes, it is the one I have avoided, just due to the sheer anxiety of what making it would mean.

Once, inside John's mom's condo near the big suburban mall, making the mistake meant a spiderweb of glass stretching across a wide-screen television on a Friday night in '03 when most of us boys were too boring and too broke to do anything but try and call some girls and then break out the stack of cards when they didn't pick up. John's mom was out of town, but that didn't mean shit to us except for the fact that some of us could drink the beer stashed under the sink and play spades like we sometimes saw the old heads play it: loud and drunk, cursing every movement of the game. Me and Shawn were partners, playing a tense game against Trevor and Josh, and I could tell the moment Josh reneged, because he confidently threw a spade down to cut my ace of hearts, but then looked back at his hand with a sense of dread slowly washing over his face. The game was close, and he'd gotten far too excited about the prospect of stealing one precious trick away from us. By the time hearts came back around, Josh, defeated, laid down an eight, and Shawn, who had been helping himself to the warm beer from under the sink, leapt out of his seat, pointing furiously at the table and yelling, "Yo nigga! Yo! You tried to slide like you ain't have hearts a few hands ago! Nah nigga! Nah!" Josh could not protest what we all knew, the homies who were once bystanders now crowding around the table as Shawn took a handful of already won tricks from Josh and Trevor's pile while yelling, "We take six where I'm from! We taking six! Game over!"

I am not sure if it was the impending doom of loss, or the ambitions raised by the steadily cracking cans of cheap beer, or if it was the fact that none of the girls we knew answered our phone calls, but I remember the moment when Trevor jumped across the table to wrestle Josh to the ground while they threw lunging punches at each other, missing wildly each time. And there was John himself, joining the fray to split up the brawl, which, by this point, resembled one of those cartoon tornados of arms and legs. Everything else was a blur until the exact moment when the cluster of boys col-

lided with the entertainment center and the television resting
atop it trembled a bit before beginning its long descent to the
ground.

And in the months after we all pooled our money to pay
John's mom and even after we had to find a new spot to hang,
I most remember the laughter that drowned the walls as Josh
and Trevor sat, out of breath, on the floor next to the shattered television screen. I remember the deck of cards, scattered on the ground, and I remember Shawn, composed as if
none of this ever happened, picking up the cards slowly and
shouting out, "Who got next?"

In that night from a long time ago, when me and my crew
were too poor to do anything but stay inside with some cards
and whatever was in the fridge, I do remember playing spades
until the clouds brightened with the promise of a coming sun.
I do remember someone I love falling asleep with their face
on the table, among the pile of scattered cards. And I do remember the moment when they woke, there was a single card
stuck to the edge of their forehead. I never looked to see, but
I told myself whatever card it was, it had to be the lucky one.
House rules.

My Favorite Thing About Don Shirley

DIDN'T GET MUCH screen time in that movie *Green Book,* or maybe it did in the moments after me and my pal walked out of the theater because we had seen enough of the old gag about how white people and Black people are different and ain't that just the weirdest thing. And besides, it wasn't like the movie was about Don Shirley anyway, so we bailed about an hour in and chalked up the twenty bucks each of us lost and tossed the butter-slicked popcorn to some kid walking into some other, better flick. Even if we'd stayed, I don't think the movie would have gotten to my favorite thing about Don Shirley, which is not that he once sat in the back of a car driven through the American South by someone white. Which is not that he, during his life, endured racism and carried on with a measured calm.

My favorite thing about Don Shirley is that he once gave up his career as a pianist in the early 1950s, after being a child prodigy. Shirley gave his first public piano performance at the age of three, and he was invited to study music theory at Leningrad when he was nine. In the mid-'40s, Shirley spent his teenage years performing his compositions with the Boston Pops and the London Philharmonic Orchestra. But by the start of the '50s, Shirley came to the realization that there might be a lack of upward mobility for Black musicians with a deep investment in classical music (stick to jazz, he was told), and so he went off to study psychology at the University of Chicago, and then he worked in the city as a psychologist.

Several factors collided in the 1950s. The U.S. population started to expand—slowly at first, then leaping up by great bounds due to the baby boom, which began in the '40s as World War II slowed and eventually ended. On top of this, there was not only an increase in income for some Americans, but also an increase in the technology that income could afford. The portable radio became a staple of the decade, and televisions became more prominent in homes. With people's access to ways of consuming entertainment growing, the entertainment itself grew. The imagination of media stretched wider, to consider all possible listening and watching audiences. With this in mind, anyone with access to a radio or television could consume all manner of media at the touch of a button: not only news, but also fictional stories of murder and theft, romance and comedy. Where the radio was once primarily a vehicle for music, it now served multiple purposes. Between this evolution and the sheer number of young people flooding the economy and growing up with the times, an organic generation gap sprang forth. Young people were taking in more information than had ever been available before, and it was of course influencing their behavior in ways that the older generation couldn't understand.

This collision course became the most common thing to blame for the panic over juvenile crime, which ticked upward in the 1950s and became the blueprint for law enforcement's "tough on crime" stances that still reverberate today. The logic was that young people were hearing and watching stories that painted criminals as "cool," and so they were naturally moved to carry out acts of crime themselves. Like most panics, the concerns themselves were rooted in an idea that things were worse than they actually were, or at least that they could get even worse. *What will we do if young people continue to watch these stories and read these books? How will we survive it all?*

This led to a different type of approach to "calming" young people, one rooted in behavioral studies in the hope of crime prevention. In 1954, during his psychology studies at the University of Chicago, Don Shirley was given a grant by researchers interested in studying the relationship between music and juvenile behavior, looking for a link that might present an opportunity to cut the growing problem short. Although he'd been out of the music scene for a few years by that point, Shirley took up residence in small music clubs, planting teenagers in the audience but otherwise playing piano to a crowd of people unaware of the experiment he had been tasked with.

During his sets Shirley would play with sound, measuring the responses of young people to the different combinations and compositions he put together. Oblivious to the science going on underneath the performance, the audience was awed by Shirley's original ear, the way he strung together sounds as if each note filled the air in search of a sonic companion to link arms with. Shirley's aim was to prove that when music was composed with unique enough arrangements, there were tonal compositions that impacted the behavior of young people. The audience's visual responses were observed when certain runs of music would play. Researchers in the club discreetly watched their eyes and bodies, taking note of what appeared to calm them: what music made a fist unclench, or an eyelid grow heavier, or the firm tap of a foot give way to the gentle swaying of the body. The experiment and surveillance were both somewhat nefarious in nature, of course. The aim was to find out what type of music should populate the airwaves in order to put the impulses of young people at ease. A bad-faith experience born out of panic. But Shirley's investment in it was in reaching out and seeing how music—his music—could actually have an impact among the people, after years of being told that what he was doing wouldn't reach anyone at all.

And so, in a time of national panic about young people listening to the wrong things and watching the wrong things, Don Shirley set out to see if he could stem the tide of crime by playing the instrument he knew how to play in a small room with young people watching. And it was in this way that Shirley fell in love with music again. By 1955, he released his first album, *Tonal Expressions*, on the Cadence label. It was met with rave reviews, even though it didn't make Shirley the international star he maybe deserved to be.

This story doesn't make for as good a movie, because there is no conclusion at the end of it all. Shirley's experiment "failed." Crime kept on happening. Youths kept on rebelling. But the mere idea of the project relied on a special type of musician. One who was willing to attempt the unknown, and be comfortable walking away with a problem unsolved. For that, I love this small sliver of the life Don Shirley lived. That in a country still obsessed with Black people solving problems they didn't create, Don Shirley walked away, answering only to himself and his own musical curiosities.

AMERICANS LOVE TO say that things that are distinctly American are not American at all. You get what I mean, or if you don't, wait until the next time someone commits a hate crime or shouts out something racist or otherwise phobic during a TV interview or on a press tour for an album or a movie. Within cycles of frustration or outright rage or comedic coping, there is inevitably a person or set of people who come out and decry the original sin with some boilerplate language about unity and choosing love over hate. These messages are oftentimes punctuated with some version of the same sentiment: This is not who or what America is. As I write this, it is almost election time in America again, and politicians are singing the old familiar song: America is better than anything their political enemies do. The separating of children from their families, the waves of drone strikes, the very violence beckoned by the presence of borders, any casualty that is the logical conclusion of the relentless desire to expand an empire. America is better than all of it, we're told.

America, of course, is not better than this. When the entire architecture of a land is built on a chorus of violences, it takes an unnatural amount of work to undo every lineage of harm and then honor the harmed parties with anything resembling equity. Some of the first steps in that direction almost certainly rely on an honest assessment of not only the history, but the ways that history has generational impact.

To insist that violence and any form of bigotry isn't American is to continue feeding into the machinery of falsehoods and readjustments that keep this country spinning its wheels and making the same mistakes when it comes to confronting the way its past has burdened its present and future. There are people who talk about Martin Luther King, Jr., as if he lived a long and healthy life and then chose to die peacefully at the end of it. There are those who treat the political landscape as if it has only local ramifications rather than the global ones it has had for the majority of my lifetime. The very concept of "choosing love" is privilege, based on an ability to have the idea that there are only two options: love and hate, as Radio Raheem had emblazoned in gold across his knuckles in Spike's *Do the Right Thing*. But the very concept resting at the heart of *Do the Right Thing* is that all this love ain't created equally. The love I have to give is malleable, but it has its limits. All of our love has its limits, and it should. I choose to love my people, and their people. And sometimes I might also choose love with your people. But other times, I choose whatever keeps me safe, and that isn't necessarily hate, but it might be if it gives me a comfortable enough distance.

And since we are talking about movies, after all: the whole thing I'm kicking around here is how movies have been so relentless in their quest to sanitize race relations in America that it has almost become its own genre entirely. Period pieces, usually. Some story about a time when violent racism was permeating every corner of a community, except for the one where a Black person and a white person learned to get along by toppling the odds and seeing the shared humanity in each other after being forced to share proximity because of work or love or an altogether accident. These movies don't really work to deconstruct the design of racial superiority, or how a country arrived at the point it arrived at. They're films that start a few inches away from a perceived finish line and then spend two hours slowly crawling across it before throwing up hands while the waves of applause rain down from the sky.

I did not walk out of *The Help*, though I might have if not for the fact that I was on a long-coveted first date with someone who wanted to see it, so I pretended I wanted to see it. By the time it finally ended, when we walked back into the noisy exterior of the mall, my date confessed that she zoned out halfway through the film, and we laughed together. *The Help* was first a book written by Kathryn Stockett, about Black maids working in white households in Jackson, Mississippi, during the 1960s. Stockett wrote the book because it mirrored her life: when she was a young girl in Jackson, she grew up close to the Black workers in her family's home. *The Help* was a bestseller even before the film rights were picked up, and in the months after the film, it won critical acclaim—particularly for the performances of Viola Davis and Octavia Spencer, who played the Black maids in the movie. *The Help* is sort of like white savior *Inception*, as it is a story written by a white woman about Black workers telling their story to a white woman writer, who sells the book containing the stories to great success. The film drowned in awards and critical praise, except from most of the Black people I knew and talked to.

I was too young to analyze *Crash* back in '05, but I know it made a lot of people cry, because I remember walking through movie theaters to see some other shit back in the spring and summer of that year, and people would pour out from the theaters where *Crash* was showing, and they'd all be wiping tears from their eyes because it turns out all of the racists in the movie were cured or dead by the end or some epiphanies rained down upon them or their sense of duty outweighed their otherwise overwhelming senses of racism. *Crash* won all of the awards that mattered and I watched it in a room of people who all cried but then nothing in the world changed.

There are the sports movies, based on true stories but also not. *Remember the Titans* or *Glory Road*—movies that play on the notion that obstacle is the great unifier. If there is a game to be won, or a shared opponent to triumph over, the concept of racial difference can dissolve. The sports movies often have a large swelling moment of clear unity, when the racial hostility breaks and, through a montage, siblinghood is formed. Like in *Remember the Titans,* in which Black defensive end Julius Campbell and white linebacker Gary Bertier alternate shouting "Left side!" and "Strong side!" into the air over a nighttime practice field while standard-issue inspirational strings swell. And then, at the height of excitement, the two smash helmets together. And like that, the niggers aren't so bad to play football with after all.

And I do admit that I have gotten emotional at that scene, foolish as I know it is. I admit it even now, as I looked at the scene once more while writing this, and then took it back to the start so that I could watch it again. It's the greatest trick: the reveal of a high-emotion resolution. It doesn't show the interior lives of the Black players who still live in a town that was certainly still bubbling over with racism. It doesn't show the distance between the full lives of the white players and Black players or the white coaches and Black coaches. Or what happens inside the walls of a newly integrated school. I know this, and yet the trick still, briefly, works on me. The grand solution to racism, riding on the back of a well-placed Marvin Gaye tune.

Green Book won a whole lotta awards too. And, like clockwork, people wrote about how the movie winning awards was a signifier for what was possible if America could just piece together some kind of bridge for its tricky and persistent divisions. Whenever these films triumph, the bill of goods that gets sold is that the country triumphs. It isn't that America loves films like these because they think the films themselves will fix racism. It seems, instead, that there is a love for these films because they make Americans believe that racism being fixed is something that can happen with a journey through some idyllic half-retelling of history. That it is a matter of proximity, or the shared need to solve some problem on the periphery of racism. Movies like these never approach the simplest and most honest idea: that racism is about power, and the solving of it relies—in part—on people being willing to give up power. But that doesn't make for as much of an interesting film as having a white person joke with a Black person about chicken.

And there are Black actors often at the center of these movies, many of them showered with awards and nomina-

tions, along with the films themselves. There's a tricky negotiation here, I imagine. The recognition Black actors receive
from the public after these performances goes a long way in
validating not only the actors themselves, but also the film.
Even if the performances are singular, to push those performances to the forefront prioritizes a cycle that gives value to
the roles Black people play when they are a part of work that
reframes and recasts racism in service of white comfort. The
awards, the notoriety, it all aims to soften the landing. History,
both the arm holding down the drowning body and the voice
claiming the water is holy.

THE NEGRO MOTORIST Green Book was published and up-
dated for a stretch of thirty years, from 1936 to 1966, during
the era of Jim Crow. It was initially created by Victor Hugo
Green, a mailman who traveled often and saw an opportunity
arising as more and more Black people gained access to auto-
mobiles and wanted to explore the vastness of the country, to
chase down their version of an American Dream. The problem with the American Dream—always, but particularly in
that moment—is that it manifests itself in different times
and places and ways for different people, depending on any
number of identity factors. For Black people in America during Jim Crow, this meant the possibility of being denied service while on the road. For many Black people who were new
to traveling great distances, they knew best the interior of the
places they lived and frequented most, but they had no guide-
line for how the rest of the country might treat them. At best,
there could be an embarrassing interaction at a restaurant or
gas station, but at worst, there could be a hostile or violent
reaction to their presence.

   The Green Book started out as a small green-covered
handbook, which grew as the years went on. It was a travel

guide that listed all of the places its Black readers and travelers could feel safe in: diners, guest homes, museums, hotels, grocery stores. Anywhere along the road, in every direction. The book spanned three hundred cities in the United States, Canada, Bermuda, the West Indies, and more. It relied on its readers to provide information on the conditions while they traveled. It was a user-created database, which circulated quietly throughout Black homes for its entire run. A run that came during a time when there were no established freeway systems in the country, and so motorists had to rely on long, winding roads to get to their destinations. The Green Book was vital in alerting travelers to what towns and cities might welcome their presence and what towns and cities they might want to be more cautious in.

Of the many things America loves to pat itself on the back about, one of the things is an obsession with exploration, or the desire to seek places beyond the places you are from or the places you have been. It is one of the many parts in the overwhelming collage of American Freedom that Americans are told was fought for and won. The Green Book is fascinating as a not-so-distant relic because it pushes back against that particular American notion. For whom is exploration treacherous? When is it a good idea to maybe not venture out into the vast unknown, and what is the return on the investment of curiosity?

Because I love a road trip myself, and have often taken to road trips recklessly and with no direction, I once found an old copy of a Green Book in an upstate New York antiques store. I was there because I knew I was on the verge of getting fired from a job I hated, and I had enough cash in my bank account to afford some gas to get lost for a weekend. The Green Book was tucked into a shelf, next to old caricatures of Black maids and vintage magazine ads with people in blackface pushing toothpaste. It was, it seemed, the "Black history" portion of the antiques store. The version I found was from 1952, and by that point, the book felt somewhat like a magazine. It had advertisements for products like lotion and car wax. It had promotional materials for tours to take in while on the road. It seemed to be catering to a very specific type of American Black person. One who, perhaps, had found some financial freedom during the boom of the postwar economy and the technologies that it introduced. Black people who maybe believed that if they worked hard enough, they could get the America they felt they deserved.

Of course, that made my handling of the book all the more bittersweet. This book, bursting with ads, promising a chance to invest in America like anyone else. Pictures of Black travelers, grinning with enthusiasm and a rush of possibility. But even with all of this, one cannot escape the literal function of the book, still present in many of its pages: offering routes for safe travels for Black people in a country that could still swallow them whole at an unpredictable moment.

The movie *Green Book* isn't about The Negro Motorist Green Book at all, unless one imagines Don Shirley's white driver, Tony Lip, as a type of Green Book of his own, shepherding the musician through the South, fighting when he's needed, and presenting a barrier between Shirley and the racism of the world he was in. This seems to be the general idea that the film tries to sell. That anyone who stands in the way of Black people and harm might represent what the Green Book was, but that isn't it. The Green Book was about a communal passing of information to shepherd people to safety through autonomy, not about the watching over of a Black person by a white person in the role of savior. The Green Book was compiled with sometimes hollow hope, but an understanding that no one could save the Black people reading it from the world outside.

Even with all of the shine and gloss added to the Green Book in its later years, it was still a book that served this single function. Black people have been making ways for other Black people to arrive someplace safely for as long as there have been Black people in America and danger for them to run into, I suppose. I stop at a gas station in one of the last cities flowing into a small Ohio town, and the Black dude behind the cash register asks me where I'm going, how long I'm going to be there. Nods slowly and tells me what routes to take and where not to stop, even if it seems like I have to. I'm often thinking about this while driving through unfamiliar parts of the country. How I rely on the kindness of Black people who know the terrain and who have, perhaps, suffered on the terrain for years before they run into me. Particularly how sometimes the warning is a knowing look, shared as I exit the restroom someone is entering, or as we lock eyes in the potato chip aisle of a convenience store. The physical, hard copy of the Green Book was needed less urgently, it seemed, as civil rights laws went into effect and as highway systems began to develop. But the actual, living needs of the Green Book don't ever actually vanish as long as there are still some places in America where Black people are less safe. The work of the Green Book now is the work of humans who know and understand where they're from and what those places are and aren't capable of accepting. Some of the small towns that rely on Black people to do their most public-facing labor: cashiers and front-desk attendants and clerks of all sorts. The new idea of the Green Book echoes the original idea of it: a conversational network that echoes from one person to the next, until a clearer road is carved out.

And the need for this type of network may never change. Funny to see a movie bearing the name of an iconic text that helped Black people realize their own dreams of safe travel and American exploration. Funnier, I think, that such a movie exists in a time when Black people are still finding their own ways to make safer pathways through remote parts of the country. *Green Book* is the type of movie that allows people in America to think about all of the gentle ways racism can be blown away, and for that it is adored. Don Shirley died in 2013, but his family spoke out against the movie's release and the acclaim it received. They disagreed with the story, and the representation of Shirley and Tony Lip's relationship, stating that Shirley viewed Lip as an employee—someone tasked with driving him around and not much more. The family's resistance to the movie didn't stop it from being praised and adored. The Black relatives of Don Shirley had to take a back seat to the coronation of the film's white creators, one of whom was Nick Vallelonga, the son of Tony Lip.

That's just the way it goes, I guess. The easy part plays well. The people who loved *Green Book* got to feel good about their America for a little while, and with enough of those good feelings strung together, it might be easy to forget that there was ever a fire, or that the fire can still burn.

IN THE MOVIE I'd like to make about Don Shirley, I want a room with four corners and a black piano in each corner. I want the piano keys to be whatever Don Shirley's favorite color was, and if he didn't have a favorite color, then I want the keys to turn whatever color he might see when he closed his eyes while listening to his own compositions. In the movie, I don't want Don Shirley to have to be driven through the American South, but from the windows of this room, I want whatever Don Shirley loved most about the South to be seen.

Far away enough to be adored, but never close enough to be dangerous.

I want two hours of Don Shirley in a room where no one can call him a nigger, or no one can tell him where he can or can't get water from. Where no one can act surprised about how well spoken he is, or how gifted he is, or how he can invent new languages by caressing an instrument's keys.

I want Don Shirley in a movie and in that movie I want his songs on the handheld radios carried by young children, and I want the old people wringing their hands about crime to get a grip for once, and I want no one in jail. I want a gathering at the door of the room where Don Shirley plays and I want each person, one by one, to press their ear to what is happening inside.

I want a movie in which Don Shirley is driven but doesn't feel the need to speak to the white driver. A movie in which we don't even know the driver's name, but we know what Don Shirley's favorite flower is by the way he rolls down his window and cranes his neck toward a field when the car drives by. I would watch the landscape change with him, in our shared silence, humming every now and again at something we found familiar.

Mostly, I want a movie about Don Shirley that allows for him to be seen through worthy eyes. One that doesn't manipulate his story to serve the American thirst for easy resolution. If only all movies about Black people struggling against the machinery of this country were, instead, movies about Black people living. I want a movie in which Don Shirley sleeps for a while. I want a movie in which Don Shirley goes to the store and holds a magazine in his hands, thumbing through the pages before sighing and putting it down. I want a movie in which Don Shirley goes to the movies and watches a movie in which no one Black suffers for the imagined greater good. I want a movie in which Don Shirley visits the grave of someone he loved dearly and lays a haphazardly arranged handful of flowers on it before going home and speaking to no one. I want a Don Shirley movie that isn't tasked with solving any problem it didn't create.

My favorite thing about Don Shirley is not that he was a genius who led a sometimes spectacular life. It is that in the moments in between, he likely led a life that was very normal. And that is spectacular too.

I want a movie cast entirely with the unspectacular but still happily living Black geniuses who have pointed me on a safer path out of the goodness of their own hearts. Perhaps scenes in whatever clothes they wear after they take off their Sunday best. I want them to be absolved, but no one else. There can be no solution without acknowledgment, and so I don't want anyone to watch this movie and consider themselves clean. Everyone else will have to earn it.

I Would Like to Give
Merry Clayton Her Roses

WHILE WE'RE ON the subject of desire.

And I would like to do it now, while the singer is still here and still with us, not at all too old to take whatever flowers she can into her open palms. I would like to give Merry Clayton her roses now, while I can still hear her haunting the corners of my sonic memories, or while I can still look at pictures of a younger version of her and not feel sadness. The old photos with her arms outstretched, hair in a perfectly picked afro, fur coat adorning her shoulders. I would like to do it in this moment, while her old solo records remain on a shelf or in some record store bargain bin and while the owners of record stores all around hand over copies of *Let It Bleed* to young rock 'n' roll fans and talk about the Stones, the Stones, oh, the Stones. When I was coming up and eager for some real rock 'n' roll like the kind I'd been reading about but not listening to, all of the record store dudes wanted to talk to me about the Stones, and so I dug Mick and Keith and the boys. I liked that in all of the photos from the '60s and '70s, they somehow looked exactly as old as they did in the '90s. Like they'd been preserved in some kind of rock machinery. I loved that in all of the old videos of performances, Mick looked entirely possessed in the midst of some controlled fury. I said I liked Mick Taylor more than I liked Brian Jones and so the older dudes would push *Let It Bleed* on me since that was the album where Jones made his unceremonious exit before ending up at the bottom of his swimming pool.

The opening track on *Let It Bleed* is "Gimme Shelter," which kicks off the album with a gentle crawl and pop of guitar flourish before beginning its rampant and breathless relay of clashing drums and voices pulling at each other for dominance among the cacophony. "Gimme Shelter" is the kind of song that gets used in movies and television shows to signify that some *real shit* is about to happen, or in a messy and hectic montage of violence and geography, like in the opening scene of *The Departed*, where Jack Nicholson's character, Frank Costello, laments the New Boston and fantasizes about the Old Boston, while clips of riots and overhead shots of the rolling and roaring city jump to the screen. The song kicks in as Costello muses on power and respect. "That's what the niggers don't realize," he says. "If I have one thing against the Black chappies, it's this: No one gives it to you. You have to take it." And then the drums rush in.

"Gimme Shelter" is one of those songs that churns and churns, invites you in and then shakes you up. It's the perfect entry point for an album, because it is an ominous point of entry. A song that lets you know something bad is maybe coming, and it is maybe coming for you, or someone you love. It's in the scenes where young kids get dropped into some war they don't want to be fighting, just in time to see their best friend killed. The biggest mistake some people make about songs that open albums is that they imagine those songs should be welcoming or warm. Set a tone of comfort before jarring the foundation. An album's opening song should be a loud and all-consuming stretch of madness. The thing that drags a listener to the edge of a cliff, holds them over, and asks them to choose what they think is safer: the unknown of floating to the bottom of some endless height, or the known chaos of solid ground. I like my albums to start by asking me what I think I can stand.

The record store dudes who put on *Let It Bleed* would play "Gimme Shelter" countless times before skipping to the next track. There was something about the way the drums sounded when they were beat out on a table or a steering wheel. *Let It Bleed* is a damn good record—particularly its side two—but there was nothing else on it that matched the sheer immersion and exhaustion of "Gimme Shelter," for me. When these record store dudes homed in on the vocal performance of "Gimme Shelter," they would never talk about Merry Clayton by name, only by the mercy she could offer to the music.

And what mercy it was, I suppose, the way she and Mick wrestled with each other for space on the song, first her voice on top and then his and then hers, before it was most certainly hers and no one else's. The Stones were so established by 1969 that it probably didn't matter that they started their album with a track on which their lead singer gets blown out of the water by, essentially, a background vocalist. But it is worth saying here and everywhere it can be said that Mick Jagger is merely an accent on the tune, and this might as well be Merry Clayton's song, except that no one I knew who talked about it said her name. They would speak of her performance, and how it summoned all of the darkness in one hand and all of the light in the other. But, in the era slightly before the Internet was what it is now, I did not see or hear Merry Clayton's name until I opened the record and unfolded its liner notes.

I would like to give Merry Clayton her roses because I have seen her name and cannot unsee the whole life she's lived every time I close my eyes during the chorus of "Gimme Shelter." I would like the roses to be luminescent shades of red, or yellow, or white, or whatever color reminds Merry Clayton most of the churches she learned to sing in. I would like to do this now, before she is again relegated to the name-less and faceless tragic backup singer. I would like to scale some mountaintop and hold stacks of her solo records in each hand, like a messiah summoning the deprived masses to drink in what they've been missing. I want Merry Clayton to live forever, but I will settle for people speaking her name when they speak of what impossible force blew through "Gimme Shelter." I will settle for people not being able to walk from the wreckage of that song without an immovable haunting.

IN THE FALL of 1969, Merry Clayton didn't know who the Rolling Stones were, and they didn't know her. All Mick Jagger knew was that he'd written the line "rape / murder / it's just a shot away" on a lyric sheet for the song that would become "Gimme Shelter," and he needed someone to sing those words like they feared them. He needed someone to sing the word "murder" like they were trying to squeeze something precious through barbed wire. The Stones needed a good break, since they had been fighting to make *Let It Bleed* for the better part of a year, fighting with the mental collapse of Brian Jones and the brutality of the world around them. Martin Luther King, Jr., and Robert Kennedy were both assassinated during the early moments of the album's recording. The Vietnam War seemed endless, and opposition to it swelled as the Stones wrestled with minute album details, changing titles, or single bass licks. *Let It Bleed* was descending into a darkness that hadn't been approached in previous Stones albums, as it became tasked with capturing the haze of dread and uncertainty that was hanging over the global landscape.

It became clear that "Gimme Shelter," with its sense of apocalyptic rattling, had to open the record. And in the middle of the night in a Los Angeles recording studio, Mick Jagger realized that he needed a woman to sing "rape, murder" and he needed those words to be sung like they might shake the walls of a Black church during a funeral.

Merry Clayton could sing her ass off and so it might not be a surprise to know that she was born with a man of God as her father. The Reverend A. G. Williams, Sr., oversaw New Zion Baptist Church in New Orleans, and Merry sang there first, in a church choir where everyone could sing, but not everyone could match her volume, her vocal fury, or the way she could push a listener to the edge of their most coveted emotion and pull them back right before they could fully grasp it. Clayton went to Los Angeles at the age of fourteen and Bobby Darin put her on his song "Who Can I Count On?"—sweeping in on the chorus while Darin wailed longingly in the background. In 1963, Clayton was the first to record "The Shoop Shoop Song (It's in His Kiss)," but her version didn't approach the charts. The song's most notable version, sung by Betty Everett, became a Top Ten hit the next year, in one of those inexplicable miracles where the right song is sung by the right person at the right moment. Everett's version isn't markedly different from Clayton's, but it's just a bit softer, more gentle, so the song's narrative feels instructive and not demanding. Clayton went on to sing backing vocals for Neil Young, Linda Ronstadt, Phil Ochs, and others, but by 1969, she hadn't caught much solo success. She would come into the studio and blow people away, but never enough to get a good solo song sent to her. There were people who thought Clayton's great flaw was that she could never pull away from her instincts to take people to church, no matter what a song's content was asking of her. Imagine that, your greatest flaw being that you sing every word as if it were delivered to you by God.

"Gimme Shelter" required the divine. Particularly in the late '60s and early '70s, rock acts from the UK often found themselves mimicking their ideas of American music, latch-

ing on to whatever gateways allowed their concepts to flourish. With the Stones, Jagger cultivated a faux accent from the
American South and sang about blues bars. Rod Stewart sang
about hard times working on the Mississippi River for a white
boss. In American rock music, women were almost inter-
changeable, products of a producer's whims. Though girl
groups were on the rise, roles in many of them were uncertain and—as in the case of the Crystals—a whole group could
be replaced in the middle of recording songs. For some Black
women, there was stability in being a background singer,
even if the notoriety wasn't there. It was leaning into the
fragile nature of being a Black woman who wanted a singing
career. If you could sing like Merry Clayton could sing, bands
from across the pond would come calling, wanting to replicate
the sounds they'd heard about, rising out of the Southern
churches.

This perfect storm is what got Merry Clayton's phone
ringing at midnight in the fall of 1969, while Mick Jagger
stared at the words "rape, murder" and knew he couldn't
bring the terror of them to life. Stones producer Jack Nitzsche
woke Clayton up out of bed and asked her to come to the studio. There was a group there from England, and they needed
a singer bad. Clayton didn't necessarily need the work, but her
husband urged her to go. Clayton showed up to the studio in
silk pajamas, with her hair still in rollers. She put on a fur
coat because she refused to show up to the studio not looking
at least a little bit fly. Clayton was also very pregnant. When
she got to the studio to sing, a stool had to be set up in the
booth for her to sit on, since it was late, and the weight of her
pregnant belly felt especially heavy at that hour. She was
skeptical of the lyrics Jagger showed her, but she did one take
of her part and got ready to go home. And then, after a play-
back, Mick Jagger asked her if she wanted to do just one more

and *really* give it everything she had. And when you can sing like Merry Clayton can sing, you don't turn away from an offer like that.

"GIMME SHELTER" WAS released as a single on December 5, 1969, the day before Meredith Hunter was stabbed and beaten to death by a group of Hells Angels while the Rolling Stones performed onstage at the ill-fated Altamont Free Concert. Hunter was an eighteen-year-old art student from Berkeley, a flashy dresser with a huge afro. The Hells Angels were hired as security for the concert and paid in free beer. As the Angels got drunker and the crowd got more high, more drunk, more irate with the trappings of large outdoor shows, the vibe became more aggressive. The Hells Angels threw full cans of beer at audience members, or struck them with pool sticks in an attempt to get them to move back. When the Rolling Stones took the stage after the sun went down, the tension was at a breaking point. By the third song in their set, Jagger was forced to stop the performance while a fight between the crowd and the Hells Angels had to be broken up. After a long pause, the band tentatively continued their set without further outbreak. Until they got to "Under My Thumb."

They'd prefaced the song with Jagger, again, pleading with the crowd for peace. Some long bit about unity and showing the world that we're all one. "Under My Thumb" is a bouncy blues drag, which on that night Jagger decided to stretch out and pull even wider along the crowd. Lingering on each lyrical sentiment, hoping for some salve to be found. He sang "Say it's all right" and "I pray it's all right" over and over, until it became an ominous incantation.

Meredith Hunter didn't even like the Stones all that much, but he wanted to be close to them. It may have been the drugs he'd taken throughout the day, or it may have been the desire for closeness that festivals can organically thrust upon their participants, or it could have been a combination of both, but by the time Hunter climbed one of the speaker boxes next to the stage, it didn't matter. He'd drawn the ire of the Hells Angels tasked with guarding the stage, drunk and still ripe for conflict. One of them pulled Hunter down from the speaker box and threw him on the ground. When Hunter shook free, the Angel punched him in the face. Two more Angels joined the fray, knocking Hunter into the dirt every time he tried to spring back up.

The entire idea of "Gimme Shelter" and its chorus is that sometimes it is just the one thing. A shot fired can unleash a country's desire for violence, or a fist thrown can incite a riot. All of us are just hanging on the edge of someone else's lust for power. That needle moves from time to time, depending on who the "us" is and who the person eager for power is. But the entire song was driving the point home. There is no reprieve from the machinery of violence, and everyone is a trip-wire away from setting off the wrong type of explosion.

For Meredith Hunter, it was surely when those two Hells Angels came over to join a beating already in progress, pressing him into the beer-soaked ground until Hunter decided he was in a losing fight and he'd have to retreat into the crowd. But Meredith Hunter was Black at a festival where not many people in the crowd were Black, and so there was no space in the audience where he could have found some saviors to blend in with. It is the old problem of being invisible until you are the only thing that someone can see.

Hunter ran, and the Angels pursued him, first three and then another and then another. Hunter had a pistol on him, and he pulled it out, thinking that might scare his pursuers away. When the Angels got to Hunter, one of them attacked him from behind, knocking the pistol out of his hand, then stabbing him twice. The Angels were all upon him now, stab-bing him repeatedly in the back. When he dropped to his knees, they kicked him in the face until he fell down in the grass, where he was kicked by a chorus line of steel-toed boots. With him on the ground and weakening, the Angels became even more furious, kicking him in his head and hit-ting him with a metal trashcan. Hunter's final words were a useless correction, directed at the Angels: "I wasn't going to shoot you."

When Altamont is written about now, it is said that Hunter was stabbed to death, which is only partially true. There are fewer details about the vicious beating that followed the stab-bing, or Hunter's lack of desire to engage in the brawl with the Angels prior to the stabbing. Fewer details about the fact that Hunter was carried to a Red Cross tent in his dying mo-ments, but his nose was so completely destroyed that he couldn't breathe, gasping for air through his mouth, trying to speak some words beyond the fruitless plea for life beneath the boots of his attackers.

Meredith Hunter's family could not afford a tombstone, and so he was buried in an unmarked grave in East Vallejo, California. He was a footnote to the land, as he'd become a footnote to the Altamont, the victim of that concert's logical conclusion. Running for his life while Mick's "I pray it's all right" still echoed among the stars. Pleading for his life while DJs in some other part of the country dropped the needle on the new Stones single about how death is but a kiss of the wind away for all of us. The grave the calmest shelter, even if the people who love you cannot find your name.

IT'S THE SECOND syllable of "murder" the third time it's sung. This is the part of "Gimme Shelter" that people have probably told you to listen to. The part of the song where

Merry Clayton's voice bends, and then breaks, a door slowly giving way to the army of noise pressing up against it. Clayton's emotional and vocal intensity had been rising as the song progressed, and around the 2:48 mark, when she got a chance to take on the song's lines that were meant for her all on her own, she seized the opportunity. It is good to sing the word "murder" like you fear it, but better to sing the word like you aren't afraid to commit it. It is best, though, to sing "murder" somewhere in between those two extremes. In the first turn of "rape/murder," Clayton sings the word as if she fears it. On the second turn, the word is sung just a touch too eagerly, ending with an expressive "yeah!" as a bookend. In the run-up to the third rotation, Clayton's voice cracks slightly on "it's just a shot away," but she is already too far in, careening toward the obvious crescendo. It's the third time "murder" rolls around that encompasses every emotion: fear, anger, a slight undercurrent of glee.

What people love to talk about is the way a listener can hear Mick Jagger in the background let out an exclamation of awe and excitement. But in the isolated vocal track, even beyond the shouts and yelps of the Stones in the studio, you can hear a slight hesitation as Clayton makes the transition from the voice-cracking howl of "murder" to the next line. The Stones kept it in the final track, but it's a subtle pause between "it's" and "just a shot," throwing off her rhythm ever so slightly. As if some spirit entered her body and then left before anyone could notice.

MERRY CLAYTON NEVER gave birth to the baby she showed up to the studio pregnant with. Shortly after getting home from the session, she miscarried. There are those who say that the physical strain Clayton exerted in the studio contributed to the miscarriage, though she herself has never blamed the

song or the Stones or the studio, which may be her way of
keeping her grief her business and not aligning it with another piece of rock 'n' roll mythology. I don't know anything
about what it is to carry or give life, but I know that when
Merry Clayton's voice cracks in "Gimme Shelter," a part of
me wants to jump as if it is the shot that begins the war itself.
A part of me hears Mick shout and wants to know what he
saw in that moment. A pregnant Black woman balancing on
a stool, summoning all she had in order to leave behind something memorable. The backup singers, man. They get to be
memorable for a few minutes at a time and forgotten in all of
the minutes in between. I want to know if Mick saw every
wretched tooth in the mouth of the world's most wretched
beasts trembling and falling to the ground. There is some
awful reckoning to be had in a song like that. Some awful
things to be lived with.

IN 1970, MERRY Clayton released her debut solo album. In
an attempt to ride the wave that her contributions to "Gimme
Shelter" had afforded her, the album itself was titled *Gimme
Shelter*. The first single on the album was her own version of
the song—her first single to crack the *Billboard* Hot 100,
landing at number 73, in part because of the momentum
from the Stones single. Clayton's solo career consisted of a
burst of five albums in the '70s, none of them rising any
higher than 146 on the U.S. charts and 36 on the R&B charts.
Clayton's version of "Gimme Shelter" is restrained,
drowning in horns and a churning bassline, swelling with a
gospel chorus backing her. On the album cover and the single,
her afro fills up most of the frame, and two large hoops dangle from her ears. A half-smile pushes up her face, and her
eyes squint slightly, giving off a knowing, satisfied look. The
song's lyrics are the exact same, but under Clayton's solo care,

it becomes less ominous; more of a prayer. It is a song of optimism in cynical times, which I suppose is what anyone who was raised singing worship songs can do with some lyrics in front of them. Clayton, for once, gets to revel in the role as conductor, with the wave of voices behind her following her vocal whims. At the end, Clayton repeats, "It's just a kiss away, Lord, a kiss away" before cutting directly into a plea: "Stop that shooting / Stop that shooting / Love is just a kiss away."

She only sings the words "rape, murder" once. So fast that if you were tapping your foot with enough ferocity, you'd miss it.

In an interview from the middle of the '80s, Merry Clayton says that she couldn't listen to "Gimme Shelter" for a long time, but she's trying. She had taken to singing uncredited commercial jingles by then, because once you get used to being both present and not there at all, it is easy to transfer those skills to a way of life. She had also started a gospel group with Della Reese and O. C. Smith. They called themselves Brilliance. It made Clayton's father happy to hear her singing the songs he once taught her in church, but Brilliance never released an album. Clayton spent much of the '80s peppering songs on soundtracks for big films like *Get Smart* and *Dirty Dancing* where she was, again, secondary to some larger, all-consuming part. Even the greatest singer who is relegated to the background has a hard time expanding out of it. To be known in this way is to be barely known at all. To be buried in history, in a grave with no marker for your name.

I THOUGHT MERRY Clayton was going to get the comeback she deserved in 2013. The documentary *20 Feet from Stardom* had come out that year, detailing the lives of backup singers throughout rock history, and Clayton had a major part in it, giving her career enough renown for her to land some backup singing gigs with contemporary musicians like G. Love and Coldplay. Shortly after the documentary was released, a compilation of her solo work also hit the market, boosting her profile even further.

But then there was the car accident in June 2014. A near-fatal wreck on a Los Angeles highway that claimed both of her legs and left her stuck in hospitals doing months of physical therapy.

When people talk about Merry Clayton now, they talk about things like luck, and how bad it can be for some folks. And it is true that Merry Clayton sang a song about the thin border between love and tragedy and then became known for being only on one side of that border and never making it over to the next. But fewer people talk about what it must have been like for an artist like Merry Clayton to give so much of herself to an industry that had already made a box for her before she'd even arrived to be put into it. She was going to be the big-voiced singer who pushed songs over the edge, but never got to immerse herself in the fame and infamy that she so eagerly provided to others. Merry Clayton, most known for how her voice bent around a single word and then known for all that she lost.

I WOULD LIKE to give Merry Clayton her roses. I would like roses to burst forth from the walls of every room Merry Clayton is in. I would like to give roses to every singer who had a name tied up in liner notes and not on the tongues of people who sang along to their pristine vocals. I would like to bring roses to the doorstep of the house Merry Clayton walked out of at midnight in 1969 and I would like to lay roses on the stool where she sat, her pregnant belly hanging over the edge while she sang *murder, murder, murder*. I would like roses to come out of the ground somewhere any time a person's voice cracks under the weight of what it has been asked to carry. I would like to do this while the living are still the living, and I don't want to hear from any motherfucker who isn't with the program. I would like roses for Merry Clayton to fall from the sky whenever a gunshot echoes above and I would like roses for Merry Clayton in the hands of whoever could throw the first punch but doesn't. I want the small red fists to come from the earth and slowly open wherever Meredith Hunter's body is, or wherever his body had been. I want Merry Clayton to be as big as the Rolling Stones. I want teenagers to wear her face on T-shirts, and I mean her good face with her good afro and her fur coat and her father's eyes. I want record stores to stock the solo records of Merry Clayton in the front case and I want them to play all of the songs she sang alone, with no one else. I want enough roses to build headstones for everyone I love. I want the moment when the drums kick in on any version of "Gimme Shelter." I want that feeling in my chest to always remind me what I'd miss if it were taken from me. I want shelter, and I don't even know what that means anymore. I want nowhere, nothing sacred.

Beyoncé Performs at the Super Bowl and
I Think About All of the Jobs I've Hated

FIRST OF ALL, the one in 2016 wasn't even Beyoncé's show to headline, but so few people remember that, myself included. She'd had her headlining run at the halftime of a Super Bowl just three seasons earlier, and she had put on a show that was above standard for the often stiff, uninspiring Super Bowl halftime performance. Which exists largely to foster excitement months out before serving as a mundane bridge between the pomp and circumstance of choreographed violence. Beyoncé's 2013 performance was great, though her performance in 2016 is the one that seems to be more memorable. A fact that is talked about with Beyoncé both enough and somehow not enough at all is that her evolution as a performer is tied directly to her evolution with regard to vision, to seeing what might be possible in the world. She is not the only Black woman performer who Americans have gotten to watch transform into different versions of her vision over the course of nearly two decades. There is a history of Black performers—specifically Black women—seamlessly reinventing and evolving without the clumsiness that seems to sometimes plague artists who make grandiose artistic shifts. Our Josephine Baker, for example, who spent the '30s and '40s building up the gravitas that she took into her later career in the '50s. Beyoncé, though, has maintained a foothold as a major and visible pop music star for a longer tenure than most of her peers. And, like Baker, as she's gotten older, Beyoncé has found ways to insert the political into the performance. The attempt being not only to start a conversation but to be a driving force and a guiding hand within the conversation.

In just three years' time, Beyoncé went from an already showstopping entertainer to someone who had a foot in two worlds of performance: being memorable, and delivering a message. And so yes, it did not matter that in February 2016 the Super Bowl had technically commissioned Coldplay to be its headlining performer. No one I know remembers that Coldplay was even there. They should never have invited Beyoncé to come if they were invested in being memorable headliners. It is perhaps a fool's errand to ask Beyoncé to accent your show if you want it to remain your show. Particularly this performance, which was styled as an homage to the Black Panther Party, as 2016 marked the fiftieth anniversary of the organization's formation.

Cloaked in a black jacket with a bandolier of bullets lining it, Beyoncé took to the halftime stage channeling *Dangerous*-era Michael Jackson. Though not Jackson's greatest album, *Dangerous* did serve one of his greatest moments, visually and aesthetically. The one in which he was giving himself completely to the gods of grandiose gestures. The era when he knew his shit was going to sell anyway, so why not give the people something to look at. Beyoncé and Jackson are very different performers but seem to come from a similar lineage of knowing what they know: that humility is a fine way to ease the hearts and minds of the folks who cannot fathom the heights you operate at. But if you are Black, and you are twice as good as a lot of people doing it, it serves you to remind the public of your greatness from time to time.

Beyoncé walked onto the grass at Levi's Stadium in the Bay Area, flanked by at least two dozen Black women, each of them dressed all in black, perfectly coiffed afros radiating from beneath their black berets. For those familiar with the Black Panthers, or even for those who only vaguely remembered some photos they had seen somewhere once, it instantly made sense. And for those not at all familiar with the Black Panthers, the image was still clear. The intent was to foster either joy or freedom or discomfort or rage, depending on which eyes were taking in the scene.

It was a gesture that overshadowed all other moments in the halftime show—even the songs themselves were secondary. On one of the biggest stages in the American consciousness, Beyoncé paid tribute to one of her people's most revolutionary movements, in the place of that movement's birth.

By 2016, Black people had found new ways to say "I am angry about every measure of American violence" without speaking the words themselves out loud. It became abundantly clear that the people in America perpetrating violences were aware of what was happening and aware of their role in it, and so the very presence of Black people noticing and understanding was enough to make these people uneasy. It is why, in response to "Black Lives Matter"—as a statement, not even a movement—a chosen response was to break apart the sentiment and apply it to all things. Not just different races or individuals, but foods or shoes or hair products. Commodify into silence. And so when there were Black people who decided to use their platform to not so subtly reclaim that which had been commodified and sanitized in the name of American Comfort, the pushback was often irrational, coming loudest from those who were the most afraid.

After Beyoncé's appearance on the halftime show, Rudy Giuliani insisted that the performance attacked police officers, despite none of the performance explicitly angling toward a criticism of law enforcement. But that's the trick, isn't it? Power, when threatened, pulls an invisible narrative from the clouds that only others in power and afraid can see.

The Super Bowl is not a radical platform, no matter what performance of radical politics can be projected onto it for a brief spell. And so it was also hard for me not to think of Beyoncé's moment at the 2016 Super Bowl as a conscious decision about how to show up to work. Obviously, there is an understanding here that for the biggest pop star of a generation clocking in isn't the same as me, you, or most of us walking to our computers and trudging through the password before starting our daily tasks. And, of course, that even this type of performance on this large of a stage is divorced from the work of the people. I want to be clear in saying that the aesthetics of revolution tied to the violent, capitalistic machine of football and carried out by one of the wealthiest musicians in the world is a far cry from any actual revolutionary work happening in marginalized and neglected communities by the people on the ground there. But the labor of performance and presentation is still labor. One must clock in, one way or another. And Beyoncé chose to clock in with a chorus of picked afros at her side and at her back, with mock bullets across her torso, and with a message so loud it didn't have to be spoken in order to be heard.

AT THE HIP healthcare start-up, no one knew how to spell my name. I worked tirelessly to correct people at first, like when my name was spelled wrong on my offer letter, or when my email was rendered unusable because my last name had a few extra and wrong letters in it. Eventually, I just gave up, figuring that if I spent all of my time correcting the spelling of my name there, I'd never get anything done. I got the job at the hip healthcare start-up on Craigslist in 2012, in a time when job searching on Craigslist was becoming even more fruitless than it already was. Between the scams and uneven expectations around pay and experience, opportunities on the website for potential good work in my city were dwindling. But still, it was a place that felt most approachable for me. I didn't have to answer a bunch of questions, or upload a résumé. I could find a job one or two clicks away from where I found a dodgy but useful old couch. It was like a one-stop shop for wayward desires, and I simply had to adjust my expectations accordingly.

The job description for the hip healthcare start-up seemed definitely like a scam. Boasting of not only salary and benefits, but also an office where employees enjoyed a free in-house hot lunch daily and a relaxed dress code. For my interview, I was told to wear "whatever I wanted." With all of this in mind, I was surprised to show up and find a functioning office with real people working in it. When I got the job, it felt like I had leveled up to a more real version of adulthood, but on my own terms. A salary and benefits, but also jeans, jerseys, and sneakers in the office.

My first job at the hip healthcare start-up was to take calls and chats from doctors and medical professionals who had questions about the healthcare software the start-up invented—a software that makes the tricky process of obtaining prior authorizations easier. On the phone, doctors asked me to spell my name twice, or sometimes three times. Upon the second or third spelling, some exclaimed, "I'm not even gonna try to say that one." These are people who, I imagine, went through several years of school. During product demos, where I talked to a group of doctors or nurses, there were days where we spent more time on my name and where I'm from than we did talking about the product itself. If you have a name like my name and you get asked its origins enough, you can tell when the line between eager curiosity and skepticism is being blurred, mostly because the people who imagine themselves good at hiding the tonal difference between the two are not actually that good at hiding the tonal difference between the two. When I told people that I'm from Ohio, they wanted to know where my parents are from, or where their parents are from. It is amazing, the weapons people disguise in small talk.

At the hip healthcare start-up, I put a Black Lives Matter sticker on the inside of my cubicle in the early days of the movement, when it was starting to pick up steam after George Zimmerman's acquittal. After a week, the sticker had vanished. I came into work on Monday, and it was gone. At the hip healthcare start-up I am one of two Black people but it's a small and growing company and surely there would be more of us eventually. I don't smile as much as the other Black person, who has an infectious warmth that I aspire to but cannot reach. It doesn't seem like a comfortable space to ask what happened to a sticker affirming Black lives, and so I don't. There is beer and a pool table, though, and sometimes we have parties. I got called a nigger on the phone once by a doctor in Maine, and so I hung up the phone and stepped outside to take a long walk. When I came back, my boss asked if I'd finished the call.

During July 2016, I decided to take a day off. It was July 7, and on July 6 Philando Castile had been murdered by police officers in the front seat of his car. On July 5, Alton Sterling had been shot six times at close range by police officers who had wrestled him to the ground. On July 4, fireworks unspooled their bright and brief magic over buildings and rivers all around America in celebration of a desire for noise and light. In celebration of a country as spectacle first and everything else second. And so on July 7, I decided I could not possibly go to work.

A thing that I've come to find is hard to explain is the immediate aftermath of Black people being shot by police. The visuals are jarring, but they have become easier for me to avoid. What is larger and more looming is the idea of fear, and how to track with and explain that fear to people who might not be feeling it in the immediate moments. Even people who I decided are good, caring people, who just don't have access to unlocking the very particular fear that exists in not only the deaths, but the country's reactions to the deaths. It isn't that I find myself afraid of a police officer coming into my house while I sleep and shooting me in my own bed. But I do think about the things on the body that could be mistaken for weapons, including the body itself. I think about how I sometimes run with headphones on and thus might not hear a command yelled by a police officer with their hand already reaching to unlatch their holster. I think of how quickly moonlight can carry infinite mistakes. In the moments after these shootings, when Black people say, "I am afraid the country is trying to kill me," a rebuttal from people without this particular fear is often rooted in what the country has given, and not what it can take away without consequence. "Don't you have a good job?" reads one tweet, in response to a Black woman who expressed fear, frustration, exhaustion. "Don't you have degrees?"

I have had many jobs and none of them can stop a bullet. I have been told how smart I am, but when I get pulled over in rural Ohio because I'm told my music is too loud, I know not to attempt an intellectual debate when there are no other cars visible for miles. I have yet to be given enough in this country that might silence the ache that arrives when a video of a Black person being murdered begins to make the rounds. I am interested most in a reparations that is rooted in the structural: abolition, reformatting and reimagining ways to build a country on something other than violence and power. But if I can't yet have that, I just need a place to be afraid and comfortable in my fear until I can bury it with another emotion.

I can't tell the people at the hip healthcare start-up this on July 7, when I woke up and didn't want to get out of bed. I don't even know if any of them have thought about Philando Castile or Alton Sterling. There are police sirens outside my apartment and I don't want to move. I send an email to my boss with some generic language about needing a day off to rest, coming down with something or the other. I never get a response. When I return to work the following day, people ask me for notes on the meeting the day before. Someone asks if I was able to get to some task that was sent to my email. It becomes clear that no one even knew I was gone.

THE DAY BEYONCÉ dropped the video for "Formation" I was in the Houston airport, which I remember not because of the serendipitous nature of being in the birthplace of an artist on the same day they release a world-stopping piece of art. I remember it because of a white man in a wrinkled shirt with his blazer slung over the back of a bar chair. We were placed next to each other by circumstance of long layovers in a busy and crowded place. I can often tell when someone has a desire to talk, especially in situations centered on travel: in airports, on planes, or in shared cars. There's the way a quick glance lingers, looking for something or anything to enter conversation with. The man and I are both traveling for work, but in vastly different work uniforms: his a suit, mine sweatpants and an old Tribe Called Quest shirt. I'm going to read some poems in California, and he's going to a sales conference in Seattle. His laptop has some spreadsheets on it, while mine is littered with open Word documents. We wear our labor on every inch of ourselves. I like the way that two strangers who likely will never see each other again fight to find some small common ground first, then see what echoes from there before parting for an eternity. If we must be confined to our unwilling clusters of closeness, I suppose, let us find something to banter meaninglessly about and save the hard conversations for the people we believe in and trust. I find myself noticing the white people who do this more carefully and cautiously with me, and this man is one of those.

SportsCenter is on the TV above our heads. He asks what I think about the upcoming Super Bowl, which is slated to happen in about twenty-four hours. I tell him that I'm rooting for the Panthers, I guess. I like Cam Newton, who by that point had become the latest in a long line of poster boys for Black athletes who are too arrogant, too flashy, and don't know their place. I lob my affection for Cam Newton out, just to see where we stand, and the man nods gently, approvingly. He's a bit older than me and insists that he's old school as a fan but really likes watching Newton play. He's still going to root for the Broncos, he tells me. He's got money riding on the game, and he thinks their defense is just going to be too much to overcome. He jokes about how he's going to force himself through watching the halftime show. His wife loves Coldplay, he says. She's gotten them to grow on him.

Working in and around music for long enough, a person can get a sort of sixth sense for when that universe is shifting, particularly if a space falls suddenly quiet, or if you look around and see masses of people hovering over their phones with looks of joy or excitement and not fear or grief. I notice this happening around me while sitting in the airport bar with my new companion, and I excuse myself from our conversation to look down at my phone. I pull up the "Forma-tion" video, and there is Beyoncé, squatting on top of a half-submerged New Orleans police cruiser.

The video draws from many images—a Black boy in a hooded sweatshirt dancing in front of a line of armed police, a long lineage of images rooted in Southern Blackness, from men on horses to flowing and billowing antebellum dresses. But in those initial moments of taking the video in, all I see is the water. As the song unfolds, the police car sinks deeper and deeper. I can tell the man next to me is watching the video along with me, first out of the corner of his eye, and then more intently. The car is mostly underwater by this point, but for the top of its windows and its unmistakable siren.

The Houston airport was renamed after George H. W. Bush, the father of George W. Bush, who once flew over the drowning city of New Orleans and looked mournfully at the submerged landscape from the window of Air Force One while photographers took photos, and there is so much lan-guage packed into certain moments of silence, I guess. At the end of "Formation," the police cruiser disappears into the water completely and takes Beyoncé with it—and the entire George H. W. Bush Intercontinental Airport around me be-gins to flood. There is water seeping through the cracks in the walls. Water rising out of the floor and soaking the feet of all the Black people at their gates staring at their phones. Water pouring into and out of planes. Water that no one is answer-ing for, or that answers to no one. When the video ends, the man next to me turns slightly more to his right, a sign that maybe our flirtation with common ground has ended. I have found the divide between us, it seems. So much language packed into certain moments of silence. I imagine everything feels distant when you are drowning. Even the things once imagined as shared comforts.

WHEN HUEY NEWTON fled the country on the back of murder charges in 1974, Elaine Brown was appointed to lead the Black Panther Party. She was the only woman to ever do so, despite the fact that by the early '70s the majority of the party's members were women, some of them working to forge community education and activism programs, and some of them fighting on the front lines against police brutality and government violence. Brown was the chair of the party for three years, from 1974 to 1977. She focused heavily on working the group toward electoral politics and continuing its firm tradition of community service. She developed the Panthers' Liberation School, which pushed to bring excitement about education into the lives of Black students who were often neglected by the school systems they found themselves in. Through it all, though, Brown maintained that she was working against a dual type of resistance: both exterior and interior. In her memoir, 1992's *A Taste of Power*, Brown wrote:

> A woman in the Black Power movement was considered, at best, irrelevant. A woman asserting herself was a pariah. If a black woman assumed a role of leadership, she was said to be eroding black manhood, to be hindering the progress of the black race. She was an enemy of the black people. . . . I knew I had to muster something mighty to manage the Black Panther Party.

Late in 2016, after the election results had come back and the demographic voting breakdowns began to circulate, the most jarring of all the stats was that white women voted for

216]   H A N I F   A B D U R R A Q I B

Donald Trump over Hillary Clinton at a 52 percent to 43 percent clip. Resting underneath that, however, was that Black
women overwhelmingly voted Clinton, at 93 percent. A lot of
the conversation centered on the intersection of gender and
power, and how white women will vote in the interest of the
latter if it means ignoring all else. But what also began was a
groundswell of appreciation for Black women that read as
disturbing to me, largely because it was rooted primarily in
their ability to fix the country, or labor on behalf of a mess
many of them didn't ask for. The discomfort was most visceral because a majority of people engaging in this narrative
in its early stages were white, and potentially "well-meaning,"
but not considering what the building of those ideas might be
doing. Or not considering the motives behind these actions.
To shout "Black women are going to save us all!" might feel
good to type out to send in a tweet, but it reads as less good
when one stops to consider that Black people—specifically
Black women in this case—are not here in this country as ves-
sels to drag it closer to some moral competence. The American obsession with immorality and a willingness to push its
hardest labor off on its most marginalized is integral to the
Black American experience, and so it occurred to me that
maybe Black women were simply attempting to save themselves. That many Black people in the country have to go to
jobs they don't love, or deal with waves of microaggressions at
work or at the coffee shop or at the gym, and still know that
voting won't save or stop any of this but did it anyway because
the bet was already bad but the dealer had the cards in his
hand to make it worse, and so many of us knew it.

And so sometimes, it is simply about alternatives. What
marginalized people can do with the space we make our own
until someone else makes it theirs. Elaine Brown and the
women of the Black Panther Party endured, I imagine, be-

cause the alternative seemed like a more difficult path toward liberation. Bree Newsome scaled a flagpole to take down a Confederate flag with her bare hands because the alternative was living underneath its vile shadow for another day and there had already been enough days. Beyoncé got five minutes as a supporting act at the Super Bowl and donned gold bullets and had Black women pick out their afros and adorn themselves in black leather because the alternative was America's comfort. A Black person leaves their loved ones or their own personal space of comfort to go into an office where their ideas aren't taken seriously, but they show up the next day still, and the next day after, because the alternative that capitalism has made for them is a lack of security, or the inability to pay for whatever small freedoms make them feel more human at the end of it all.

And I know, I know I said that clocking in to a job or casting a vote isn't the same as performing at the Super Bowl or opening a school in the name of Black Liberation or the messaging of laying one's body against a police car, slowly vanishing into dark water at the end of an expensive music video. But the idea of this Black Excellence that I keep returning to is what a person does when faced with these alternatives. What better living is seen beyond the living currently constructed. Beyond the job, or beyond the emails, or beyond the days where some of us must take walks to shake off the hovering specter of fear, or beyond the videos of how quickly a life can be swept away, or beyond a voting system that fails everyone underneath it, but some of us more than others. Beyoncé had a whole career before her appearance at the Super Bowl to leverage and earn the public's trust, then demand more from those watching. The end result isn't the excellence, even if it is excellent. The excellence, for me, rests in the mundane fight for individuality, or the excellence rests in the moments before the moment. Excellence, too, is showing up when it is easier for you not to be present, especially when no one would notice you being gone. When those same people arise only to applaud you for what they see as your desire to save them from themselves and the growing tab on their endless damage. When your mark is your own, defined by rules of your own making, you build the boat wide enough for your people and whatever you need to survive. You save yourself first.

ANATOMY OF

CLOSENESS //

CHASING BLOOD

On Times I Have Forced Myself to Dance

WITH THE BLADE tenderly edging along the line of hair creeping unevenly down my forehead my barber says *and listen man, gay people got more rights than us Black folk these days* & I can't say that I know what prompted this & I stopped listening to this nigga speak 5 haircuts ago & we ain't cool but I live in Connecticut & I don't trust any of the barbers here & they all white & this dude got a shop near the apartment I hate & pay too much for & up to now he been easy to tune out & he can cut a mean line & few people speak about a haircut as an act of intimacy & a way to give oneself over to the whims of another person & when my barber says *and listen man, gay people got more rights than us Black folk these days* my head is cradled gently in his left hand & his thumb stretching out the skin near my left eye & who is to say what is an act of love and what is not & I think this even though I clench my fist & tighten my jaw after my barber speaks & it is true that I arrived here and asked to be made into a new image & what is that if not an act of love & I trust a man I barely know and do not like with the sculpting of my look & my self-worth & ain't that some shit & I trust my barber more than I have trusted girlfriends & brothers & the oldest homies & it's because if he does his job right I can always find new love somewhere & we are in a waltz now & by that I mean there is a negotiation one enters into with a blade to their hairline & I have a widow's peak & it was passed down from my mother

who got it from her mother who got it from somewhere worse
than I live now & so I'm saying I am of a particular hairline
& it deserves all of the affection I couldn't give the women
who blessed me with it & I tell my barber *There are people
who are both Black and gay though man* and he just says *Nah
I ain't with that bullshit* & I don't know what *that bullshit* is &
my fist is still clenched & he is still tracing a line along my
forehead with a sharp blade & maybe now is not the time to
fight & we contain multitudes is all I was saying like how I
can want to fight with this nigga but also know it's the only
trustworthy cut in town & I am failing again when the stakes
are high & when I write about the romantics of the barbershop it is never this part & it is never the men who dismiss the
violences we revel in for the sake of a laugh or the sake of not
feeling lonely & it is never the women who walk in the shop
or work in the shop & it is never this part where everyone
under a shop's roof is expected to bend toward the politics of
the person holding a head in their gentle palms & it is always
about the familial romantics of a place where niggas come to
get fresh & I suppose that is the problem I think & I suppose
even the tightest families gotta scrap some shit out once in a
while & my barber says *Yo unclench your jaw, I can't get your
beard like this.*

The Beef Sometimes
Begins with a Dance Move

A WALTZ IN a circular chamber of your homies and not-homies, shouting chants of excitement. There are whole seasons where the people I grew up around didn't want to throw fists, but might do it begrudgingly. These seasons are never to be confused with the seasons where people charge into all manner of ruckus until a playground or a basketball court is a tornado of fists and elbows and sometimes legs. In those seasons, one might have to fight once or twice just so people know they aren't afraid to. Run the white tee through a light wash so the stain of blood might take on a copper tint when the summer sunlight spills onto it.

These seasons don't align for everyone. Sometimes, if the hands are fresh from burial, or from planting roses on a grave, calling them to make a fist seems impossible. In school, if any sports team was relying on your presence, a teammate would likely pull you away from whatever your emotions were dragging you toward.

What I have loved and not loved about beef is that it becomes more treacherous the longer it lies dormant. When I was coming up, particularly in school, sometimes the performance of beef was in two people who didn't particularly want to fight, inching toward each other's faces, airing out a set of grievances ferociously, hands clenched at their sides. If you have had beef that careened toward a violent climax, you know when someone is and isn't down to scrap. I knew if someone locked eyes with mine—unblinking and unmoving—then there wouldn't be much of an actual physical fight to be had. Just the performance of perceived dominance. I wish more people talked about the moments that build up to a potential brawl as intimacy. The way it begs of closeness and anticipation and yes, the eye contact, tracing the interior of a person you may hate but still try to know, even if the knowing is simply a way to keep yourself safe.

There were the real beefs of my neighborhood: over territory or someone coming back to the block with too much product or not enough cash or any long string of retaliatory violence. Those were the beefs that might end in a funeral, or a prolonged hospital stay, or a parent trembling under a porch light and yelling their child's name down a dark street only to have the darkness lob their own voice back to them.

The secondary beefs—the ones that most consumed me and my pals growing up—were almost exclusively about the trials and tribulations of romance. Particularly when it came to the boys. Someone had a girlfriend, and then they didn't. If someone kissed someone else outside the Lennox movie theater while we all waited to be picked up by parents on a Friday night, by Sunday, who knows what the perceived slight could be built up into. This was the era before widespread cellphone use among teenagers, before camera phones and the boom of the Internet. Everything seen was passed along in a slow chain of information, the story being accessorized with salacious details as it bounced from one ear to the next.

And so we either threw fists or didn't, mostly over our broken hearts. To "win" meant nothing, of course. A part of this particular brand of beef meant the brokenhearted fighting or not fighting in an attempt to heal the ego, but not to bring themselves closer to being back with the person who broke their heart. A person they maybe loved but probably just liked a little bit, in a time when love was most measured by proximity and not emotion. It's easier to circle someone in an endless waltz of volume and eye contact than it is to tell them that they've made you very plainly sad. And so, there is beef, the concoction of which at least promises a new type of relationship to fill the absence.

THERE ARE MANY ways the beef can begin with a dance move and then spiral outward. Just ask James Brown and Joe Tex, who both kicked their microphone stands and did their splits and there's no real telling who got to it first, and it is safe to say that neither of the two invented legs or the high kicking of them. But Joe Tex definitely got to the song "Baby You're Right" first in 1961. He recorded it for Anna Records at a time when he was searching for a hit. Tex first came to prominence in 1955, after he stormed into New York from Rogers, Texas. In his junior year of high school, he won a talent show in nearby Houston; the prize was $300 and a trip to New York, complete with a weeklong hotel stay at the Teresa, situated in close proximity to the legendary Apollo Theater.

Amateur Night at the Apollo Theater was the first and truest proving grounds for young artists, because there was no real barrier between the performance and the audience's expression of pleasure or displeasure at the performer onstage. The audience was empowered to display their distaste for a performer's act, both vocally and even physically, with demonstrative actions like running into the aisles and shouting while pointing fingers, or—if pleased—pretending to faint with joy. The Apollo existed in the days before paneled judges would offer feedback, when even the rudest of comments from a judge seem scripted and a little too made-for-television. At the Apollo, the audience was there to perform just as much as the person onstage. Like any good audience in a schoolyard escalation, they could dictate the arc of a night, or a whole life, right in the moment. It can be argued that no roomful of people should have this much power, but the crowd of largely Black people was there to give mostly Black performers what they needed: honesty from their kinfolk.

In a moment, I will return to foolish-ass James Brown, who stole "Baby You're Right" from Joe Tex and so maybe it could be said that he also stole the dance moves or at least had the theft of his own dance moves coming. But now is the time to mention that when Joe Tex arrived for Amateur Night at the Apollo back in 1955, Sandman Sims was the person who had the honor of playing the role of the Executioner. The audience loved the Executioner, but performers didn't want to see his ass while they were onstage, because if that nigga is coming out after you, that means your time is up. By the time you see the Executioner, the boos are probably so loud that the audience can't hear whatever shoddy rendition of that thing you were doing anyway. The Executioner's job is to cleanse the audience of whatever it was they were enduring, by running onstage and tap-dancing the performer off while the boos gave way to cheers.

Howard "Sandman" Sims once wanted to be a boxer out in California but broke his hand twice as a young man, and you can't box if you can't keep a fist closed, but the joke with him was that he wasn't much of a boxer anyway. He was known for how he'd move around the ring. The age-old idea of the desire to dance outweighing the desire to actually get into the messy throwing of punches. He'd look almost like he was floating, dodging and ducking and juking. The sound his feet made as he bounced around the ring, shuffling the rosin around the wood. Like sand being kicked up everywhere. When he figured out dance as a career alternative to boxing, he tried to glue sandpaper to his shoes or to his dancing mat, in an attempt to reproduce the sound of his shoes moving around the boxing ring. When that didn't work, he sprinkled sand on flat platforms to create soundboards. This was in the '30s, when movement was king, and sound and the body were becoming one. Tap dancers like Sandman carried shoes with them everywhere they went, and if they spotted someone else carrying shoes, one dancer would throw their shoes down on the ground, initiating a challenge, which would take place right there in the middle of the street.

Sometimes the beef begins with a clatter of shoes against pavement.

Sandman left California and moved to Harlem in the early 1950s. He'd swept through all of the street dancers in Los Angeles, then he heard there were ones in Harlem who could dance on dinner plates without breaking them, or tap atop newspapers without tearing them. Those challenges were more than worthwhile, but Sandman had his eyes set on Harlem for the famed Apollo Theater. He'd heard word of the Wednesday night show, where amateurs could seek glory on the stage. He would go on to win the competition a record-breaking twenty-five times. After the twenty-fifth time, a new rule was made: performers were no longer allowed to compete once they had earned four first-place prizes.

The Sandman had conquered the Apollo and rewritten its history but had nothing particularly tangible to show for it. He still didn't have steady work as a dancer, or much of anything else. In the mid-'50s, the Apollo decided to hire him as a stage manager. Shortly thereafter, he began his role as the Executioner. He revolutionized the role, not only dancing performers offstage but adding comedic elements to it, like chasing them off with a broom or a hook while wearing clown suits or diapers. It was all a trick to pull the audience back from the brink of their displeasure and give them something satisfying in between acts. Story goes that once he got the performers safely backstage, he would drop the act and console the people who needed it. Sandman was the longest-running Executioner at the Apollo, staying in the role until 1999. The entire time, despite having a job that paid, he'd still carry his dancing shoes with him on the streets of Harlem, throwing them down for a fight whenever he saw fit.

But Joe Tex never met the Executioner during his time on the Apollo stage, because he never got booed off the Apollo Stage. He won Amateur Night four weeks in a row before he'd even graduated from high school. When he did graduate, in 1955, he immediately got signed to a record deal with a label called King Records, out of Cincinnati, Ohio. They were known best among Black people as Queen Records, which distributed a run of race records in the '40s before folding into King, where the focus became making rockabilly music, and Joe Tex seemed like a star in the making. He was charismatic, a sharp songwriter, with a voice that hit the right kind of pleading—like a gentle and trapped bird asking for escape.

The problem was that early on in his career, Joe Tex couldn't channel any of that into a hit. He recorded for King between 1955 and 1957 but couldn't break through with any songs. In an old label rumor, it was said that Tex wrote and composed the song "Fever," which eventually became a hit for King labelmate Little Willie John. Tex sold it to King Records to pay his rent. This was, I imagine, the first sign that Tex's time at King was in need of coming to a close.

Tex moved to Ace Records in 1958 and continued to be unable to cut a hit, but where he could always eat was on the stage. There he was a step ahead of his peers. He garnered a singular reputation for his stage acts, pulling off microphone tricks and dance moves that hadn't been seen before. Including his main gimmick: letting the mic stand fall to the floor before

grabbing it, right at the last moment, with his foot, then pro-
ceeding to kick the stand around, on beat with the song he was
singing. His onstage stylings got him cash and a few choice
opening gigs. He would open for acts who were also ascending,
as he was, but were seen as having more star potential. Acts
like Jackie Wilson, or Little Richard. Or James Brown.

This of course is not to say that James Brown waited in the
wings and watched Joe Tex, studying his dance moves and
mapping them out for his own use. But James Brown sure
could make a mic stand do whatever he wanted it to, and so
could Joe Tex, and some would say—again, there's just no
telling. Back to "Baby You're Right": Tex recorded that tune
in March '61, when Anna Records was owned by Anna Gordy,
Berry Gordy's sister. Tex was looking to build a pipeline to
Motown, and so he recorded "Baby You're Right" for them,
and a few others. The song was unspectacular for its era, with
a slow finger-picked guitar backbone and bursts of horns
punctuating the lyrics, affirming to a lover that she is missed.

Here is where James Brown enters again. Later in 1961,
James Brown recorded a cover of the song, altering the melody and changing the lyrics slightly. Brown's lyrical melody
drags out the words, adding a palpable urgency to the questioning. "Yooooouuuuuuuu think I wanna love you?" hangs
in the air for a touch longer than Tex's version did, while the
listener—even if they know the answer—eagerly waits for a
response. Tex was singing to convince his beloved, while
Brown was singing with the understanding that his beloved
was already convinced. It was enough to catapult James Brown
to the pop charts and the R&B Top Ten. Brown chose to add
his name alongside Tex's as a songwriter in the credits.

Tex, who hadn't been able to break onto the charts at all in
his career, finally got there. A small circle of light inside the
shadow of James Brown.

* * *

I LIED WHEN I said winning meant nothing, and this is how you can tell that I have lost enough fights to know I should stop fighting. The ego's ache calls for bandaging, and that salve could come in the way of dominating an opponent in a physical fight, or getting to a song before they do, but the ego will call for the salve nonetheless. A dancer throwing their shoes at your feet is attempting to push your pride past the point of no return. To say they know you and what you are capable of better than you know yourself. It is good to know you are feared. It's what kept the Sandman running into the streets, and what kept performers on the Apollo stage from clocking him one when he ran out in the middle of their performances with a broom. Winning sometimes means you can opt out of whatever violence comes for you next. Winning sometimes means you get to go home with a clean face and no questions from your worried kin.

It was the wedding scene that kept *New Jack City* out of some theaters in my city when the film touched down in the late winter of 1991. The whole film is about the depths the powerful will go to in order to maintain power, but the wedding scene is specifically harrowing. While walking down the steps after the ceremony, one of the young flower girls drops one of the wedding accessories. As she retreats back up the steps to get it, the kingpin, Nino Brown, bends down to retrieve it and hand it back to her, a smile mapping its way along his face. Something was always going to go bad because Nino's in all black at a wedding, dressed like he's prepared to bury or be buried. And anyone with half a mind could peep the scene and know that the caterers closing the doors of their van at the bottom of the steps were actually the Italian mobsters, looking to settle a score. But it's already too late, even if you knew what was on the horizon. The mobsters have their guns out and start firing, the way guns are fired in movies— haphazardly but not really hitting anything.

If the scene were to simply spiral into your run-of-the-mill movie shootout from here, it would be unspectacular, and unworthy of controversy. But there is a moment that lasts about four seconds. As the young girl's father runs back up the stairs to protect his daughter, as bullets kick up small kisses of smoke from the concrete, Nino snatches the screaming girl and holds her over his face and torso, using her as a shield. Even within the precedent of horror set by the film, it is an especially horrific scene, clearly situated within the film to push the boundaries of violence but also to draw a line in the sand on Nino Brown as a character who could be redeemed by any reasonable audience.

Parents in my neighborhood caught wind of the scene when reviews came out. There was pressure for theaters to drop the film from their lineup, and some did. Local news panicked about the movie inciting violence—a threat that would be bandied about later in 1991, when *Boyz n the Hood* dropped, and in 1993 when *Menace II Society* came out.

Those who could snuck out to see the movie anyway. I was too young to see it in theaters, but not too young to hear the older hustlers and hoopers dissect it on the basketball court across the street from my house, or listen in on my older brother talking about it with his friends. If it's *real* beef, the kind with bodies left bleeding out in a city's daylight, then the stakes become different. Someone is dead, and so someone else has to die. But even among the streets there is a code, usually revolving around women and children, funerals and weddings. Nino Brown was unsympathetic because he didn't have a *code,* I'd hear. And to see the lack of a code played out in the manner Brown chose rattled the foundation of those who did tend to their beefs with a firm understanding of who bleeds and who doesn't.

The full shootout lasts just over a minute, but the part of it that is not as memorable to most as the child-as-shield moment comes at the end. As Nino Brown and his crew hide behind tables and wedding gifts, firing their own parade of reckless bullets in the general direction of their foes, the mobsters slowly begin to retreat. Somewhat inexplicably, Keisha, the lone woman member of Brown's gang embroiled in the shootout, runs out to the center of the steps with her gun and begins firing. Expectedly, free from the cover of the wall she was hiding behind, she is hit with a stream of bullets, each painting a small red burst along her cream-colored suit. She collapses to the steps, and Nino Brown survives. It is the part of the film that most clearly articulates that power—particularly for men—means having access to bodies that are not yours as collateral. Countless options for remaining unscathed.

For James Brown, that option was Bea Ford. Ford was a background singer with a sharp and inviting voice. She was married to Joe Tex until 1959, and in 1960, James Brown recruited Ford to sing with him on the song "You've Got the Power," a slow, horn-soaked ballad that opens with Ford singing:

I'm leaving you, darling
And I won't be back
I found something better
Somewhere down the track

By the time Brown's voice enters the song, his and Ford's vocals are stitched together, inextricable, as if they'd known each other an entire lifetime.

At some point after the song's release, Brown sent a letter to Tex. The letter insisted that he was "done" with Ford and that Tex could have her back. In response, Tex recorded the song "You Keep Her," which opens with the lines:

James I got your letter
It came to me today
You said I can have my baby back
But I don't want her that way
So you keep her
You keep her because man, she belongs to you

There are many ways to poke at a person over a long stretch of time, digging the knife into their worst insecurities and then twisting the blade. The word "belongs" is the blade here, I suppose. If one searches wide and far on the Internet, there isn't much about Bea Ford to be found. The only recording she's ever credited for is the duet with Brown, and she didn't last on the James Brown Revue much longer after the song was released. The first photo in a search is of her standing at a microphone singing while a young James Brown watches, expectantly.

One of the many problems with beef—as it has been constructed throughout history—is that bystanders are used as a currency within the ecosystem of the disagreement. When the beef is between two men, those bystanders are often women. Women who have full lives, careers, and ambitions but are reduced to weapons for the sake of two men carrying out a petty feud. This is the downside to it all. Beef is sometimes about who has and who doesn't have, and with that in mind, even people can become property.

And so, in the midst of all the fireworks, and all the thrilling talk about fights and the public rubbing their hands together to see who will spark the next match, I don't want it to get lost that Bea Ford was a woman of talent. A woman who perhaps had career ambitions beyond the men she found herself in between. A woman I have to largely speculate about, because the only information easily found about her is that she was once married to one singer until she was singing a duet with another. There is something damaging about what happens in the periphery of two men fighting with each other. The ego of a powerful man detonates, and in its wake is a land that looks nothing like it did before the explosion. Even the clearest memories become wind.

THE NOTORIOUS B.I.G. said *Beef is when you roll no less than thirty deep* and it is tough to say how many people were with James Brown when he rolled into an after-hours juke joint in 1963 with a few shotguns on him and his crew, but that is when the shit got too real to be anything but beef. Beef is at its most thrilling when the two people engaged in it are performers, who perhaps have something at stake and are therefore committed to dragging their disagreements out over long stretches of time. People who have a flair for the dramatic built into their DNA. A rapper who grew up with the dozens and holds close both language and the ability to humiliate with it. A tap dancer who throws their shoes down in the middle of a crowded street and dares someone to take them up on the challenge. Or a soul singer with a whole audience of people trained in on their every move.

By 1963, Joe Tex and James Brown were absolutely fed up with each other, Tex mocking Brown at every turn. Still, because the world of Black soul and rock 'n' roll was still relatively small and segregated, Tex and Brown couldn't avoid each other on the road. So when the two performed together in Macon, Georgia, at James Brown's homecoming show, Tex took the opportunity to really dig his heels into the feud. By this point, James Brown had perfected his now well-known cape routine. Becoming seemingly consumed by sweat and emotion at the end of a performance, Brown would have someone throw a cape over his shoulders and begin to escort him off the stage. He would take a few exhausted steps with the cape on his back before throwing it off and running back to the microphone, straining his voice to the final levels it could reach while the audience went wild. It was the old dancer trick, which is the old beef trick, which is simply an old crowd trick: let the people believe you can't take any more, and then give them a newer, better part of yourself.

In Macon, Georgia, Joe Tex opened the James Brown homecoming show with a tattered blanket on his back. While the audience looked on, he fell to the ground and rolled around mimicking agony and shouting, "Someone, please! Help me get out of this cape!"

This was in the place James Brown was born, where people knew him and loved him before the fame. Before there were stolen dance moves, or dance moves to steal. To be loved somewhere before the fame is real. And so to come into someone's backyard and challenge their greatness is something, I imagine, that cannot be allowed to stand. Not now, and not in 1963, when there were places where Black artists couldn't play their songs anywhere but home. Home was where they could still be seen.

There is a code to beef, until there isn't.

Joe Tex went out to Club 15 after the show to see a late-night gig by Otis Redding and the Pinetoppers. That's where James Brown and his crew showed up with shotguns and fired several shots into the joint. Otis Redding dove behind a piano and stayed there. Joe Tex ran out the back door and hid among the trees. Six people were shot, but no one died. This story

never made it much further than that night, because someone
from James Brown's crew went around giving hundred-dollar
bills to folks in exchange for silence.

And I suppose there is nothing left to be said once the bullets talk and make their intentions clear. Joe Tex and James
Brown were in the beef for one thing, until it became another
thing entirely, and there is a point where one must tap out or
pay a price they don't have the wallet for. Joe Tex finally got a
hit in 1964 with "Hold On to What You've Got," and then he
placed six Top Forty hits in 1965 alone. Up until the early to
mid-'70s, Tex finally had the career everyone thought he
would.

In 1972, James Brown released an eight-minute track with
Bobby Byrd and Hank Ballard called "Funky Side of Town."
There is a call and response portion of the track that involves
Byrd and Ballard calling out the names of soul music stars
and Brown responding affirmatively.

"Aretha Franklin!" one yells. "All right now!" responds
Brown. "Joe Tex!" another shouts. "Who?" Brown replies.

"Joe Tex!"

"Who?" Brown replies again.

The song plays on with no vocals for a handful of seconds
after, and I think this is where the beef ends: with a type of
forgetting. One person telling the world that their once-foe is
now as inconsequential as dust.

IN THE 2000s, it felt like there was always a movie out
about dancing, and dance battles. I didn't live in a place where
I'd ever see anything like that unfold in real life. Everyone I
knew who could dance could also scrap, and they weren't exactly keen on dancing their way out of a mess when they
could just as easily fight their way out of it. By the time the
2000s rolled around, me and most of my crew were done

beefing over love. Some of us were good at sports, others had jobs, or nice cars, or hustled to keep money overflowing from our pockets. Even the idea of love wasn't scarce. Besides, around that time, so many of us had heard the story of the neighborhood that was not our neighborhood but was close enough. How a young man was shot on a Friday night, and by Sunday morning, in retaliation, a church was shot up while people praised inside. No one was killed, but the church shut down. The stained glass from its shattered windows littered the ground for months after. It was a different time for conflict. Every season was a season someone could be coaxed into chasing blood. We were done meeting at the center of our friends and circling an opponent, searching their eyes for desire. At some point, every person has to know when a mode of conflict has had its way with them. When you are maybe the dancing type, and maybe the fighting type, but not yet the killing type.

The Sandman left the Apollo in 1999. There were stories of how, even in his early eighties, he would sometimes go outside in Harlem, walking the streets with his tap shoes. Unfamiliar with how the world changed. How the battle became something different while he wasn't looking. I think about this part often. What it must be like to have defined yourself by how the body can move. The fear your feet can strike into the heart of someone else. What it is to go looking for beef in the only way you know how, inside a world that has moved on from what you know. Everything is a show, until the show moves on without you. And there you are with all of the weapons, but no fight. Beef doesn't ever change, until it does. Until you throw your shoes down in the street and nothing meets you but an echo.

Fear: A Crown

IT WAS THE way Mike Tyson entered a ring that told me he was of a different mind and spirit. In the old VHS tapes from the years right after I was born, the static crackled unevenly along the television and the sound of the commentators was warbled, like they were speaking with their heads half-dipped into a river. But when the arena lights dipped and cloaked the stands in a vast and endless black, the cameras would wobbly zoom in and out on the tunnel. Among the crowd of yelling men and security guards, there would be Mike Tyson. Draped in a towel, a circle cut big enough to fit his head through, so that the towel could be worn like a shirt. It hung loosely off Tyson's body, almost begging to be removed. Sometimes he'd enter to Public Enemy's "Welcome to the Terrordome," dropping himself into the most frantic of the song's movements: the scratches, the grunts, the chopped sirens. Other times, he'd just come out to a cascade of assorted noises. Chains rattling, or jail cells closing. The boxing entrance is art.

The boxers I loved most trended toward opulence: an attempt to declare themselves regal at the entrance in hopes that they might remain that way by the time of exit, a clean face and a gold robe thrown over their shoulders. It was the simplicity of Tyson's entry that haunts. I do not fear harm as much as I fear the man who takes pleasure in doing it.

//

* * *

AS MUCH AS I fear the man who takes pleasure in doing harm, I might still have thrown myself to the wolves of the high school hallways during the earliest moments of my ninth grade year because I was small & came from a place where you had to know how to fight even if you didn't want to fight & so I threw slow & looping fists at my own shadow in the backyard with the sun sitting high enough to make the shadow version of myself a large & towering machine & I stayed rolling with the kinda kids who never *actually* fought but swore they could if they had to & I guess they just never had to & sometimes it is just an expression of willingness & sometimes it is just in knowing what damage you might be taking in & how the body might recover or not recover from it & once a woman whispered *I am going to break your heart* into my ear on a dance floor & I still allowed her to lead me by the hand into the night swelling certain with the promised grief of some morning beyond the next one & some might say that fighting is not about victory but about how vigorously one takes to the chaos & this is why when set upon by four boys on the last day before summer I still stood & threw fists even as my vision clouded with my own blood & to practice violence on your own shadow is to say there is no winning, but to pray for that which might shrink you or make you large.

   //

PRAY FOR THAT which might shrink you or make you large, depending on the stage and what particular mood has gotten into the crowd on any given night. At the Def Comedy Jam in the early '90s, the crowd could get hostile if a comedian didn't deliver from the moment they took the stage. Bernie Mac worked odd jobs, doing comedy on the side at the Cotton Club in Chicago. The night he got his big break, the crowd at the Def Comedy Jam was on edge, booing off multiple comedians despite host Martin Lawrence's pleas for them to calm down. What is tucked underneath the exchange between the comic and the audience is a desire not only to laugh, but also to make sense of the otherwise unexplainable absurdities of the world outside. The stakes are higher for a comedian, who is all at once a vehicle for jokes, a therapist, and a storyteller. The Def Comedy Jam could make or break the early career of a comedian, which Bill Bellamy told to Bernie Mac backstage as the boos and shouts from the crowd carried yet another comedian off. Mac, who had surely seen enough and who also surely wasn't going to return to the life he had had before setting foot in this ring, told Bellamy *Fuck it.* Before storming out onstage, tearing the microphone off the mic stand, assessing the crowd, and shouting *I ain't scared of you motherfuckers.* Laughing into the aisles, bodies fell.

//

INTO THE AISLES, bodies fell over bodies, reaching for the last of something or the first of something. The supermarket is a museum of human reaching. It was once a sprawling field of brick buildings, leaning, but strong enough to hold families of working Black folks packed into apartments. The basketball courts vanished and so the kids nailed a milk crate to the top of an old wall, but then the wall got torn down too. It is easiest to think about gentrification in terms of what once was standing and what no longer is. But I think of it more often as a replacement of people and their histories. The way a shifting landscape can obscure what once was, so that a person can't take someone to their old neighborhood and show them where they learned to shoot baskets. For this, I love the hoods that still stand, no matter the cost to remain standing. Even in my hood, which wasn't the safest on the eastside of Columbus, people still bristled at the idea of setting foot in

Windsor Terrace, a few blocks to the north. TV anchors would wring their hands and talk about the crime, the gangs, the gangs. None of them considered that the gang operates in multiple ways. One of the ways, for that neighborhood, was to keep unwanted hands off the land. To keep the buildings standing for as long as they could. Even if it meant wearing the face of the dead on a shirt.

   //

IF IT MEANS wearing your living face on a shirt, I suppose a nigga must stand out one way or another. That is, when being Black and loud won't get the job done on its own. Bernie Mac had his whole-ass face spray-painted on his blue jeans, and it must be said that this was the early '90s, when such decoration was not at all surprising. People would pack the halls of middle and high schools with anything airbrushed on them. Dead homies, living homies, the name of the block they come from. Onstage, as it was with the entirety of Bernie Mac's career, it wasn't what he was saying, but how he was saying it. His deliberately jumpy, breathless, and sometimes half-mumbled mashing together of words sounded like no one else. Even if the audience couldn't unravel language from the sonic jambalaya, they'd laugh at how it arrived to their ears. Every time a joke landed, Mac would turn to Def Comedy Jam's house DJ, Kid Capri, yell, "Kick it!" and then dance for a few seconds while Capri played a clip of Terminator X's "Buck Whylin." Then Mac would slice a hand across his own neck, signaling Capri to cut the music so he could stare at the crowd and yell, "You don't understand! I ain't scared of you motherfuckers!" one more time—each rotation of the phrase delivered with more confidence and ferocity, sending the crowd gasping with more and more laughter. Never let people forget that you are untouchable.

//

NEVER LET THE people forget that you are untouchable, as
Muhammad Ali insisted upon. Which is why when I didn't
grow past five foot seven and I realized I didn't like going to
the gym, I decided I was going to be fast. My middle name is
Muhammad, but I am named after the prophet, not the boxer.
The prophet is described with a series of descriptors that
could belong to any man. Al-Bara said *Once I saw him in a red
cloak and I had never seen anyone more handsome than him.*
Anas said *When Allah took him unto Him, there was scarcely
twenty white hairs in his head and beard.* I do love carrying the
Good and Holy Name of a man who might have looked like
any man. I can better explain all of the ways I have disappeared. I thought I was in love enough to stay, but then the
sky opened up and I became a kaleidoscope of butterflies. I
thought I might live a life in which I let no one down, but
that was the other man who is not me but who I think I have
seen before. Muhammad is one of the most common names
in the world, some variation of it passed on to more than 150
million people. When I was a child, people would joke about
my parents having me, the youngest of their four children,
and running out of ideas. But I inherited a desire to make
myself too fast to be touched. All pain inflicted upon this
body must be earned. I'll keep my blood with mine. A red
cloak, never worn outside.

//

OUTSIDE, A RED cloak dresses the sky above boarded-up
houses and apartment project towers. Buster Douglas came
out of Windsor Terrace in Columbus, Ohio, years before this
one. He was a better ballplayer than brawler, but most people
don't know that. At Linden-McKinley in the '70s, he got him-

self a state title in hoops. Could dunk so hard on Friday night that the whole block would still be shaking Saturday morning. But his daddy was a fighter. Dynamite Douglas, who made his name getting knockouts in Columbus at the old state fairgrounds in the late '6os. Would've been a champ if it wasn't for what some called a lack of desire and focus—same thing they said about his boy Buster, even after Buster plowed through his early opponents. He lost a title fight by TKO in 1987 against Tony Tucker before reeling off six wins in a row, which gave him what many assumed was the honor of losing to Mike Tyson, who swaggered into rings quickly and without fanfare to dispose of his opponents in a similar fashion. Douglas was seen as a brief speed bump before Tyson took on Evander Holyfield, the real prize. Buster Douglas lost his mother, Lula Pearl, twenty-three days before the fight. Those who don't understand death may not understand how it flushes the system of any fear that might exist. Even before I'd buried anyone, I knew. During interviews, I saw his eyes change.

//

DURING THE INTERVIEW, the eyes of Robin Givens change. In 1989, sitting across from Barbara Walters, the actress sat on a couch in a blue suit. Her husband, Mike Tyson, was in a blue sweater, an arm resting around her shoulders. Barbara Walters wants to talk about Tyson as if he's not in the room, and as if he was not, at the time, one of the most feared men in America. There had been rumors of Tyson abusing Givens. Tormenting her and her mother. When Walters asks about this, Givens tenses up. She turns away from Tyson entirely, as if only she and Walters are in the room. She talks about fear—about how Tyson shakes her and swings his fists at her. She talks with the understanding that the world viewed Tyson's body as a vehicle for violence. The more she talked, the more she offered, calmly, about her life with Tyson. It is haunting to watch someone unravel the details of abuse in real time, on national television. Critics of Givens pointed to the calmness in her voice but didn't notice much else. The way she held her hands to stop them from trembling, or the way her eyes locked in on a single spot. Or, more important, the way Tyson does not speak at all, but begins to breathe deeper and deeper, the blue of his sweater puffing and stretching along his wide shoulders. A man trying desperately to hold himself in check.

    //

A MAN TRYING desperately to hold himself in check has to learn to stare through an opponent. I learned this, too, at an early age. The fight can be won or lost in these moments of silent tension. The trick is to pick a spot to focus on, like an ear. Then start zooming in on all the small nuances of it: curve, shape, the beads of sweat dropping from the lobes. No other eye will be able to tell that you are staring through and beyond a person. Of all the foolish tricks of dominance, the one that is perhaps the most foolish is the way immovability is celebrated when another person is in your face. Boxers are better at this than almost anyone. In the center of the ring, Buster Douglas didn't even bother to look at Mike Tyson, who was doing a stare-down of indifference. Tyson often looked directly at his opponents with disdain, but he couldn't even muster it for Douglas, who fumbled with his gloves a bit while a referee gave instructions. In the house where I was a child watching the fight, someone announced that this is how they knew Douglas was cooked. I suppose I didn't know then what I know now about fear, but I imagine that moment represented the opposite. Douglas knew the trick inside the trick.

If you know I see you looking, but I can't be bothered to look, which one of us is truly indifferent? In the old clip of the fight that I watch now, this is when I knew. He was never scared.

//

THE BIGGEST JOKE of all is that he was always scared. Bernie Mac was scared and lied his ass off about being scared because lying is what the scared do best. There is a way to make fear a mirror, I think. And what better weapon is there than a mirror—that which carries back the echo of good news or bad news. Each time *I'm not scared of you motherfuckers* was sung into the air, and after each fresh chorus of screaming and clapping, Mac got a new bounce to his step. Came with something a little edgier. People were wanting to laugh before he even opened his mouth again, waiting for him to speed to a dance break and tell them how unafraid he was of their silly asses. And do you see now why I can't unravel the jokes from the violence of the boxing ring? Have I made it clear enough that I come from a place where if you had good enough jokes, you might be able to talk your way out of a potential beating? What if I told you that when my parents were angry, and contemplating all modes of punishment, I would try to make them laugh? This is the first and only fight. On the ground floor. The one that says *I would like to avoid my worst impulses, and I want you to help me.* Bernie Mac said that if they were going to boo him offstage, he was at least going to make them remember him. If they insisted on carrying him off, he was at least gonna land a few.

//

AT LEAST LAND a few for the weary & trembling milk carton tumbling to the grass with every good brick shot from the

hands of kids who could be fighting in a schoolyard somewhere, but not today. At least land a few for whatever rested
in the milk carton before it was emptied & a hole was cut into
its bottom so that it could become a vessel for keeping the
devil away from idle hands. At least land a few for the horizon
swallowing the buildings where you came from & replacing
them with stores you can't afford to shop in. At least land a
few for the way some of the living do not wash their airbrushed shirts, so the faces of their dead do not fade. Land a
few for the people you have smiled in front of and then
dreamed of killing later. Land a few for the times you have
spun yourself out of some danger & held court until your enemies doubled over in laughter & forgot that they once might
have wanted to tear you apart. Land a few for all of the times
you didn't land any & walked home to some parent who won
street fights back in his day & didn't dream of raising someone who couldn't. Land a few for where you come from & how
where you come from ain't always gonna be where you came
from. Land a few for the knowledge that around the corner of
every victory, there is still someone who can tell you—with
their whole chest—that you better *watch your mouth.*

//

YOU BETTER WATCH your mouth and the plastic crescent
fastened to the inside of it when the action inside the ring
gets hot. Looking back, it was certainly the right jabs Buster
Douglas was landing all fight that did it. Douglas was almost
six inches taller than Mike Tyson and had a longer reach,
which meant Douglas could sling his signature right jab from
distance and stop Tyson from getting inside, where he often
did his damage. Tyson knocked Douglas to the canvas in the
eighth, but Douglas got up and had Tyson staggering against
the ropes in the ninth. It was in the tenth when Tyson fell,

knocked to the canvas for the first time in his entire career with an uppercut and then a flurry of punches to the head. But as a child, all I remember was the mouthpiece, flying out of Tyson's mouth and skipping along the canvas. Tyson made the mistake of fumbling around for the mouthpiece on the ground while referee Octavio Meyran stood over him, counting to ten. Tyson, attempting to close his gloved hand around the mouthpiece before rising. When he finally rose, Tyson stumbled into Meyran's embrace while the old referee told him, "It's okay. It's all right," over and over. The count to ten was over. I remember the mouthpiece and I remember how lost Tyson looked on the ground. I wondered where, in his descent to the unknown canvas, he came to grips with being mortal.

//

IT IS ALWAYS in descent when I come to grips with being mortal. On airplanes, it is easiest for me to forget I'm in the air when the hum of movement is consistent, sometimes buried underneath the ruckus of headphones or unsettled children. I fly enough now to have methods for cloaking my anxiety. A therapist once told me that it isn't heights that I fear, but the idea of falling from a high place. It feels to me like those are two rivers flowing into the same terrifying body of water, but who am I to argue. Still, it is knowing the plane is making an intentional and controlled plunge back toward the earth that sends me gripping the sides of my seat. When the clouds outside the window get thin and then break apart to reveal the tops of trees and houses, I imagine this is where something could most likely go wrong. Always at the end, when I think I've survived the worst. There is also, these days, the business of turning my phone back on. After a year of landing and far too often seeing a wave of terrifying news, I

began to just pay for Wi-Fi on planes, even if I didn't use it all
of the time, just so the news could come in small bites. Where
the guns went off this time. Where the living loved ones will
be mourning their dead. I am most anxious about the living
world I know best when I am miles above it but coming close
to the horrors of returning.

//

THE HORRORS OF returning to the world make for desirable
escapes, but also a shrinking window to enjoy those escapes in.
If I turn away too long, I might forget what it is to mourn.
The newest thing that cloaks me in fear is the idea that I've
become too numb to a world that increasingly demands furious engagement. I went to sleep again, and when I woke up,
there were fifty Muslims dead in New Zealand and people
once again arguing over who deserves to live a full life and
how those people deserve to live a full life. In all of my group
chats, no one really knows what to say, and so no one says anything. I have run out of jokes to break the silence with. On the
Internet, someone mentions all of the things our collective
grief can turn into: rage, hope, something useful against the
exhausting scroll of violence.

Friends, I come to you very plainly afraid that I am losing
faith in the idea that grief can become anything but grief.
The way old neighborhoods are torn to the ground and new
ones sprout from that same ground, it feels, most days, like my
grief is simply being rebuilt and restructured along my own
interior landscape. There is not enough distance between
tragedies for my sadness to mature into anything else but another new monument obscuring the last new monument.
When the interviewers asked Buster Douglas what his plan
was in 1990, days before the fight, he responded *I'll just hit
him, I guess.* And trust, I have dragged myself back to the

walls of my fears and thrown my fists into them, hoping a crack might open for the sunlight to gallop through. But it turns out I'm not the fighter I once was, and I was never much of a fighter in the first place. It turns out all of my fears have become immovable.

I am afraid not of death itself, but of the unknown that comes after. I am afraid not of leaving, but of being forgotten. I am in love today but am afraid that I might not be tomorrow. And that is to say nothing of the bullets, the bombs, the waters rising, and the potential for an apocalypse. People ask me to offer them hope, but I'd rather offer them honesty. Black people get asked to perform hope when white people are afraid, but it doesn't always serve reality. Hope is the small hole cut into the honest machinery. The milk crate is still a milk crate, but with the right opening, a basketball can make its way through. If I am going to be afraid, I might as well do it honest. Arm in arm with everyone I love, adorned in blood and bruises, singing jokes on our way to a grave.

On the Performance of Softness

IT WAS THE summer my living mother sat unknowingly on the doorstep of a sudden vanishing. It was the summer of the funeral and my boys not knowing what to say to me after, so it was the summer of playing videogames in silence but for the occasional crack and hiss of a tab being pulled back on a soda can. It was the summer of me and my brothers freestyling in our basement at night even though none of us could rhyme but each of us wanted some reason to stay awake a little bit longer. To not go to our rooms, which were different than the rooms they were before the funeral. It was the summer each of us wanted to suspend our reality and pretend that any sound we made would replace the echo of a mother's laugh vibrating the walls. And so we slap our open palms on our bare thighs or bang sticks on the drums I would steal from the house years later or kick a few sloppy rhymes while laughing at each other until someone fell on the floor, holding their stomach from laughing so hard.

It was the summer the Wu-Tang Clan came back out and dropped their second album and the lead single for it was over six minutes long with no chorus. It was the summer when you could still sit in front of a television and watch a music video premiere like it was the biggest event on the planet, and when the video for "Triumph" dropped it was theatrical and massive and fire danced on top of Method Man's head while he rode a motorcycle down a New York street consumed by fire and U-God hung upside down from barren trees while flames lapped at his hair and RZA wore massive black wings in the midst of a prison riot and none of it made sense really but everyone I know loved that shit because Wu-Tang was back, our boys. This band of brothers who linked arms to fight their way out of Staten Island through the underground rap ecosystem with their affinity for old kung fu films and absurdist album skits.

Older heads at the park tell me they like Wu-Tang because the group fashioned themselves into whatever the fuck they wanted to be and I don't know what that means really but I do know that I liked most when they called themselves the Wu-Tang Killa Bees and I know that I love the "Triumph" video, and how each of them exploded into a colony of CGI bees after each of their verses and at the end of the song, Raekwon and Ghostface are trading verses in a cage and this was the summer where you were defined by the member of the Wu-Tang Clan you liked the most and the popular kids liked Meth cuz he was tall and looked like he was the one that might most command the attention at a party but I like Ghostface because nothing he says makes sense to me in the moment but it sounds good and I tell all the dudes on the bus that I understand everything because when nothing makes sense everything can make sense. And in Wu-Tang no one is tighter than Ghostface and Raekwon, who might as well be kin or who seem to love each other in a way that few kin have ever loved me.

And in the final verse of "Triumph" Raekwon is rapping his ass off while Ghostface gestures wildly behind him, throwing arms in every direction with a smile stretching across his face, something like an honest and overwhelming pride consuming this single corner of a video otherwise cloaked with fire and hollow and haunting futuristic landscapes. Ghostface and Raekwon, locked away from a world drowning in flames and bees, playing off each other as they always had. And there, in the final moments of the song, on Raekwon's final line, Ghostface throws his arm around his boy and kisses him on the side of his head and it is the kind of kiss unlike the messy and clumsy ones I'd known to this point and it is also unlike any kiss I understand two friends could give each other. Ghostface pulls Raekwon close and holds his lips to his friend's head for a few seconds longer than I'd ever been kissed by anyone and Raekwon smiles and I have never seen two men kiss in any capacity before and so I tell myself *This must be love* and then they and everyone else in the scene all become bees.

August 2016

YOUNG THUG IS wearing a dress on the cover of his mixtape *Jeffery* and the Internet wants to argue about what it all means for the future of masculinity and I need a haircut tomorrow but I'm not going to the shop to hear them talk about this shit and I go because it's the only shop in town but I hate their politics but I gotta stay fly because I don't feel like myself without a fresh cut. Let me try this again. I don't feel like myself without something that makes me desirable to people I don't know, and to know this is to know that the future of masculinity is probably not in the shape people want it to be. But Young Thug is wearing an expensive dress on the cover of his mixtape, and on the Internet, there are people insisting that this will be the thing that pushes *the conversation* forward. Someone shares a video of Young Thug flashing guns and this is the juxtaposition: *You can still be hard and wear a dress* is the sentiment. I scroll through comments and see variations on this theme, but I don't see anyone mention the idea that perhaps one problem is the public's concept that the masculine antithesis to wearing a dress is showing that you are willing to enact violence. Within an hour of the cover art's release, outlets write about it, labeling the art as controversial. No one suggests that the very idea of gender norms themselves are controversial, or that any binary aggressively enforcing itself through rigid definitions is controversial. Young Thug wore a dress on the cover for a mixtape that had some good songs about that same shit Thug had been rapping about forever and no one I know really listened to it all that much because the talk about the dress eclipsed all else. About a month later, a man walked out of the train station near my apartment wearing a crop top, a full face of makeup, and tight jeans that flared wide at the bottom. The papers say he was chased by another group of men until they caught him on a corner two blocks from where I lived. He was beaten bloody by one man while the others stood over him, mocking the way he curled up in a ball while being kicked. This story made the last five minutes of the local news. I wonder what clothing masculinity could cloak itself in that might drive it further away from an obsession with dominance through violence. I don't get my hair cut for three weeks.

March 1998

UPON MY HANDS is the blood of a boy I wanted to like me once, probably even mere hours ago. I am guessing the blood came from his nose, but it could be from anywhere, and it is certainly mixed with my own. I haven't said "I love you" to anyone out loud since my mother died. I have no language for affection, but I do know how to throw a fist. The way my father taught me some years ago, when he took my hand in his and curled my fingers into my palm gently. This is another type of romance, I suppose. The rules of engagement handed down from a man who learned them from a man before him. Don't leave your thumb out. Don't hit anyone wearing glasses in the face. I was told to fight only when I had to, but who is to determine when one has to, really? I have to fight because I do not have the language for anything else but violence, and so when the boy I wanted to like me took my basketball and kicked it into the fields behind the school, I want to tell him *How could you do this to me* or *I want for us to play videogames in silence* but instead, I wrestle him to the ground and this is a demand for closeness. Even out of anger, I know that I want to be held. Even though I have not spoken a word out loud about love, I throw my fist back and swing it down on the face of someone I could imagine myself loving, not yet knowing if boys could even be capable of loving each other. We swing and swing at each other until we are cloaked in portions of each other's blood, gasping for air on the ground. No one was there to watch this fight, and so no one was there to declare a winner, and so there was no currency gained or lost. And it is only when I am on my back in the grass looking skyward that I realize I am trembling. It is only when the cloud above our head splits itself into the shape of my father's hands that I understand the sound next to me is the boy crying, in small leaps of breath, and I touch my face and realize that there is a tear of my own crawling its way toward the split in my lip and I think the pain we've inflicted on each other is not the pain we are hurting from but there is no way to say this either and so we don't talk and we get up from our makeshift battle-ground and I walk home and see my boys on the way and they look at my swelling lip and the red clawing its way through the dark skin of my cheek and they ask *Did you win* and in the summer the boy I fought moved out of the neighborhood and never came back.

A Tour Bus, 1994

IN THE DEF JAM—backed 1995 documentary *The Show*, Method Man is telling a story about where he grew up, as unspectacular as most stories about where someone comes from when they come from a particular type of place. Though no two hoods are the same, the overarching concept of the hood—when told by someone from there—can feel somewhat monolithic. Still, Method Man is holding court, telling stories of Park Hill, the Staten Island projects where he grew up. Some story about ball, about streetlights, about fear. The year of the video is undefined, but Method Man has settled into his role as the clear star of the group, which he seemed always destined to be. The B side of the group's 1993 breakout single "Protect Ya Neck" included Method Man's "Method Man"—an introduction to the artist in hopes of breaking him out and setting him apart from the rest of the group early on. The Wu-Tang record deal was unprecedented when they came into the game. RZA had them sign with Loud Records as a group, but worked a deal that allowed for each member to sign with his own individual label for his solo career, and Method Man was scooped up early as a darling of Def Jam Records. He was the most personable, which led to him often taking the lead during interviews, as he is doing on a tour bus while all of the other members of the group look on with some mixture of frustration, annoyance, and exhaustion. Finally, while Method Man gets really into the story, Ghostface chimes in:

"Man, kill that shit, man. Nobody wanna hear that shit."

Inspectah Deck and U-God chime in, affirmatively. Method Man jumps to his feet, insisting that the group always derides him when the cameras are on. An argument starts, and then escalates. The kind of argument that is not actually about the thing that they're all arguing about. Broth-

ers store things. Especially ones who rely on each other for a
livelihood, or a verse, or an appearance. There are endless
places to tuck damages to the ego when the performance of
love is how you and yours get your checks. The argument on
the tour bus is fascinating because it is so decidedly not about
interviews, or who talks the most. It's about people who grew
up together knowing one another, and the world starting to
know one of them differently. There is no way to plainly articulate that pain but this, perhaps: yelling about how few
minutes someone gets on camera compared to someone else.

When the camera focuses on U-God, complaining about
an interview in the UK where Method Man gave all of the
answers, a viewer can pick up on another character in the
shot. There's Raekwon, looking longingly out of the tour bus
window, not saying a word.

Summer 1999

MY OLDER BROTHER got a dark blue 1992 Ford Thunder-
bird and tinted the windows and threw some rims on it. It was
his first car, and I wouldn't be able to start driving for at least
another year, I was told. When I could get my temporary per-
mit and start taking classes. My brother and I are only about
seventeen months apart, but in between those seventeen
months is an entire ocean separating the two lands of our
adolescence. My brother was cool and I was uncool. This was
established pretty early on in our childhoods, and I think we'd
both decided to lean into it, for better or worse. It dawned on
me when we shared the halls of our middle school, one grade
apart, that I was not going to get any cooler and would perhaps only serve to make him less cool. And so we chose separate high schools, and separate paths to reshaping our
identities. He became a football star. I played soccer and
joined drama club.

When we were younger, we'd argue all the time, and sometimes we'd get into physical scuffles that all usually ended with me on the receiving end of a lost battle. He was bigger, stronger, more aggressive. We were also both trouble-makers by nature, which simply led to our being grounded together a lot. And so, in between our arguments and physical standoffs, we shared a lot of childhood time in the intimacy of punishment, banished to our room, having to make the most of our imaginations. Our love for each other was forged by our parents, who—I imagine—didn't know what to do with two boys who couldn't stop finding themselves in foolish mishaps. In the rare moments we weren't in trouble together, I found myself missing him. If I could go outside and he was grounded, I'd ride my bike around or shoot basketball at the park alone. An older brother, especially one that close in age, can be a lot of things. For me, mine was a type of north star. I set myself by him, and by his movements. When our older siblings or parents pulled us apart after a fight and asked us why we couldn't just stop fighting each other, I imagine the answer I had but never gave was that I loved my brother too much to allow myself to be afraid of him. Even though I knew I could never beat him in a fight, I hit him back to show him that I was still going to be here, no matter the crashing of fists, no matter the thrown toys across a room neither of us was allowed to exit, no matter the nights spent not speaking.

In the first year after my mother died, we fought less, and then not really at all. We were getting older, sure. But we were also maybe coming to terms with the fact that thrashing up against the wall of grief was all we had energy for. In that year, I went to high school. I got suspended for fighting. I got sent to detention often, and became a fixture in the princi-pal's office. I found myself trying to fill the space of violence born out of discord. I didn't particularly understand the calm of harmony that blanketed the oldest relationship I knew, and so I found chaos elsewhere.

My brother spends an entire afternoon polishing the rims on his car. He gets a stereo system installed: two huge subs in the trunk weighing down the car's long backside. When he pulls up to the house, you can hear him coming from at least a block away. For the first few weeks he owns the car, whenever I hear the faint sound of bass beginning to rumble down the block, I run to the window to watch him pull into the driveway. And then he starts to stay out later, so I stop coming to the window altogether. The thing that was always hardest to acknowledge was becoming clearer: he was always better than me at making friends. He was, always, going to outgrow the part of our relationship where we had each other and only each other as windows to the outside world. Everything we saw and took in and loved was lensed through our love for each other. A love that was tenuous, held together by both violence and a resistance to it.

It isn't the car itself, but the widened view of possibilities that the car provided. He could opt out of our home, and I couldn't any longer. He could exit the spaces where we felt our closest bond, outside a world that measured the two of us up and found me leaving much to be desired. I spend most of the summer at home, watching old recorded versions of *Rap City* that we'd archived on the days we'd get home from school too late to watch it. I define loneliness by the way the water between my brother and I grows, and becomes more treacherous.

The Source Magazine, 1993

IN THEIR FIRST major interview as a group, the Wu-Tang Clan is asked by the interviewer how they manage to stay so tightly knit despite the fact that there are so many of them, and with success, there would be no way for them to keep ego at a distance while navigating the fame that seemed to be surely coming. Raekwon replies to the question:

"It's easy. Love your niggas. Love them."

As if it could be so simple.

May 2017

WE FOUND SOME dive in some district of one of those cities that began to give gentrified areas pretty names to distract from the upheaval of the people who were there before. The Pineapple District or the Old North District. We're in a part of town where there's one of those bars that looks old but is certainly new. I tell myself it's cool because at least the juke has some hip-hop I can scroll through and find some shit that might, at the very least, foster some discomfort in the people at the edge of the bar drinking expensive beers and wearing thick black trench coats despite the temperature outside flirting with midsummer heat.

My boys and I find a corner booth and I play "Can It Be All So Simple" because I'm feeling nostalgic for a very particular brand of Wu-Tang Clan, and this is it. One of those Wu songs that really isn't about anything other than the fact that none of us can be as we were when we were young. That a great deal of us have seen too much or heard too much or lived through too much to wrestle our innocence back from whatever cynicism or heartbreak has grown in its place. The song is just Raekwon and Ghostface reaching for each other over the vast expanse of memory, wound tightly around a Gladys Knight sample. It isn't the best song for a night out with friends I don't see that often, since we live scattered across the American landscape, pulled together only on occasions like these: someone is getting married, someone is having a birthday or anniversary, someone died and requires burial. It's perhaps too melancholy and not the kind of thing a joyful glass would be raised to, but here we are, kids no longer.

At the end of the night, I hug my boys and tell them I love them. The words come out easy and the hugs linger with the knowledge of not knowing when the next hug will be given. We punch each other's chests after hugs, lightly, before getting into our separate cabs or cars and speeding off toward a few hours of sleep before our separate airport trips. From the back of my car, underneath waves of glowing neon lights flooding into the windows, I think about how often me and the boys I knew and know were taught to love each other through expressions of violence. How, if that is our baseline for love, it might be impossible for us to love anyone well, including ourselves.

Spring 2002

I GO TO tell my girlfriend I love her and the words become a flood of bees. I come home to hit my father up for money and I turn to tell him I love him but the walls become bees. We bury Shawn and the dirt poured onto his grave becomes bees. We bury Trenton and I try to walk up to see his body in the casket dressed in a suit he would never wear, but the casket becomes bees. Derrick dies and his mother cries when she hears the news, each of her tears becoming a hive of bees. The churches where I ask forgiveness for all of my misdeeds become bees once my prayers enter them, and so I am never forgiven. The bees won't leave my apartment. I can't afford to fix the muffler in my shitty car, and so every song I play in the shitty car stereo system is backed by a low buzz. I kiss a girl at a party and we pull long strands of honey from our tongues. I drive to some vague western landscape and the sand is littered with dead bees. My pal Brittany tells me a story about how bees don't want to sting people. *They don't want to die,* she tells me. *They want to live as much as we do.* And I think of all of the friends I've loved who didn't want to live at all, and how I never told them I loved them enough when they were alive. How they chased something worth stinging until they finally found it.

December 2014

THE WU-TANG CLAN release a new album and the bees are dying. The bees have been dying for a while, it seems. I don't understand the science, but at some party, a woman tells me that if the bees keep dying, we're all going to starve to death. I make a joke about being consumed by a swarm of bees being the best way to go, and she walks away, nervously. The Wu-Tang Clan hadn't released an album in seven years, and the group had splintered in the kind of unromantic way that groups sometimes splinter. There was no massive fight or dramatic exit. They simply grew up and grew distant, not willing to be on the same page anymore, since all of their solo careers had taken them in vastly different directions, with varying results.

Still, RZA seemed determined to put his head down and craft one last Wu-Tang album, and so the group got back together for the messy, disjointed *A Better Tomorrow.* RZA and Raekwon fought publicly over the album's direction, RZA pleading with Raekwon to join the recording sessions and Raekwon proving to be skeptical. Though he did eventually record verses, they sound especially distant, detached from the project. The album itself got mixed reviews and was seen as one last exhausted effort to capture magic that had long been lost. Still, nostalgists and hip-hop heads got some comfort in seeing the gang back together again. The performance of appearances. They all seemed to love one another for just a little while longer. It is funny, the things that give people comfort. Even a group of men gritting their teeth and tucking in long-held resentments can bring joy to people who don't even know them but have built a monument to their closeness in their heads. I listen to the new Wu-Tang album and know that it wasn't made in harmony, but I pretend it was, because these were the first men I knew who weren't afraid to love each other loudly and publicly, even as messy and unrefined as it was, and I'm trying to learn a better way. I'm trying to reach across the shallow expanse of gendered rigidity and walk the walk of affection rather than just live the highlights of it. The parts of it that aren't hard. I imagine it is hard to live an entire life with your brothers even when you don't want to. To be angry or resentful or just exhausted, but to have your name always linked with theirs. On posters, or on T-shirts plastered to the chests of people who don't know what getting up every day and having to love through the overwhelming world of fame, of visibility, is like. Oh, could it all be so simple as "Love your niggas." Oh, could it be a kiss on the head when the excitement for sharing space with someone becomes too much and there's no other way to express it.

I eventually look up the science of colony collapse disorder, which is killing the bees. It is when the worker bees vanish and leave behind just a queen and a few nurse bees to care for the young bees, who eventually die because the workforce that keeps them alive has disappeared. I am fascinated, considering how the lone few remaining bees must scramble to keep themselves and their beloveds breathing. And with what propelling force? It isn't love alone, I imagine. Love alone is a warm but hollow cavern. It is where the once-living bodies are stored.

December 2019

OH BRANDON, OH Tyler, oh Trenton, I miss you all. Oh
Kenny, oh MarShawn, oh Thomas. Oh Demetrius, oh Trey, oh
James. From the cliffs where you were reaching, I wish my
hands could have appeared. Oh you dearly departed band of
brothers, there are so many ways to leave the earth and my
name will surely land upon one of them on a day I perhaps
want to still be here, but I will think of you. My loves, I want
to know if heaven is real only if you are promised to be in it.
I do not fear death as much as I fear the uncertain dark. An
eternity that doesn't include a chance for me to make amends
for all of the things that kept me from holding you close while
you were breathing and telling you how much I didn't understand about love. I know now that I have always loved you and
now you are gone. I am trying to love better in your memory.
I am trying to have less to apologize for. I have drawn the tat-
too a thousand times, boys. I haven't yet found the skin worthy of your names.

Board Up the Doors, Tear Down the Walls

IN BETWEEN SONGS during the Fuck U Pay Us set in their hometown of L.A., guitarist and singer Uhuru Moor lets his guitar swing freely while spreading his arms wide in front of an audience, still buzzing from excitement as the band's previous song rattles and echoes around the room. A grin creeps across Uhuru's face as he starts to sway. "For those who don't know," they begin, "we are Fuck U Pay Us, and that means we are looking for reparations for Black folks." The crowd—mostly Black people and people of color pressed up close to the stage—begins to cheer. The band lets the applause linger for a bit before sprinting into their next brilliant cacophony.

This is my second time seeing Fuck U Pay Us, after a pal convinced me to go out and see them in 2017, when I happened to be in the same city where they were playing a show. To be fair, it didn't take much convincing beyond my friend saying, "This is the band you've always wanted to see."

It is hard to put to words what seeing FUPU for the first time feels like, particularly if you are Black and came up in punk, aching for a band like this one. They are a band that really step into their fullest selves live, and anyone watching them is encouraged to follow suit. Their between-song banter blends humor with a scroll of truths. Nudges about white supremacy and reparations that make sure to let any white people in the audience know that they're not off the hook—that their presence in the space doesn't equal absolution. The banter is spoken to the audience without preaching, but with an expectation that there is an understanding in the room: if you came out tonight, you knew what you were getting. And if you didn't, here's what the program is.

The band is made up of drummer Tianna Nicole, bassist Ayotunde Osareme, guitarist Moor, and lead singer Jasmine Nyende. For all that can be said about their stage presence, or the way they hold a room together until the exact moment they want it to come apart, all of that has to begin with their songs. The way Osareme's bass digs into the ribs, and Nicole's drumming is distinct and piercing, hammering a smooth path for Moor and Nyende to make a delightful mess of the soundscape. And I do love a band that wastes no time. That tells you, up front, what its concerns are, and never lets up. FUPU does this in their band name, in their song titles, in the presentation of their sometimes sparse lyrics. During their Los Angeles show, when they launch into the slow march of their song "Burn Ye Old White Male Patriarchy, Burn," Nyende leans forward, repeating the song's title, chanting it while an audience member near me throws up a fist and shouts, "Burn!" after each rotation. It becomes almost like a prayer, the words all folding into each other until the sentence becomes one word. A meditation, shouted with equal measures of rage and hope.

A FUPU show is unmistakably a punk show, though it is less about spectacle, which makes the show itself more urgent. The people on the stage are on the front lines of the very politics they are espousing. They're among the people most at risk if the change they're searching for doesn't come to fruition. Yes, of course, the group are also performers— artists who know how to move along a stage just right, or when to turn on a moment of flourish for the greater good of a viewing public. But the band feel so closely tied to the stakes of their own creation that there isn't much of a put-on. The show and the songs feel like they're doing the work of attempting to unlock a fearlessness in the audience. By the three-minute mark of "Burn Ye Old White Male Patriarchy, Burn," Nyende spirals into a rhythmic chant of "burn ye old / burn ye old / burn ye old" and it is all at once mesmerizing, rage-inducing, and empowering. The people around me, in different tones and timings, all shouting "burn," intoxicated by the understanding that this is a kind of space where one could call for such burning and remain unscathed.

There is a love and affection among the audience at a FUPU show that drew me in the first time I saw them, and drew me in further when I saw them in Los Angeles. There isn't as much jostling to claim space, though their songs do call for movement, like the sprawling, multilayered tune "Root," which sent me and the folks around me first into a slow nod, and then a complete thrashing of the upper body. Still, even with the sometimes frantic tossing of arms and heads brought on by the spirit of crashing noise, there is a respect for space—a decency not always afforded to the marginalized folks at punk shows I've been to. The gift of FUPU and their music is that it is made clear who they are making music for and why they are doing it. They don't have to announce it (though they might stop for a between-song break just to reiterate). Many artists—myself included—talk about making art for their people, but do it with the understanding that when the work itself enters the world, we lose control over it to some extent. Even someone we might not want to have access to it may get their hands on it and find something useful. But the live show of FUPU is direct and confrontational, and it seems to be this way out of a protective affection. They are creating with the people at the margins of the margins in mind. Black people, sure. But specifically Black women, Black trans folks, sex workers, survivors. Black people and people of color who are made most vulnerable by systemic violence. There is something within the confines of the show that pushes people past a collective rage and into a kind of loving safety. There were people close to me who began the show shouting, and by the show's end, they had fallen into the arms of another person who was once shouting. I am far beyond my most demonstrative days of concertgoing, but at the show, I felt a very distinct type of expression being pulled out of me. All of the frustrations or micro-angers I'd pushed down to another place could live outside my body. And the feeling on the other side of that was where the healing was. The exhaustion, the beauty, the comfort of knowing I could find a release here. This isn't to say that anyone not at the margins can or will feel out of place at a FUPU show. To the contrary, because the band states its boundaries and aims so freely, I felt held in a way I rarely feel at concerts anymore. I felt safe. There's a beauty and generosity in that. Though a foolish outsider looking in might only see Black folks shouting and imagine it as rage.

I CAME UP around Black folks who were angry. Sometimes, or often, angry at whatever foolish mishap I had found myself in. Or at least that is how the anger manifested itself. The people I loved and the people they loved were likely mad at some other, more immovable injustice, but to yell at some unruly child let off enough steam. I loved Black folks who were angry, loved them not in spite of their anger but because of it. Because it was a part of who they were. My pal Jason had a mother who people thought was mean because of the way she'd materialize on the sidelines of the basketball court if J lingered too long once the streetlights began to tiptoe through the darkness, shouting for him to get his ass in the house. And by the way she would glare at anyone who dared laugh as her boy shook his head and walked sullenly toward her. People thought she was too strict because of the way J called her "Ma'am" instead of "Mom," or "Umi." But I loved her as I loved too many of the elders on my block, even the ones who shouted me down when I tracked mud in their houses or yelled at me from their porches when I sped my bike across their freshly manicured lawns. Some Sundays, when J's hair had grown too unruly for the hallways of his school, we would sit and play videogames in his living room while his mother would take a comb to his head and tenderly untangle the wreck of it before braiding it back together, humming an old song that I'd heard hummed in my own home.

And so I don't know if I believe in rage as something always acting in opposition to tenderness. I believe, more often, in the two as braided together. Two elements of trying to survive in a world once you have an understanding of that world's capacity for violence. Of course, this isn't true of every manifestation of anger—I'm not upholding abuse, or a replication of violence. What I'm talking about here is the fact that my own mother was a loud woman. When she laughed, it could be heard from two houses away, and when she yelled, it carried further. In our old, noisy house, you knew when my mother was coming, and you knew by the tone of her steps what mood might be on the other side of her arrival. When she was at peace, her steps were calm, gentle, and slowly taken. When she was excited, she would take steps quicker, almost barreling down the stairs from her second-floor room. When she was angry, the steps were heavy, and ominous. But she did nothing silently.

When we were young, and in a state of perpetual mischief, my brother and I often had to wait anxiously while our parents determined which one would be responsible for rep-

rimanding us. Each outcome had its pros and cons. When
both of my parents were still alive, my brother and I preferred to be reprimanded by our father, who was more prone
to calmly lecturing, sometimes for hours on end. As punishment, he'd often hand us massive, dog-eared books, or give us
large research projects to undertake, sometimes themed to fit
whatever it was we had gotten in trouble for. If I got caught
stealing candy, for instance, I might have to research the history of that candy and write a paper on it. This brand of punishment was exhausting, and undeniably unenjoyable. But it
somehow felt gentler, more restrained. We would simply have
to sit through a long talk and then go off to complete an as-
signment. College students pay money for my father's idea of
punishment.

To be punished by my mother was a much shorter experience. It wasn't the work of enduring my mother's anger as
much as it was dealing with the understanding that my
mother was mad at me. She'd yell a little bit, and then banish
us to our rooms. But because she was a woman who wore
every emotion outside herself, she couldn't hide when she was
angry with us, or disappointed in us. This punishment was
somehow far worse than a hand cramping while handwriting
a three-page paper on the history of chocolate. When someone loves loudly, with everything they have in them, the
withholding of that loud love, even briefly, feels impossible to
endure.

The upside to being punished by my mother was that she
could rarely bring herself to stay angry for long. She softened
significantly quicker than my father, who was eternally stoic,
and more challenging to read. It was my mother who often
caved, letting us off punishments earlier, who allowed us to
grab treats during shopping trips when we weren't supposed
to. There is something about the way that rage interlocks

with love, which interlocks with a need to protect. To protect the people you care for, but also to protect yourself.

I was twelve when I had my first and only seizure. The night before, I had been grounded for something I couldn't recall if I tried, and I have tried. It was the day before the start of spring break, so I can only imagine that I'd acted a fool in some class and a teacher called my mother at work. I was grounded, by both of my parents—the idea being that I'd spend my break inside, working as I might during school. Turning in assignments each day and doing chores. The first night of punishment, I went to sleep in my room on the top bunk, with my brother on the bottom. When I woke up, I was sitting at the kitchen table. I was told that my eyes were open, but I couldn't see anything. Someone was attempting to push a glass of orange juice into my mouth. My head hurt, and I wasn't prone to getting headaches. I am sure seizures impact people differently. But for me, it felt like I was being wrapped in black electrical tape from the neck up, tighter with each rotation.

I think, even now, of how frightening it must have been for my family, in the moment. My brother, who woke up to discover me in the midst of the seizure, twitching in bed. My parents when I was unresponsive, shouting that I couldn't see when I finally began to speak. When my eyes finally started to work again, it was as if the static had been pushed to the bottom of a TV screen. There was my mother, standing at the head of the table, relieved, smiling, holding back tears by clenching a trembling fist.

ON THE PLANE back home from the FUPU show in Los Angeles, I still feel the charge of their music, and their environment making its way through my body. I will tell people that this is what I got into punk music for, though I know that is a lie. When I was younger, I got into punk shows because I thought it might help me release all of the anger I held inside me. After my mom died, after I got suspended for fighting, after I stole things from my own house and from my own family members. I figured the problem was that I didn't have an outlet for my anger, and my pals would go to shows where they threw themselves around and felt a little better afterward, and so I started to join them.

The Midwest punk scene in my little corner of the Midwest existed in a circle of cities, and destinations were almost always a financial decision. If you could pool enough money for a few tanks of gas, Chicago was always the dream. At the time, the scene was dense, and shows with packed bills could run all weekend long. Places to crash were plentiful, and if not, my pal Tyler had a van we slept in. But if your bread was a bit lower, Detroit and Pittsburgh were also hot spots with high-quality scenes. If your bread was the absolute lowest, Dayton was just a short trip out of Columbus. And of course Columbus itself more than did the trick.

The thing with all of these places, though, was that if you were rolling with mostly Black punks, and especially if you and your Black punks were from out of town, the spaces you pulled up in might not be safe for you and whatever release you might be looking for. There are places you start fights, and there are places you don't. There are places you fight back in, and there are places you get thrown out of. There was a shifting scale for this, being Black in a place where people might be more likely to test you, or feel more entitled to your space. Fighting itself was never a catharsis for me when it felt like it was tied to my immediate survival. Throwing my body around in a mass of bodies didn't do much to bring me to some emotional resolution when it felt like the people around me didn't always see me as one of them and therefore cared less about damage. Even in my fucked-up youthful understanding of violence and rage as catharsis, I knew that it was best felt when the perceived enemy had some level of respect for, or understanding of, my person-hood. If I traded punches with a kid on my neighborhood basketball court, we'd see each other the next week, and the week after, and the week after that. And so we go into our throwing of punches with the understanding that while we might not be pals, on the other side of this is a world where we will have to interact—to find some common ground among our shared vulnerable lives.

That was a bit less common on the scenes I'd pop into, and sometimes even less common on the scene I lived in. When I'd see other Black punks out and about at shows, we'd some-times commune, sometimes ending up huddled in the back of a venue. If there were enough of us, we'd push to the front and form our own small nation.

If I'm being honest with myself, what I like about bands like FUPU, Big Joanie, the Txlips, the Muslims, and others now is that they fly in the face of what my younger self seemed to be asking for on stages. In my late teens and early twenties, when I'd clamor about wanting to see someone who looked like me onstage, that is—at its base level—all I was looking for. Someone Black and male to replicate the perfor-mance of ferocity that it felt like the white artists I saw had endless permission to do. I wanted to see a reproduction of a very narrow and masculine idea of how to release anger, be-cause all I knew was that I hadn't figured out a way yet, and I'd hoped someone might show me. And, of course, there were bands at least in the spirit of FUPU waiting for me the whole time, but I'd just never thought to look, be it due to my youth, or my narrow ideas of what permission for open expressions of rage (and love) looked like. There were bands waiting that not only upset my initial ideas about gender and representation but turned a direct address to an audience and challenged them in real time. Bands that appear invested in real-time emotional liberation, something beyond the much-needed anger of pointing to open wounds. When you find yourself chasing the tail of representation at all costs, you'd be surprised what speeds past you while you aren't even looking. And you'll be surprised by what you'll accept for yourself when you get the narrowest idea of representation fulfilled.

I am older now, and I go to far fewer shows than I used to. I'd guess that I still go to shows more than most people of my age and with my level of responsibilities and lack of free time. But I attend shows differently. I am now happily a fixture in the back of most rooms. I lean against a wall, or a pole, or a bar. Anywhere that allows me to take a brief load off while still being able to get a small sliver of the stage to watch. If it is an outdoor seated concert, sign me right up. And yes, I know how this sounds, as I have spoken it out loud to many of my pals who I used to cram into shows with five nights out of seven. And they laugh and laugh before realizing that they're about the same. We were often in shows where we had to fight for every inch of what we got, where we sometimes lovingly crashed ourselves into strangers, but sometimes not so lovingly. For over a decade, I kept searching for a way to rebuild myself through these acts of misguided rage, until I found newer and better ways. Until I grew too old, wounded, and cynical to keep searching, or when I asked myself *At what cost?* and could no longer endure the answer. I accumulated funerals, clung to old T-shirts from dead friends. Friends I loved who got spit on by the white straight-edge punks in Illinois or fought in Pennsylvania because someone called our pal a nigger. Yes, of course, it wasn't like this every time, in every place. But it was sometimes, somewhere. It dawned on me eventually that I was accumulating more anger than I could shake myself free of.

And so, at a rare punk show at the end of 2018, at the very back of the venue where I am the only Black person in my line of vision, a white dude stands directly in front of me and begins to comfortably walk backward, until I have to physically put my hand on his back, alerting him to my presence. When I tell him gently that he is crowding my space, and has blocked my entire view of the stage, he turns to me, and matter-of-factly says, *I can't move, sorry. I've been waiting for this show for months.*

In my younger days, I might have pushed or fought or begun some pointless shouting match. But another thing I learned long ago is that scenes benefit from the appearance of diversity, because that appearance gives them a space to not change any actual behavior on the interior of the scene. It's a model known all too well, where a company or an organization has some large public fuckup or gets called out on some long-known truth, and their first instinct is to bring in a Black person to help calm the noise. A politician who is charged with being out of touch with America's Black population tweets a poorly constructed Kwanzaa greeting. Blackness, or a proximity to Blackness, is America's favorite balm for a painful conscience.

But what rarely gets addressed is the full life beyond the performance of presence. The punk scene is a soft target, sure. Your scene is too white and will probably stay too white because when the Black kids come to your shows, people make sure to include them in the photos but shove them outta the way once the songs start. Your scene will stay too white because all shows are is a negotiation of space, who deserves it and who doesn't, and there's no way you and your crew are gonna make space for people who don't look like you when most of the room already looks like you.

But still, white dudes in band tees still tell me they've got Black kids at their shows now. They've got some queer folks there too, well hot damn. They maybe don't know any of them by name, or anything like that, but lord knows they're there and so the crisis over what to do about this goddamn mess is over.

It must be said that it feels selfish to tell young and unhappy punks of color to stop going to shows. I've had my fun, and if anyone older than I was at nineteen had told me to stop going to shows instead of fighting for my corner of freedom at a show, I'd have laughed in their face. And it ain't exactly my place to tell the disgruntled young punks of color to start their own thing, either. It's dismissive, first of all. It ignores the root of the problem and assumes everyone has the same access and ability to just spring up and do their own thing. But it also ignores the fact that many of them already have. There are Black and brown punk festivals sprouting up all over the States and beyond. But that all still leaves several young (and not-so-young) folks in certain areas running up against the same or similar walls I ran up against over a decade ago. I see these people. I talk to them after I do readings, or I get their emails. And I want to tell them to divest. To stop giving themselves to scenes that aren't interested in serving them, or acknowledging them, or scenes that render them invisible when a song starts. But I know that isn't fair, and it doesn't serve me to issue directives from on high. So I listen, and nod, and tell

them I understand because I've been there. We talk about
bands we're excited about, and I tell them to keep in touch if
they need to talk. And then we're back to our worlds.

When I talk about my personal divestment, I am not just
talking about removing myself from spaces. That is a part of
it for me now, but it's also the easiest part of it for me now, as
someone more excited about my couch than any pit. I'm also
talking about divesting from giving a scene my energy and,
specifically, my rage. The withholding of rage is a powerful
tool—one that I have found more useful than the withholding of love. It is rage that propels me most vigorously to the
work of serving my people, and so I don't feel it useful to
waste it in front of or in service of people I do not have an
investment in.

The brilliance of a band like Fuck U Pay Us is in the understanding of this, I think. A fool might come to their shows
or cycle through their songs and see only rage, or only anger.
Anger at whiteness, at patriarchy, at empire. All worthy
sources of anger, to be clear. And yes, of course there is anger
directed at these institutions and societal frameworks. But the
rage that is in the songs, and the rage that is upheld on the
stage, feels so permission-giving. *This* is what I had been
looking for. Rage to the untrained eye and ear, yes. But also a
deep, deep love for anyone who knows better. Anyone in a
room, shouting about burning it all down while being af-
firmed by the people around them. Anyone who has beaten
their fists against a wall, hoping it might crack and reveal to
them a place for their people to live unburdened, whoever
their people might be. What else carries anyone to that type
of rage but love? Or hope, maybe, though not the empty hope
of ads and political campaigns. Hope for a promised land and
the knowledge of what must be torn down to get there. I have
witnessed a Fuck U Pay Us show, and I have not been able to

stop thinking about it ever since. Black people shouting be-cause there is no other way for them to hold what they know. There is no other mode of expression for understanding all of the things that have held people back from understanding freedom, and there is no other volume at which one can say to their people, *I want all of us to be free, and I cannot do it alone.*

Movement V

CALLINGS

TO REMEMBER

On Times I Have Forced
Myself Not to Dance

I HAVE WANTED to die enough times in my life to understand the idea that wanting to die is not a foolish thing. My pal Donika and I once sat at a table together in Washington, D.C., because we had both written books that were up for awards. That in itself is a miracle, given that we both are Black in America, a place where our people could not always read or write without fear of punishment. When Donika won the award for her book, she gave thanks for the fact that she had survived all of the things that have tried to kill her, including herself. I have yet to be able to pull that small and simple statement apart from the fact that I am still alive, knowing there were once days when I didn't want to be and knowing that there might once again be days I don't want to be. I don't mean to prop up the idea of wanting an exit, but for me, not to imagine it as foolish means that I am, by default, tasked with taking it seriously. I can't live as I once did, telling people that I was doing fine and desperately wanting them to wade through the language and see that I was in pain.

I am called to remember this today, in this moment where I am still breathing and can deliver the news of my living, which is sometimes good and sometimes not. I am called to remember this today, while a text message from my brother sits on my phone that I am eager to respond to. My brother who once, in a year well before this one, left something he was doing to drive to a side of town he did not live on and knock on the door I was sitting on the floor behind at the end of a summer where everything had broken bad. I am thankful for what it is to grow up with a life fastened to another life, even as you both age upward and outward from whatever paths you began on. I am thankful for how the fastening of those lives creates a type of understanding of the unspoken, and I am thankful for how the fastening of those lives creates a type of urgency around that understanding.

I am called to remember all of this when I think of how my brother knocked and did not leave, knowing that I was sitting on the floor, holding the doorknob with a trembling hand and refusing to turn it. I am called to remember how, when I finally did turn it, there was my brother, who did not bother to ask whether or not I was doing all right. Who knew only that he couldn't get hold of me in a week where things went bad, and I mean the kind of bad that feels insurmountable. And I remember, most of all, how my brother—larger than me in every way—held me while I cried in his arms and did not speak at all, not even to reassure me that things were going to be fine. Rather, in silence, to help me understand that things were not fine, but this was him, dragging me back from the brink. Holding me until the ledge became solid ground again. Staying in that old, cheap apartment with me until it became so dark inside that I had to finally get off the floor and turn on a light. I am in praise of this today, a day when I will text my brother back and make some time to talk to him on the phone.

We have never talked about this, my brother and I. After that day, it was just another memory in our long and sometimes complicated tapestry of memories. My brother, who, even before the day he saved my life, once visited me when I spent a week in jail for stealing and lying and stealing again.

I have grown weary of talking about life as if it is deserved, or earned, or gifted, or wasted. I'm going to be honest about my scorecard and just say that the math on me being here and the people who have kept me here doesn't add up when weighed against the person I've been and the person I can still be sometimes. But isn't that the entire point of gratitude? To have a relentless understanding of all the ways you could have vanished, but haven't? The possibilities for my exits have been endless, and so the gratitude for my staying must be equally endless. I am sorry that this one is not about movement, or history, or dance. But instead about stillness. About all of the frozen moments that I have been pulled back from, in service of attempting another day.

ACKNOWLEDGMENTS

THIS BOOK WAS made possible with the patience and grace of many people, and the generosity of those who shared labor, resources, and time. Endless thanks to Maya Millett for steering this book in a newer, better direction. To Dart Adams for the fact-checking. To Kambui Olujimi for all of the dance marathon archives. To the vast team at Random House, who not only worked on this book as it shifted but helped it to live a wonderful life as soon as it entered the world: Ben Greenberg, who remained open to believing in what it could become. Maria Braeckel, Felix Cruz, Ayelet Durantt, and Shauna Carlos, who did an immense amount of lifting to give this book the opportunity to thrive, and who put up with my absentmindedness, my haphazardly arranged schedule, and my general anxieties around the world of publishing. Kaeli Subberwal, who was the engine behind the immense (and many) undertakings of this book's journey. Thanks, also, to Alia Habib and everyone at Gernert who fought for this book behind the scenes before it was even a book. Chances to work with such a singular team to bring something into the world don't come along often, and I am glad I got to do it here.

Like everything else, this book is a happy culmination of the many people, books, ideas, and energies that have informed my living to this point. Writers I look up to, yes, but also my friends in Columbus who make the time to sit with me in the comfort of our shared tenured affections. The people in my various group chats who put up with my overeager ramblings. The organizers in Columbus and beyond, who do the work of stretching my imagination, of making me think the world is worth writing in and writing about. I am thankful to all of those people.

This book is dedicated to the memory of MarShawn McCarrel, of Amber Evans, of Rubén Castilla Herrera, of Gina Blaurock, of Bill Hurley.

CREDITS

INDEX

magical negroes (*cont'd*):
  making money appear and, 62–63
  as The Prestige part of magic tricks, 51–52
  as replaceable, 66
magic tricks
  deconstructed into parts, 51–52
  Ellen and John Armstrong, 62–65
  role of viewer, 63
  sacrifice and, 55–56
Martin, Trayvon, 125–26, 127–28
"Mary Don't You Weep," 39
Master Juba
  Barnum and, 71
  dancing of, 69–70, 79–80
  death of, 87–88
  Diamond and, 71–72, 79
  portraits of, 81–82
McCain, John, 31–32
McDonald, Carrie, 144
McDonald, Freda Josephine. *See* Baker, Josephine
McMillan, Terry, 109
Menace II Society, 231
Merman, Ethel, 85
Method Man, 255, 256
Meyran, Octavio, 247
minstrel shows
  blackface won by Black performers in, 76–77
  Diamond, 71–72
  Master Juba (Lane), 69–70, 79–80

Miser's Dream trick, 64–65
Mitchell, Daryl, 50
Moor, 265
movies. *See also* specific titles
  primarily Black cast, 117
  sanitization of race relations in, 181–84, 188, 189–90
Muhammad (the Prophet), 242
Murphy, Eddie, 50
Murphy, Henry, 75–76
music. *See also* specific artists
  classical, as closed to Black people, 176–77
  gospel, 39, 42–43
  Grammy Awards, 92, 94–96
  invisibility of backup singers, 202
  juvenile behavior and, 178–79
  movement's link to, 13
  political inserted into the performance, 205–7, 214
  punk, 264–67, 270–75
  Soul Train (television program), 12, 14–15, 16–18
  "The Soul Train" concerts, 12
  Soul Train Line, 15–17, 19–21, 22
  Soul Train Music Awards, 97–98, 101–2, 108–10
  threatening power, 207–8, 214
  women in rock, 196
"My Prerogative," 108

white people (*cont'd*):
   pretending to be Black on
     Internet, 70–71
Whitney (albums), 93
Williams, A. G., Sr., 195
Williams, Bert, 85–86, 87
Williams, Billy Dee, 121–24
Williams, Jasper, Jr., 31
winning, meaning of, 230
women
   beefs and, 231–34
   power of, 215, 216–17

in rock music, 196
2016 presidential election,
   216
Wonder, Stevie, 31, 108
World War I, 147–48
Wu-Tang Clan, 250–52, 255,
   258–60, 261–62

Yo! MTV Raps (television
   program), 12
Young Thug, 252–53
You've Got Mail, 56

PHOTO: MEGAN LEIGH BARNARD

ABOUT THE AUTHOR

HANIF ABDURRAQIB is a poet, essayist, and cultural critic from Columbus, Ohio. His poetry has been published in PEN America, *Muzzle*, *Vinyl*, and other journals, and his essays and criticism have been published in *The New Yorker*, *Pitchfork*, *The New York Times*, and *Fader*. His first full-length poetry collection, *The Crown Ain't Worth Much*, was named a finalist for an Eric Hoffer book award and nominated for a Hurston/Wright Legacy Award. His first collection of essays, *They Can't Kill Us Until They Kill Us*, was named a book of the year by NPR, *Buzzfeed*, *Esquire*, *O: The Oprah Magazine*, *Pitchfork*, and *Chicago Tribune*, among others. *Go Ahead in the Rain: Notes to A Tribe Called Quest* was a *New York Times* bestseller and a National Book Critics Circle and Kirkus Prize finalist and was long-listed for the National Book Award. His second collection of poems, *A Fortune for Your Disaster*, won the Lenore Marshall Poetry Prize. He is a graduate of Beechcroft High School.

Abdurraqib.com

ABOUT THE TYPE

This book was set in Walbaum, a typeface designed in 1810 by German punch cutter J. E. (Justus Erich) Walbaum (1768–1839). Walbaum's type is more French than German in appearance. Like Bodoni, it is a classical typeface, yet its openness and slight irregularities give it a human, romantic quality.